# WAS HITLER ILL?

# WAS HITLER ILL?

## A FINAL DIAGNOSIS

HANS-JOACHIM NEUMANN AND
HENRIK EBERLE

Translated by Nick Somers

polity

First published in German as *War Hitler krank?* © Bastei Lübbe GmbH & Co. KG, Köln 2009

This English edition © Polity Press, 2013

The translation of this work was funded by Geisteswissenschaften International – Translation Funding for Humanities and Social Sciences from Germany, a joint initiative of the Fritz Thyssen Foundation, the German Federal Foreign Office, the collecting society VG WORT and the Börsenverein des Deutschen Buchhandels (German Publishers and Booksellers Association).

Polity Press
65 Bridge Street
Cambridge CB2 1UR, UK

Polity Press
350 Main Street
Malden, MA 02148, USA

ISBN-13: 978-0-7456-5222-1

A catalogue record for this book is available from the British Library.

Typeset in 10.5 on 12 pt Sabon
by Servis Filmsetting Ltd, Stockport, Cheshire
Printed and bound in the US by Edwards Brothers, Inc.

The publisher has used its best endeavours to ensure that the URLs for external websites referred to in this book are correct and active at the time of going to press. However, the publisher has no responsibility for the websites and can make no guarantee that a site will remain live or that the content is or will remain appropriate.

Every effort has been made to trace all copyright holders, but if any have been inadvertently overlooked the publisher will be pleased to include any necessary credits in any subsequent reprint or edition.

For further information on Polity, visit our website: www.politybooks.com

# CONTENTS

# ACKNOWLEDGEMENTS

The idea of describing Hitler's illnesses and of studying their possible effects on his behaviour came from historian and medical colleagues. As Hitler's biography still contains many gaps, we decided to study his life from this point of view. We were assisted in our task by a number of people who provided suggestions and ideas to help us with our work. When we asked her what she thought of our planned pathography in 1997, the historian and Hitler biographer Brigitte Hamann wrote in reply that she considered our planned project to be 'very important'.

Hitler's secretary Traudl Junge and his valet Otto Günsche were inexhaustible sources of information about his person, and their statements contained some hitherto unpublished details about his life. We obtained valuable information from various archives, institutes, hospitals and museums, whose helpfulness should be mentioned. We beg our readers' indulgence if we address our thanks first of all to family members, who not only helped the project through their consideration and infinite patience, but also took a lively interest themselves in the material and subject of the book, which was to be seen almost daily on one television channel or another. I (Hans-Joachim Neumann) should like in particular to thank my wife Susanne, who provided me with a wealth of suggestions. And I (Henrik Eberle) likewise express my gratitude to my mother, Sabine Ludewig, for her interest and support, which were very helpful and motivating to us.

Special thanks go to Gregor Pickro from the Bundesarchiv Koblenz, whose consistently friendly assistance and professional competence in the recommendation and provision of valuable archive material enabled us to progress with our research. Other members of the archive, such as Thomas Frank, were also extremely helpful. We should also like to thank the members of the Institute of Contemporary History Munich-Berlin, particularly its director Professor Horst Möller.

Our thanks also go to our literary agent Thomas Karlauf, who suggested the interdisciplinary study and helped to find a way of publishing it, and to Gustav Lübbe Verlag, particularly copy-editors Stefanie Heinen and Christan Stuewe, who accompanied the various phases of the project.

The experts in forensic medicine, Professor Otto Prokop (Berlin) and Professor Wolfgang Eisenmenger (Munich), were very receptive to our questions, for which we would like to thank them. We also received friendly assistance from Monika Gross, director of Landsberg am Lech Prison, Klaus Weichert, rector of the prison service, and Inga Zapka, registrar of the town of Tegernsee.

We should also like to mention a number of doctors in Berlin who read the manuscript: Professor Hartmut Zippel, Professor Volker Jahnke, Professor Walter Briedigkeit, Dr Swetlana Möller, Dr Karin Salmon and Dr Doris Schmidt all provided useful critical comments.

Various historian colleagues provided information about the scattered documents, as well as advice about the seriousness of the various historical assessments. We would mention in particular Dietmar Schulze (Leipzig), Matthias Uhl (Moscow), Hendrik Schäfer (Potsdam), Daniel Bohse (Magdeburg), Lydia Bittner (Dortmund), Barbara Stubbs (Dover) and Jana Wüstenhagen (Potsdam).

Our thanks go as well to Claudia Sachse from the German Pharmacy Museum in Heidelberg Castle. We were delighted to receive illustrations from Eva-Maria Flegel (Central Pharmacy of Charité University Hospital, Berlin) of medicines from the 1930s and 1940s and would like to thank her and Christoph Weber (also Charité) for their assistance in this regard. Peter-Alexander Bösel, Berlin, provided the illustration of the Kurfürstendamm and information about other possible picture sources. We also received excellent pictorial material for the book from Winfried Schultze, director of the Berlin university archive, and Elke-Barbara Peschke, head of the university library, and would like to thank them and all of the library staff in Berlin, Koblenz and Halle.

# ILLUSTRATIONS

We are grateful to the following sources for kindly granting their permission to reproduce images in this book:

(Image numbers) 3, 4, 22 – © Bundesarchiv Berlin

9, 10, 13, 14, 19, 21, 28, 29, 37, 39 – © Bayerische Staatsbibliothek München

11 – © ullstein bild – Top Foto

12 – © ullstein bild – Walter Frentz

15 – © ullstein bild – Heinrich Hoffmann

18 – © ullstein bild – Heinrich Hoffmann

27, 34, 35, 36, 43, 44, 45, 46, 47, 48, 49, 50, 51, 52, 53, 54, 55, 56 – © Bundesarchiv Koblenz

38 – © ullstein bild

# GLOSSARY

| | |
|---|---|
| aetiology | study of the causes of disease |
| analgesic | painkiller |
| anamnesis | patient history |
| angina pectoris | feeling of suffocation in the chest; sudden pain in the thorax spreading to the shoulders, arms and neck |
| aortic sclerosis | constriction of the aorta |
| Bodelschwinghsche Anstalten | confessional clinic in Bethel near Bielefeld, founded by Friedrich von Bodelschwingh |
| coronary sclerosis | constriction or occlusion of one or several branches of the coronary vessels |
| dementia | undefined loss of intellectual function |
| diastole | dilation of the heart between two contractions |
| differential diagnosis | diagnostic distinction between similar pathologies |
| dysbacteria | pathological condition caused by abnormal intestinal flora |
| endogenous | from within the body |
| endoscopic | examination of hollow internal organs using an endoscope |
| epithelium | topmost cell layer in the body |
| exogenous | from outside the body |
| floaters | spots before the eyes, also known as *mouches volantes* |
| haemorrhagic diathesis | predisposition to abnormal bleeding |
| hypertonia | high blood pressure |
| hypotonia | low blood pressure |

| | |
|---|---|
| hysteria | lack of control over acts and emotions, called today 'dissociative disorder' |
| idiopathic | without discernible cause |
| inotropic | influencing muscle contractions of the heart |
| intestinal flora | bacteria living in the intestine |
| ischaemia | constriction or obstruction of blood flow to a vessel |
| Lugol's solution | strong iodine solution, deep brown liquid consisting of iodine and potassium iodide |
| monocausal | having a single cause |
| oedema | swelling due to the accumulation of fluid |
| papilloma | benign skin and mucous tumour |
| parenchyma | functional components of an organ as opposed to the structure |
| pathogenic | causing disease |
| polyp | generally benign growth, usually of the mucous membranes |
| polypragmasy | polypharmacy, treatment with several drugs simultaneously |
| psychogenic | of psychological origin |
| psychosomatic | said of diseases having mental rather than physical origins |
| pulmonary oedema | accumulation of fluid in the lungs |
| shaking palsy | another name for parkinsonism |
| somatopsychic | pertaining to both body and mind |
| sympathicotonic | excitation of the sympathetic nervous system with heightened blood pressure and tachycardia and reduced motility of the gastrointestinal tract and glandular secretion |
| systole | contraction of the heart |
| tachycardia | fast heart beat |

# ABBREVIATIONS

| | |
|---|---|
| CIA | Central Intelligence Agency |
| ECG | electrocardiogram |
| ENT | ear, nose and throat |
| HAGEDA | Association of German Pharmacists |
| KGB | Soviet secret service |
| NKGB | People's Commissariat for State Security (USSR) |
| NKVD | People's Commissariat for Internal Affairs (USSR) |
| NSDAP | National Socialist German Workers' Party |
| OSS | Office of Strategic Services |
| PQ wave | ECG feature, complete atrial contraction |
| PQ interval | ECG feature, time between atrial and ventricular contraction |
| QRS complex | ECG feature tracing complete cardiac cycle |
| SA | Sturmabteilung, stormtroopers |
| SD | Security Service, part of the SS |
| SS | Schutzstaffel |
| ST wave | ECG feature, complete ventricular contraction |
| WHO | World Health Organization |

# 1

# MADNESS, DESIGN AND REALITY: WHY A MEDICAL BIOGRAPHY OF HITLER?

'Actually Hitler was never sick', Hitler's long-time personal physician Professor Theodor Morell is supposed to have said to Professor Karl Brandt, the Führer's attendant surgeon, in September 1945. We do not know whether Morell actually made this pronouncement in so many words, but Brandt, who was to be hanged a short while later for his crimes, certainly reported as much to his American interrogator at Camp Siebert. Brandt and Morell shared a cell in the internment camp and when they spoke to each other it was about Hitler.

Less than a year earlier, Brandt's career had come to an abrupt end on account of Morell and a bout of 'jaundice' by Hitler, which Brandt attributed to years of incorrect treatment by the Führer and Reich Chancellor's personal physician. He claimed that Morell had made Hitler dependent on 'mobilizing drugs, i.e. stimulants', and had also treated him unnecessarily with vitamins and sulphonamides. The entire medical profession had been 'embarrassed' that a person with such 'primitive conceptions' had been able to become Hitler's personal physician.[1]

The statements by both doctors are short on credibility. Brandt was attempting to curry favour with the American officers by providing detailed information about Morell and Hitler in order to save his skin. He knew that he would be held responsible for the death of over 70,000 people, since he was the person who had been commissioned by Hitler in 1939 to dispose of 'incurable mentally ill patients'.[2] For his part, Morell feared that he might die soon as a result of his heart condition; his concern was with how history would see him. In spite of frequent heart attacks and occasional disorientation, he did his best to persuade Brandt that he had not at all acted incorrectly. He

1

repeatedly defended his actions and attempted to convince Brandt that he had not treated Hitler for any serious conditions.

The dispute between the two professors[3] in a prison cell in Oberursel was to go down in history – quite literally, since their conflicting utterances have remained even today the basis for the historical discussion of this subject. Doctors, psychologists and historians still seek explanations for the genocides committed during the Nazi era and necessarily devote attention in various ways to the dictator's diseases, illnesses and supposed perversions. Hitler's contemporaries carried out even more intensive research to explain how they could have followed someone who was responsible for the greatest disaster in Germany's history. In asking this question they were referring not to the millions of people exterminated by the Nazis, but to their own suffering, the millions of dead soldiers, the division of the country, and to the flight and expulsion of millions of Germans from Poland and other parts of eastern Europe.

The explanation that Hitler was a megalomaniac who at some point lost his mind and was perhaps somehow ill was after all the simplest and most obvious. Several books after 1945 spread the idea that the Nazi regime had started well but had degenerated. There is no doubt that until 1939 most Germans pinned their hopes for the nation on Hitler,[4] and millions felt that they were understood and being taken seriously politically.[5] The disappointment with which they rejected him was all the greater when they realized the misery he had inflicted on them and the criminal acts that he had caused to be committed in Germany's name.[6] Quite often, writers asked the question 'what would have happened if . . .?'. For example, if Hitler had been assassinated in 1938 or 1944.[7] No doubt the readers of these books and their authors, including the countless writers of memoirs, were also hoping to find an excuse. The historian Hannes Heer summed up the post-war mood when he said it was Hitler's fault.[8] And if Hitler was solely responsible and people had not been completely mistaken about him, it was natural to believe in a Hitler who had changed, possibly even under the supposed damaging influence of his personal physician Theodor Morell, who is alleged to have pumped Hitler full of drugs and treated him completely wrongly.[9]

Analyses at the time came to different conclusions. The conspirators of 20 July 1944 regarded Hitler's personality as the incarnation of evil and attempted to eliminate him for that reason.[10] In 1943, the émigré Austrian psychiatrist Walter C. Langer also reported to the OSS, the forerunner of the CIA, that Hitler had sadistic traits and suicidal tendencies. He firmly believed that Hitler would not call an early end to the war and that there would be peace in Europe again only after his death. Langer's diagnosis, as imprecise as the details may appear today, was at least right on that point.[11] The result is horrific: more than fifty-five million people were killed during the Second World War through combat operations and planned genocide.

This is one of the reasons why generations of professional and amateur historians have attempted to explain Hitler's apocalyptic impact on history. The literature about Hitler includes a number of books by renowned historians, notably the British writer Ian Kershaw, whose two-volume biography has set the standard.[12] Kershaw reconstructs Hitler's decisions and actions without venturing into the treacherous realm of psychological explanations. He points out that psychologists have repeatedly attempted to find out what precisely was wrong with Hitler, but he does not believe that we have to know this. Psychohistorical diagnosis is difficult in any case, he says, because Hitler had never been psychoanalysed and we simply know too little about his childhood and adolescence.[13] In his latest work on turning points in the Second World War, Kershaw nevertheless diagnoses Hitler as having a 'personal paranoid fixation with the Jews' and describes the Holocaust ultimately as a consequence of his sick ideas.[14]

Was the murder of millions of people the product of madness or a mental illness? Attempts to determine what may be regarded as the truth about Hitler have given rise to intense discussion.[15] Since Alan Bullock, an Oxford historian and Churchill's personal assistant, published the first biography of Hitler based on original sources in 1952, the debate about the riddle of Hitler has not subsided.[16] Tireless scholars like Anton Joachimsthaler and Werner Maser have been seeking to expand the state of knowledge, as have interpretive journalists like Joachim Fest and Sebastian Haffner.[17] Countless historians have studied particular aspects of Hitler's life, considering his time in Vienna,[18] editing writings thought to have disappeared,[19] or analysing his attitude to women and sexuality.[20] German military historians have also finally started looking in detail at the role of Hitler as commander-in-chief of the armed forces.[21] Even ideologically questionable authors like the Holocaust denier David Irving or the Berlin professor Ernst Nolte have made a contribution by revealing new sources, giving food for thought and posing polemical questions that nevertheless call for refutation by serious historians.[22] But it was not until the end of the Cold War that it became possible to seriously discuss the initiation, implementation and extent of the genocide and those involved in it on the basis of a reliable set of facts

3

and insights.[23] Comprehensive descriptions of the extermination of the Jews such as those by Saul Friedländer, Christopher Browning and Peter Longerich are the results of decades of research.[24] For the first time they permit a precise reconstruction of Hitler's role in this extermination process.

Current findings now also make it possible for us to reassess the medical biography of the dictator. The most reliable study to date on this subject is probably *Patient Hitler* by Ernst Günther Schenck, a university lecturer dismissed in 1945. It has no personal signature or political judgements, no doubt because as an SS-Standartenführer Schenck was himself deeply implicated in the crimes of the Nazi regime.[25]

When Fritz Redlich's medical biography of Hitler appeared,[26] Christina Berndt wrote in the *Süddeutsche Zeitung* on 24 November 1998 that the work offered a 'comprehensive medical and psychological biography of the dictator', and Ian Kershaw described it as the 'most thorough investigation yet undertaken of Hitler's medical condition'.[27] For all the detail in Redlich's analysis, however, not all of the quotations are sufficiently corroborated and quite a few of the sources mentioned have been regarded by historical researchers as unreliable.[28] The diagnosis of Hitler by the doyen of American social psychiatry as a 'destructive and paranoid prophet' is not contested here, as Redlich clearly rejects psychiatric diagnoses as inaccurate generalizations by which 'nothing is gained other than a false sense of knowledge'.[29]

Both of us, the doctor and the historian, agree that history cannot be reconstructed in its entirety. Similarly, life-histories can only be interpreted and can never be understood in all their facets. Beyond these theoretical considerations, this observation is all the more applicable in the case of Hitler because he left no evidence himself, in the form of diaries, for example, that can be reliably interpreted. On the contrary, the ambitious politician and later dictator of the German Reich was always at pains to erase traces of the past. When he came to power, he had all written evidence of his youth and family confiscated, and he prohibited its distribution.[30] The scanty utterances in his nightly monologues on his health sound more like asides, with the result that his table talk also has nothing on the subject.[31] The only source in connection with his medical history that he recognized was *Mein Kampf*, the self-penned account of his life.[32]

As late as 31 March 1945, when personal physician Theodor Morell, 'after having attempted on several occasions to record [Hitler's] medical history', once again asked for permission to do so, he was 'roundly rebuffed' by him: 'I have never been ill. There is nothing to write up.'[33] In 2002, biographer Joachim Fest also came to the conclusion that 'the exact nature of Hitler's illness can no longer be determined' since none of the various diagnoses can be 'persuasively supported or rejected'.[34]

There are nevertheless numerous 'jottings', and these written records have been reinterpreted again and again, so it is therefore worthwhile taking a close look at the supposedly sick, homosexual or crazed dictator. Morell, who rose fortuitously to become Hitler's personal physician, kept detailed records between 1941 and 1945, not least out of fear of possible reprisals by the SS Security Service and the Gestapo if something were to happen to Hitler. As the Führer's personal physician he would have had to justify himself, as he would naturally have been the first suspect, for example, if Hitler had been poisoned. He therefore took medical examinations seriously and kept a record of all of Hitler's diseases and the medical treatments to enable them to be verified at any time.

We have reassessed these records, because previous accounts, such as those by the Holocaust denier David Irving, have often proved to be incorrect or, in the case of the former SS officer Ernst Günther Schenck, inadequate. We have also discovered new sources, such as those in hitherto inaccessible or disregarded SS files. Moreover, it also appeared appropriate to reassess certain medical diagnoses of the time and to place them reliably in their historical context.

This new evaluation was also considered necessary because the appraisal of the one-time 'traitor' and subsequent dictator is still open to discussion. This is not just a debate in the ivory tower of academia. Television gives viewers access every week, if not every day, to documentaries about Hitler and his political decisions. In some cases outdated findings from 1943 are reworked as sensational new information.[35]

Historical and medical research have both undergone a fundamental change since then, and considerable progress, if that is the word, has been made. It is now possible to give persuasive reasons for the acceptance or rejection of particular diagnoses. To do this, however, it has been necessary to reconstruct the research and to mark incorrect interpretations as such – not least as both medical and historical judgements are influenced by the state of knowledge and the *zeitgeist*, the spirit of the times.

The collaboration between a historian and a doctor has been extremely profitable as a way of trying to understand Hitler as a person who in retrospect can be interpreted only through a mixture of historically verifiable facts and informed interpretations.[36] A study of Hitler's medical biography touches both private and highly political aspects of his life. There is considerable dispute as to the relative importance of these two aspects and the role they played in Hitler's rise, the outbreak of the Second World War and the death of millions of people. We hope that this book will make a constructive and interdisciplinary contribution to an understanding of these processes.

*Hans-Joachim Neumann and Henrik Eberle*
*Berlin and Halle, February 2009*

# — 2 —

# THE DISEASED HITLER: A HISTORIOGRAPHICAL PROJECT

## Psychohistorical Aberrations: Anti-Semitism as 'Madness'

Numerous attempts have been made to attribute the crimes committed in Nazi Germany to mental illness on the part of the dictator Adolf Hitler. Not all of the claims can be simply dismissed. Hitler's anti-Semitism, for example, does indeed appear to have been irrational. Ian Kershaw said in 2006: 'The Jewish tragedy was based on the fixed idea by the Nazis – most strongly represented by Hitler himself – that the Jews needed to be "eliminated" in order to "cleanse" the German nation and to pave the way towards a new, "racially pure" order in Europe that would overcome the centuries of supremacy of Judeo-Christian values and beliefs.'[1]

The fascination that Hitler exerted might also be explained in terms of a 'religious mania'. Hitler's supporters repeatedly emphasized after 1945 that Hitler had communicated an overpowering fanaticism, and even beforehand letters by the German population had made reference to the 'saviour'.[2] Retrospectively, there can be no doubt that Hitler himself was affected by a kind of 'redemptive anti-Semitism'. In his own words, the eradication of the Jews was nothing other than a 'surgical intervention' to remove a foreign body or infiltrating neoplasm from the body of the German people.[3]

Like every form of xenophobia, anti-Semitism is basically irrational, but the way in which various authors have described Hitler as 'mentally ill' or 'mad' deserves closer analysis. In many cases it is a media rather than a historical phenomenon. The evolution of this attributed madness is a product solely of modern media culture and is not supported by the verifiable facts. Former comrades-in-arms, for example, stylized Hitler as a pervert who could obtain sexual

7

satisfaction only if a woman urinated on him.[4] Others accused him indirectly of being a paedophile.[5] In the 1970s, it was fashionable to describe Hitler as a victim of a violent father as a result of which he developed an uncontrollable hate that culminated in the extermination of the Jews.[6] Even today, popular psychological interpretations, such as the conjecture that Hitler had only one testicle, still abound.

For serious historians, the comments in 1964 by Percy Ernst Schramm, a respected professor at the University of Göttingen and editor of the war diaries of the German High Command, still apply. In analysing Hitler's thinking and attempting to penetrate into his character, we must remain on this side of the psychological Rubicon, 'where historians can still have solid ground under their feet'.[7] Schramm also called for a 'medical biography' of Hitler supervised by psychologists and psychiatrists.

A book of this nature still remains to be written. There has been no shortage of attempts to approach the 'Adolf Hitler problem' in a scientific and interdisciplinary manner, and efforts in this direction have indeed been notable for the endeavour to solve the puzzle that Hitler presents. One highly promising attempt was the book *Hitler: Karriere eines Wahns* by psychotherapist Paul Matussek, historian and cultural studies expert Peter Matussek and systems theoretician and sociologist Jan Marbach.[8]

In spite of their systematic study of the literature and available sources, the authors were nevertheless only able to present another version of Hitler's alleged 'mental illness'. Like others, Matussek and his co-authors assumed that the extermination of the Jews had been the product of an 'extermination mania', an 'early frustrated need' and a 'huge personality disorder'. They ultimately diagnosed a 'schizophrenic madness' that, coupled with a 'narcissistic fixation on his public self', led to a 'paranoid extermination programme'.[9] American psychiatrist Walter C. Langer had already diagnosed sadistic and masochistic traits in 1943.[10] Narcissistic people with a fixation on their public selves are to be found in all areas of society, however, as are people with sexual preference disorders – at least if the eagerness with which those affected declare their feelings in television programmes and the vast array of publications on the subject are anything to go by. In concluding that Hitler suffered from a 'schizophrenic mania', Matussek and his co-authors even came up with a new definition of schizophrenia.[11]

If the definition of a disease has to be modified to analyse a single 'case', there is a suggestion that the former definition was in fact correct but not applicable to the case in point. The interpretations by the psychologist and political adviser Manfred Koch-Hillebrecht might also suffer from these limitations. While his assertions about Hitler's 'eidetic' memory, as Koch-Hillebrecht describes it, might be valid, further comments by him prove to be wayward.[12] He claimed that Hitler suffered an early change of character as a result of Parkinson's disease, which more recent research has proved to be erroneous. On the basis of 'harmless examples' Koch-Hillebrecht then talks of the scale of Hitler's 'blunt eroticism', stating that 'it is quite possible that if he had not lived out his desires in the killing orgies of the Second World War, Adolf, handsome as he was, could well have turned into a paedophile and sodomite'.[13] There is more. At the end of his analysis he concludes that Hitler could have freed himself of his 'worst extermination fantasies' if he had come out and admitted his repressed homosexuality.

From a historical point of view it is unacceptable that Koch-Hillebrecht does not quote the sources for his findings. The 500-page book contains not one single piece of evidence, and those facts that might appear to be verifiable turn out to be a collection of assumptions. Without any proof he describes the Waldviertel, where Hitler's family came from, as 'no doubt also full of inbreeding' and draws wide-ranging conclusions from this assumption. The confusing text mixes up people, gives them jobs they never had and presents a series of myths that have long been debunked.[14] Psychoanalytical interpretations based on dubious sources of this nature cannot be taken seriously.

The problem of psychohistorical interpretation cannot be reduced to a single book, however. The comment by Matussek et al. regarding earlier, equally sloppy 'analyses' ultimately applies to the entire discipline of psychoanalysis: 'The main problem with such diagnoses is, as mentioned, their arbitrariness.'[15] A different question needs to be asked. If Hitler does indeed fit some psychoanalytical pattern, why was it he and no one else who caused the greatest disaster in the history of Europe? It is also questionable whether the murder of millions of Jews, Slavs, mentally ill, Sinti and Roma can be explained at all by Hitler's mental disposition, whatever it was, or whether it was caused by other factors.

## The Rational Core of Hitler's Anti-Semitism: Expedience

Walter C. Langer, the psychiatrist mentioned earlier who examined Hitler on behalf of the OSS, forerunner of the CIA, apologised to the readers of his dossier, written in 1943: 'If our study is to be complete, we must appraise his strengths as well as his weaknesses.'[16] He described Hitler as having 'extraordinary abilities where the psychology of the average man is concerned' and even 'the ability to feel, identify with and express in passionate language the deepest needs and sentiments of the average German'. As head of government he also had 'opportunities or possibilities for their gratification'. Hitler had the 'capacity to appeal to the most primitive, as well as the most ideal inclinations in man, to arouse the basest instincts and yet cloak them with nobility'. Not least, he was able 'to persuade others to repudiate their individual consciences'.

Looking back, there can be no dispute that these abilities made a decisive contribution to his success in the Party and in politics.[17] Hitler was aware of this fearful weapon in the hands of an expert, as his comments on propaganda in *Mein Kampf* confirm.[18] He consistently chose topics for his speeches that appealed to his audience: the German defeat and anti-Jewish feelings. He repeatedly linked these two themes by making 'the Jews' and their 'fateful influence' in society responsible for the defeat.

In doing so he was able to draw on a long anti-Semitic tradition in Germany and German Austria. The social climate was coloured in particular, however, by the new type of anti-Semitism that had evolved in the late nineteenth century both in Germany and in the Austro-Hungarian Empire. The historian Brigitte Hamann describes Linz, the city in which Hitler spent his youth, as a 'stronghold of anti-Semitism'. Signs saying 'Admission for Germans (Aryans) only' were no rarity, even before the First World War.[19] In the German Empire anti-Semitism was also socially acceptable.[20] Conspiracy theories, the idea of the Jews as the 'masterminds' of a policy aimed at conquering the world were not dismissed but taken seriously even in educated circles.[21] This anti-Semitism climaxed during the war, as the politician and industrialist Walter Rathenau commented in 1916: 'The more Jews killed in this war, the more their opponents will insist that they were all profiteering behind the lines. The hate will double and triple.'[22] When, at the insistence of the extreme right, the Prussian Ministry of War ordered a 'Jewish census' in the army and then kept the results secret, a rumour spread among the troops that the Jews were basically 'shirkers'. This animosity was fuelled by the defeat, the 'stab-in-the-back', for which the Jews were once again held responsible, and not only by Hitler.[23]

However deep Hitler's personal anti-Semitism might have been before the First World War, at the latest during his service as a front-line soldier he must have been exposed to massive anti-Semitic rabble-rousing, which provided a plausible basis to explain the German defeat.[24] For propaganda to be effective in bourgeois, right-wing conservative 'national circles', it therefore had to be anti-Jewish.[25] In Munich Hitler associated with radical right-wing circles such as the Thule Society, initially as an informer for the Reichswehr and then as a promising political talent. Open anti-Semitism was not only acceptable but also a prerequisite for obtaining financial and political support for political aims.[26] Moreover, his intellectual mentor Dietrich Eckart, who not only exerted an influence on Hitler but also raised funds for the NSDAP, was a radical anti-Semite.[27] Eckart also introduced Hitler to the family of Richard Wagner, whose world view was influenced by the eloquent anti-Semite and philosopher Houston Stewart Chamberlain. As the author of the influential *The Foundations of the Nineteenth Century* and de facto master of Wagner's household at Wahnfried, and having married one of Cosima Wagner's daughters he was a leading light in Bayreuth society.[28] In Hitler's view, political and economic expediency went hand in hand with personal convenience. His desire for personal advancement was inseparably linked with a demonstrative anti-Semitic attitude.

There is no doubt that Hitler adopted this attitude for himself. As Kershaw suggests, however, he was not the most radical anti-Semite. He was outdone, at least in terms of the obscenity of their claims, by Artur Dinter, a successful novelist and Gauleiter of Thuringia and Franconia, and Julius Streicher, publisher of *Der Stürmer*.[29] Within the Nazi Party, which saw itself as a collective movement, Hitler was more in the centre than at the extremes. He saw his most urgent task as unifying the fragmented populist camps.[30] His ability to do this was clearly linked with his instrumentalization of anti-Semitic feelings. Like an actor adapting his role to his audience, Hitler deliberately measured the rabble-rousing anti-Semitic content of his speeches or omitted it altogether, as in a speech in Bayreuth in 1923, where his aim was to win over 'dignitaries', or in 1932 to industrialists in Dusseldorf, when he sought support from heavy industry.[31] As head of state, Hitler also projected himself as a moderate. The Law on Restoration of the Civil Service of 7 April 1933 provided exceptions for Jewish war veterans, who were thus initially able to continue working as public servants.[32] It was not until the Nuremberg Rally in 1935 that the Nuremberg Laws defined who was to be regarded as 'Jewish'. For the first time, 'Mischlinge' in particular had clear and in some cases 'favourable' classifications.[33] There were more than 1,300 Jewish 'Mischlinge', quite an appreciable number, who were exempted by Hitler's decree from reprisals, further indication that Hitler was more interested in political, military and economic objectives than in the creation at all costs of a German people free of any 'mixed blood'.[34] As soon as the opportunity arose to liquidate the Jews in the conquered territories, however, Hitler did not hesitate to issue the necessary orders. Here, too, he could be sure of having enough 'willing helpers', not least as hundreds of thousands of Germans would benefit from the removal of the Jews and their extermination.[35]

## The Extermination of the Jews: The Holocaust as a Process

The Catalan journalist Eugeni Xammar, who interviewed Adolf Hitler in 1928, came to the conclusion that the leader of the NSDAP was a 'fool' but one full of 'drive, vitality and energy' and altogether 'immoderate but unstoppable'. Xammar described him as a 'powerful, splendid fool destined for an illustrious career (of which he is even more convinced than we are)'. Hitler stated quite frankly what he thought of the Jews. They were 'a cancerous growth consuming our German national organism'. Obviously, the best thing would be to exterminate the Jews, he continued, but that would not be possible. All that remained was the solution chosen by Spain of 'expulsion, mass expulsion'.[36]

In the very first surviving political document written by Hitler himself, a letter on the Jews of 10 September 1919, he emphasized the need for 'rational anti-Semitism', which should lead to a 'systematic and legal struggle against, and eradication of, the privileges the Jews enjoy over the other foreigners living among us'. However, its 'final objective', he said in this letter addressed to his military superiors, 'must be the total removal of all Jews from our midst'.[37] There is no doubt that this 'rational anti-Semitism' was nothing other than undisguised hatred of the Jews, demonstrating that it was the decisive political motive, and not just one of many.

In Vienna, where Hitler lived until 1913 in a men's hostel – and not, as was claimed,[38] in a dosshouse – he worked for Jewish tradesmen; his pictures were sold, among others, by a Jewish pedlar. In spite of the anti-Semitic mood in the capital of the Habsburg monarchy, Hitler apparently had no qualms about working with Jews if it was to his advantage.[39] It was only when he came into contact with the populist movement and the Wagner clan that he changed his opinion.

Like Richard Wagner in his pamphlet 'Judaism in Music', Hitler opposed the integration of a people felt to be alien. They always remained the same, he said. 'A splash of baptismal water could always save the business and the Jew at the same time.'[40] Hitler also adapted Wagner's call for the 'downfall of our Culture' to be 'arrested by a violent ejection of the destructive alien element'. And like Hitler in 1939, Wagner had prophesied the 'demise' of the 'Ahasuerus', the 'eternal Jew' in 1850.[41]

It would nevertheless be wrong to attribute the Holocaust solely to Hitler's anti-Semitism. At least 200,000 people were directly involved in the extermination of the six million Jews, as members of the SS killing units, for example. Added to this are the millions of people who were indirectly implicated in the mass murder, as members of the various administrative bodies or employees of the Reichsbahn, whose trains transported people to the extermination camps.

The time frame also needs to be taken into account: several years elapsed and there were various escalating stages between the first pogroms and boycotts in early 1933 and the start of the shootings in early autumn 1941.[12] In the first few years of the Nazi regime Jews were systematically excluded from German society. To force them to emigrate, their livelihood was methodically and gradually removed, as it said in an internal memorandum from the Ministry of Justice.[43] Businessmen were expropriated, civil servants and employees were dismissed, and self-employed persons were no longer able to exercise their professions. Non-Jewish Germans benefited considerably from the confiscated assets.[44] The November Pogrom in 1938, trivialized as the 'Night of Broken Glass', was an important turning point, when it became clear to the victims that the regime was not going to guarantee them any legal protection whatsoever. At the same time, the Party members, SS and SA men, who had taken part in this mistreatment and destruction now had confirmation that they could give free rein to their hate.[45] The German authorities stepped up their repression and forced more than 120,000 Jews to emigrate, not before having robbed them through the imposition of a Reich Flight Tax [Reichsfluchtsteuer].

The transition from persecution to extermination began right after war broke out. Hitler himself called for a 'hard national struggle', without making specific demands on the army and SS. But even in the first year of the war, improvised killing commandos murdered over 50,000 people in occupied Poland. At the same time the German occupying authorities initiated a massive population shift. Hundreds of thousands of Jews were herded into ghettos, and Polish farmers

13

were forced to move and their properties given to Germans. As historian Christopher Browning puts it, Poland thus became the 'laboratory of racial policy'. The chaotic terror of the first days of the war was gradually replaced by systematic terror.[46]

The next phase in this terror was the systematic 'evacuation', i.e. deportation, of more than 600,000 Jews and 'dangerous' Poles from the territories that were to be annexed to the German Reich. High-ranking officials from various ministries would meet regularly with representatives of the SS to discuss the organizational details. As a result of logistical problems the numbers were even reduced. The idea of resettling all of the Jews from the Old Reich and the conquered Polish territories in Lublin District also had to be abandoned in June 1940.

The victory over France opened up the possibility of settling millions of Jews in Madagascar, a French island in the Indian Ocean. The plan was abandoned after Germany had lost the Battle of Britain and failed to break the British navy's domination of the seas.[47] It was not until December 1940, after the decision to go to war against the Soviet Union, that the next phase could be considered: the deportation of the Jews to a 'territory to be determined' where, 'in accordance with the will of the Führer, a final solution to the Jewish question' could be achieved. Reinhard Heydrich, head of the Security Police [*Sicherheitspolizei*] and Security Service (SD), had already been given the order from Hitler, through Göring, to present a project for the 'final solution'. The draft version was submitted to Hitler and Göring in December 1940 or January 1941 at the latest, as can be seen from an internal memo from the Reich Security Head Office.[48] In Order No. 21 issued in March 1941 concerning directives for 'special areas', Hitler basically gave the SS mobile task forces a free hand. It stated that in the territory in which the combat operations were to take place the SS would have 'special tasks . . . that will arise from the forthcoming final struggle between two opposing political systems'.[49]

Himmler and Heydrich put together mobile units [*Einsatzgruppen*], which started on 24 June 1941 with the mass killing of Lithuanian, Belarusian and Ukrainian Jews. By the end of the year they had killed almost 400,000 people. At the same time the deportations to the ghettos in Riga, the Lublin district and elsewhere continued. The administrative authorities in these areas protested not against the deportations but on account of the associated logistical difficulties. By September 1941, however, it had become clear that it would not be possible to 'crush Soviet Russia in a quick campaign' as Hitler's order

14

for Operation Barbarossa had originally stated.[50] In other words, the Jews in these territories would not be able to be deported eastwards, where they would be dealt with by the SS.[51]

Himmler visited Ukraine on 30 September and 4 October to review the logistical aspects of the mass killings. He submitted a report to Hitler at his Wolf's Lair headquarters. A few days later, on 13 and 14 October, he met with Reinhard Heydrich and Odilo Globocnik, SS and police chief of Lublin district.[52] At the same time, some of the mobile units were trying out more efficient killing methods, such as the use of trucks into which carbon monoxide was introduced. At Auschwitz concentration camp, Zyklon B gas was tested for the first time and 250 inmates killed with it. A few days later a further 900 inmates succumbed. After these trials, work started on the construction of crematoriums, and the mass killing by gas began.

Hitler was regularly informed of the progress of the genocide. He obtained monthly reports from the SS mobile units, and Himmler also submitted regular reports, for example on 4, 5, 7 and 16 September. On 23 September, Hitler, Himmler, Heydrich, Goebbels and others discussed the deportation of the Jews to camps to be set up on the White Sea canal. On 24 September, Hitler, Lammers, Bormann, Heydrich and others considered the situation in the Protectorate of Bohemia and Moravia. On 5 October, Himmler reported on his visit to the mobile killing units. On 9 October, after having lunch with Hitler, Himmler met Martin Bormann for extended discussions. Hitler and Himmler had a long meeting on 2 November 1941 at which it is likely that the Reichsführer-SS once again reported in detail about the killing of Jews. The minutes of subsequent meetings between Hitler and Himmler indicate that the question was not discussed any further in 1941.

In a speech to the NSDAP Reichsleiter and Gauleiter on 12 December 1941 Hitler stated that his prophecy on 30 January 1939 regarding the extermination of the Jews was not a mere 'figure of speech'.[53] This resulted in ambiguous interpretations by lower instances but only concerning different ways as to how the mass killing should be continued. Himmler submitted two detailed reports to Hitler, on 10 and 17 March 1942. In the interceding week he had spoken on the phone to several high-ranking SS officers and had visited Krakow and Lublin to inspect the situation for himself. The gas chambers in Belzec started operation on 17 March 1942. By 1945, more than three million people throughout Europe had been killed by gassing.[54]

The fact that the planning of the 'final solution of the Jewish question' changed repeatedly and that the initiative for its execution often came from subordinate SS officers reflects the progressive nature of the Holocaust. Hitler intervened on several occasions in this process. He signalled his wishes by way of relatively imprecise and cryptic utterances, warnings and prophecies. He shied away from giving one or more specific orders, even when he had full details, as with the gas chambers, for example.[55] More than two years elapsed from the outbreak of war until the industrial extermination by poisonous gas, during which time others carried out the 'killing work', as they described it.[56] Hitler conferred with Himmler but never saw a mobile killing operation or extermination camp himself. Himmler in turn delegated the organization of the genocide to Heydrich, head of the Reich Security Head Office, where the threads came together, and to the commanders of the mobile units and local SS and police chiefs.

Hitler showed very few emotions. His remarks about Jews recorded during the table talk at lunches and dinners, also sound strangely distant. Although his utterances were frequently radical – as on 21 October 1941, for example, when he stated that the extermination of this plague would render a service to humanity[57] – even this hatred sounds distant and abstract in retrospect. The repeated tirades against Jews as destroyers of culture were nothing more than a continuation of his dualistic world view of noble Aryans and his eternal enemy, the Jew, which he had already sketched in *Mein Kampf*.[58]

The Holocaust was thus the realization of Hitler's personal anti-Semitism and also the result of a widespread wish within German society. Anti-Semitism formed the frame of reference within which Hitler operated both during his rise to power and later as Führer and Reich Chancellor. The deprivation of rights and stigmatization of the Jews took place gradually, and when military successes opened up the possibility for mass killing they were killed. Hitler did not need to order the genocide; it was sufficient for him to clear the way for the Holocaust, as he did with the Directive for Special Areas for Order No. 21.

This observation makes it necessary to study the plausibility of the various conjectures as to the causes of Hitler's anti-Semitism and his psychological disposition as a whole. This consideration centres around the recurrent myths and legends, whose patterns remained constant even if the specific formulations differed.

## 2007: Dani Levy's *Mein Führer* and the Scientific Basis for a Hitler Persiflage

On 28 May 2005 director Dani Levy applied for official funding for his film project *Mein Führer*. He told the committee that he had deliberately avoided carrying out 'meticulous research'. Instead of historical facts he sought to create a projection, to establish a fictional figure to be placed within the 'moral tragedy of an era'. Levy wrote a comedy about Hitler's last days in the bunker underneath the Reich Chancellery, which was nevertheless based on how he imagined the real Hitler to have been.[59] He assumed without question that Hitler 'suffered from depressions' and had him portrayed by Helge Schneider as a bundle of nerves, externally controlled and lost in a dream world. Hitler breaks down several times in the film and is restored by his (Jewish) speech trainer. When the latter's wife tries to kill him, the professor protests: 'You are doing the same as him! You are killing a defenceless man. He is also just an unloved child!'[60]

In his simple explanation of the murderous Nazi regime Levy makes specific reference to Alice Miller, 'one of the most well-known and popular psychologists of our time'.[61] He is no doubt thinking of the most influential book by the Swiss psychologist, the controversial *For Your Own Good: Hidden Cruelty in Child-Rearing and the Roots of Violence*. The book is not about Hitler, however, or a psychoanalytical discussion of the Nazi regime but an indictment of 'early childhood suffering' caused by education.[62] Like her other examples, she used Hitler only as an illustration for her general critique of society.[63] Hitler was predestined to become a mass murderer, says Miller, his life being the 'outcome of a tragic childhood'.[64] This type of analysis is now considered outdated, also in forensic psychology, but was still highly topical in 1980, when Miller's book appeared.

In any case, the evidence that Adolf Hitler was constantly humiliated as a child by his father Alois is quite meagre. Miller claims that Alois Hitler thrashed his son every day, that he was an alcoholic, emotionally unstable and that he was even admitted once to an asylum.[65] None of these claims are verified in any way apart from a report by Hitler that he had once received thirty strokes from his father.[66] Regarding the mother, Miller assumes that Hitler was not loved but merely 'spoiled'. In psychological terms, love means that 'the mother is open and sensitive to her child's true needs'. Because she did not love her son, he was 'showered with things he (did) not need' but only as 'ersatz for that which parents are unable to give their child because of their own problems'. Even if historians were to

17

allow in retrospect that Hitler's relationship to his mother was diffi-cult, Miller's conclusion nevertheless appears wayward: 'If Hitler had really been loved as a child, he would also have been capable of love. His relationships with women, his perversions, and his whole aloof and basically cold relationships with people in general reveal that he never received love from any quarter.'[67]

## Hereditary Diseases: The Fragmentary Information about Hitler's Ancestors

Psychohistorians thus seek the key to Hitler's deep-seated hatred in the family, be it through the father Alois or the mother Klara.[68] This idea is not new and there were rumours even in the 1930s that Hitler hated the Jews because his father Alois Hitler was of Jewish descent and allegedly even a 'half-Jew'. This rumour appeared to be con-firmed by a statement by Hitler's erstwhile lawyer Hans Frank, who converted to Catholicism while interned in Nuremberg and made an extensive and subsequently published confession. This transcript taken down while facing the gallows proved to be inaccurate in every respect.[69] The thesis that Hitler's father was a 'half-Jew' has now also been refuted. The alleged father, a Jewish businessman by the name of 'Frankenberger', did not exist, or at least not in places where Alois Hitler's mother, Maria Anna Schicklgruber, lived her life (between 1795 and 1847).[70]

Research into Hitler's ancestors revealed, however, that Alois Schicklgruber, born illegitimately in 1837, was possibly begotten not by Johann Georg Hiedler, who was registered as the father, but by Johann's brother Nepomuk Hüttler. (The different spellings of the name are due to different phonetic transcriptions.) Hüttler was the grandfather of Klara Pölzl, Alois Hitler's third wife and Adolf Hitler's mother. So even if Johann Georg Hiedler had been Alois Hitler's father, Klara Pölzl would still have been a first cousin once removed.[71] It was thus only a short step to the conclusion that Hitler came from a family in which 'inbreeding' or 'incest' prevailed and that he was thus probably 'mentally ill'. The assumption that Hitler possibly suffered from a hereditary mental disorder has been magni-fied by numerous television reports and uninhibited and exaggerated reporting by the tabloid press.[72]

Credence was given to this presumption by Hitler's reluctance to talk about his family. In view of the taboo surrounding incest, which still exists today, Hitler refused to answer questions about his ancestry and relationships within the family, revealing instead a manifest lack of interest, stating demonstratively that his family was the German people and not his Austrian relatives.[73] It is now also known that Hitler deceived his audience in this regard as well. As a young man he was appreciative of his family and spent his holidays with them.[74] Hitler also avoided answering why he had never married and founded a family. He said to his secretary Traudl Junge: 'I believe it is irresponsible to found a family . . . I find that the descendants of geniuses usually have it very hard in the world. They are expected to have the same stature as their famous ancestors and are not allowed to be mediocre. Besides, they are usually cretins.'[75] Was it merely the fact that he thought he was a genius that prevented him from having a family, or was it fear of the possible consequences of inbreeding?

It is not impossible that there were hereditary diseases in Hitler's family, because the Waldviertel in Austria, where he came from, was a self-contained area with a small marriage radius. In many cases, as with Hitler's parents, who grew up in Spital, both spouses came from the same place.[76] It is true that in sub-populations like the Waldviertel, where the people live in geographical, religious or social isolation, fluctuations in the gene distribution can occur from generation to generation.[77] In the 1930s, between 45 and 60 per cent of marriages in central Europe were between people born in the same locality. Before the Second World War, the marriage radius in Germany was around ten kilometres, whereas by the 1970s and 1980s it had increased to thirty-five to fifty-five kilometres. In Hitler's family the radius was very small, less than one kilometre.

It is known that physical (i.e. external) and internal features as well as certain talents and hereditary diseases are passed on from generation to generation. With monogenic heredity, there is a 50 per cent probability of the disease. The probability in the case of polygenic heredity caused by several hereditary factors and also by environmental influences varies. Generations can be bypassed.[78] The course of monogenic diseases can be determined relatively easily by tracing the heredity, but such analyses are much more difficult in the case of the more common polygenic or multifactorial hereditary diseases.

The evidence with regard to Hitler's parents, however, would seem to indicate that they were both healthy and that the children who died before Hitler's birth did not suffer from hereditary diseases. Even if incomplete, the family tree, which he subsequently demanded of every German as proof of their Aryan roots, can be traced in Hitler's case back to his great-grandfather. It reveals that his ancestors were long-lived and died of old-age complaints like 'dropsy' or 'apoplexy' but not of any recurrent disease in the family.

There are two distant relatives of Hitler who appear to have suffered from a 'mental disease'. Johanna Pölzl, the sister of Hitler's mother Klara ('Aunt Hanni'), who helped in the house and lived with the family until her death, is said to have been 'feeble-minded' or 'retarded'.[79] Besides, she also had a hump, which was alleged in those days to be an indication of mental deficiency. She died in 1911 in a diabetic coma, i.e. insulin deficiency.[80] Finally, there is a further indication of 'mental illness' in one of Hitler's distant relations, Aloisia Veit, who was born on 18 July 1891. The medical record, which still survives today, starts in 1932. The medical officer wrote that the patient, who normally worked as a chambermaid, began to behave very strangely. She claimed to see ghosts and would start to cry for no reason. She was admitted to Steinhof Psychiatric Clinic in Vienna on 26 January 1932. She often reacted aggressively to other patients and had to be sedated on several occasions. In 1938 she described herself as a 'Communist' and refused, not for the first time, to eat. Her behaviour fluctuated between restlessness and agitation on the one hand and a 'friendly' collegial manner in the sewing room on the other. She was transferred to Ybbs an der Donau on 28 November 1940 and probably killed at Hartheim Castle near Linz on 6 December 1940.[81]

When considering whether Hitler might have suffered from a hereditary disease it is necessary to determine how close the relationship was. Aloisia Veit was the great-granddaughter of the sister of Maria Anna Schicklgruber, who had married Johann Georg Hiedler, the official father of Adolf Hitler's father. Hitler and his great-great-aunt were thus three generations apart. On this basis it is not possible to infer a shared 'hereditary disease'.

There were no 'mental' diseases or 'mood disorders', as they were called at the time, in Hitler's direct ascendant line or in the families of Hitler's ancestors (Hiedler or Hüttler, Schicklgruber and Pölzl). It is possible, however, that Hitler's skin complaint was hereditary. The desquamation and inflammatory reactions on Hitler's left lower leg were known not only to Theodor Morell, who was requested to treat what he described as 'eczema' shortly after he became Hitler's personal physician.[82] It is unlikely that Hitler's skin disease was confined to his left leg, because he himself spoke of annoying eczema on both legs.[83]

According to the differential diagnosis by Professor Wolfram Sterry from Charité Hospital in Berlin, Hitler might have been suffering from psoriasis, a hereditary skin disease.[84] It can be caused by stress and medical drugs, neither of which was in short supply. The disease is also polygenic and does not therefore appear in every generation.[85] The biographies and memoirs tend to talk of eczema rather than psoriasis. Morell also assumed this to be the case but without making a differential diagnosis. It is impossible to determine whether Hitler suffered from eczema or psoriasis, whether it was a reaction to exogenous or endogenous stimuli, or whether it was recessively inherited.

## 1918: Gas Poisoning and Hypnosis

An injury incurred by Hitler and other soldiers in his unit on 14 October 1918 following a mustard gas (*Lost* in German)[86] attack by the British near Wervik, Belgium, has given rise to considerable discussion. Biographers Werner Maser and Joachim Fest believe that Hitler's temporary blindness was caused by poison gas.[87] Even in the 1920s, however, there were those who suggested that Hitler was 'hysterical', in other words mentally ill, or that he might even have been pretending. There are no medical records to verify the 1918 diagnosis.

The discussion that raged in the 1970s[88] was resurrected in 2004 by the jurist and author Bernhard Horstmann. He reconstructed Hitler's time at the field hospital in Pasewalk in meticulous detail and came out emphatically in favour of 'hysterical blindness'.[89] The arguments presented in his book *Hitler in Pasewalk* are cogent and worthy of discussion. His hypotheses regarding Hitler's treatment by the psychiatrist Edmund Forster are less convincing, however.

It has been established that Hitler suffered severe conjunctivitis and inflammation of the eyelid, had impaired vision for a time and also claimed to have been blind for a short while. Genuine blindness is irreversible, however. It is possible retrospectively to surmise that the inflammation was so severe that Hitler could not see. Inflammations of this type subside after a time, however. On the other hand, a hysterical reaction cannot be ruled out.

It is known that functional blindness can occur without an objectifiable pathological condition of the eye as a result of psychogenic causes, shock or hysteria.[90] The fact that Hitler was in the neurology and psychiatry ward at the Pasewalk field hospital would also appear to indicate a psychogenic condition. At the same time, the effects of mustard gas are reversible. It causes extreme irritation and burning of the skin and mucosa. The eye is most sensitive to this effect and

21

the eyelid swells up to such an extent that the eye cannot be properly opened, causing a temporary impairment of vision.[91]

In Hitler's case it is therefore impossible to tell whether the cause of his condition was hysterical blindness or the effects of mustard gas. The answer is no longer important today, but it was highly relevant in the 1920s and 1930s. Psychiatric conditions caused by exogenous events were not accepted by society after the First World War as they might be today. On the contrary, although there were tens of thousands of shell-shocked veterans, often soldiers who had been buried alive in the trenches, they were not regarded as war victims but as 'weaklings'.[92] Psychiatrists in the Weimar Republic attempted to rectify this situation, but 'mental illnesses' remained socially taboo and were thought to be incurable. If there had been the slightest suggestion that Hitler suffered from such a condition, his rise and the aura surrounding him after 1932 as the beacon of hope for the German people would have been seriously jeopardized.

This could be the reason why Reich Minister of Defence Kurt von Schleicher attempted to get hold of Hitler's medical records. Moreover, contemporary witnesses claim credibly that he succeeded in doing so. They were not published, however, because von Schleicher was not interested in publicly discrediting Hitler but rather in including him in a government under his chancellorship. The fact remains that everyone who might have seen Hitler's medical record from Pasewalk met a violent end. Kurt von Schleicher and his deputy Major General Ferdinand von Bredow, who is alleged to have obtained the record, were both shot in 1934. The treating psychiatrist Edmund Robert Forster, who held a professorship at the University of Greifswald after the First World War, was driven to suicide. The Jewish doctor Ernst Weiss, to whom Forster is said to have given his shorthand records of Hitler's treatment, committed suicide after the German army entered Paris.[93]

Weiss had previously turned Forster's information into a novel entitled *Der Augenzeuge* (The Eyewitness), which was not published, however, until 1963.[94] The first-person narrator discusses Adolf Hitler ('A. H.') as a former patient in Pasewalk. Although the fictional form inevitably contains inaccuracies, the historical authenticity of the characters and events is confirmed by statements and reports by contemporary witnesses. Weiss describes treatment using hypnosis that cured the patient.

A. H. Horstmann believes that this description is true to the facts and irrefutable. The first-person narrator plants the suggestion while Hitler is in a hypnotic trance that although there were no miracles

22

any more, it was possible that 'miracles still occurred sometimes on chosen subjects . . . to whom nature defers'. He, the narrator, was just a simple doctor, but perhaps his patient had 'the rare power that occurs once in a thousand years, to perform miracles'. It was thus up to the patient to bring about the cure. In the case described by Weiss, the patient does indeed manage to perform a miracle: he opens his eyes and can see again. After the treatment, however, the doctor forgets to wake Hitler from his trance and he remains under hypnosis. That, at least, is the fictional version.

It is unclear why the first-person narrator, based on the psychiatrist Edmund Robert Forster, does not wake up the patient. Horstmann attributes it to Forster's abrupt departure from Pasewalk and the confusion reigning at the time. As a result, says Horstmann, Hitler remained in a hypnotic trance for the rest of his life.[95] He concludes that 'the accumulation of Forster's will with Hitler's no doubt stronger will, combined with the liberation from the psychological handicap caused by the blindness, opened up the way for the release of the latent malice in Hitler's character'. In his view this hypothesis could help to explain the 'mystery of Hitler's incomprehensible metamorphosis after Pasewalk'.[96]

If we take this argument to its logical conclusion, it would mean that Hitler was able to hypnotize his audience because the subject who had himself been hypnotized in Pasewalk had become a mass hypnotist in his own right. The fact that Professor Forster did not wake Hitler from his hypnotic trance provided an apology for Hitler, since he was not acting according to his own will. The existing image of Hitler thus needed to be reassessed, since the future dictator had been the victim of a hypnotic cure that had been left unfinished.

From a medical point of view, however, the assumption that Hitler had not returned to reality and had remained in a hypnotic trance is 'poorly researched and unworthy of discussion'.[97] There is no reason, either, to suppose that Edmund Robert Forster, the real doctor, treated his patients superficially or without the requisite expertise. Forster had written his habilitation thesis at Charité Hospital in 1910 on anxiety psychosis. He published a paper on traumatic neuroses in 1915[98] and one on hysterical reaction and simulation in 1917. This paper does not mention hypnosis at all, alluding merely to the 'usual suggestion methods'. Forster's standard treatment of hysterics was cold showers, electric shock and painful prostate massage. He regarded his suggestion not as a treatment but as a means of turning hysterics into soldiers capable of returning to the front. His idea was to make the stay in the field hospital as unpleasant as possible.[99] His inhuman method of treatment appears to have been so successful that he later came to the conclusion that patients of this type did not need suggestion treatment at all, as they would sooner or later become healthy again of their own accord.[100]

From a historical point of view, the idea that Hitler suddenly became 'different' as a result of hypnosis is also untenable. Hitler's ideological convictions evolved slowly. His hatred of the Jews had already started in Austria and became more radical during the war. Other political agenda items were not formulated until the 1920s, during his imprisonment in Landsberg or while writing the second volume of *Mein Kampf* in 1926.[101] There was no sudden decision of the kind 'I for my part decided to go into politics',[102] as he later formulated it. In December 1918 he was not even sure that he could be the instigator of a national movement. On the contrary, Hitler's character, painstakingly reconstructed by numerous historians, developed slowly between 1918 and 1925, as he hesitated between left- and right-wing politics. Hitler belonged to a workers' and soldiers' council and worked as an informer for the Reichswehr on 'populist movements'.[103] He was not even certain of his abilities as an organizer or agitator, as his activities in spring and summer 1919 reveal. Although he made speeches to soldiers, after undergoing training himself, it was only as a member of the German Workers' Party after September 1919 that he developed his idea of influencing the masses through propaganda. His first public speech before a large audience was on 13 November 1919.[104] The 'different Hitler', whom Horstmann describes as a product of an unsuccessful hypnosis, did not develop suddenly in a field hospital in Pasewalk, but evolved slowly over a long period. Hitler expert Anton Joachimsthaler sums it up nicely: 'Hitler's career began in Munich.'

## Supposed Compulsions: Hand-Washing, Fear of Bacteria and Syphilis

Contemporary witnesses confirm that Hitler used to wash his hands frequently and that he was afraid of infectious diseases. Psychologists have interpreted this as a pathological 'compulsion'.[105] First of all, it should be pointed out that Germany – including the Führer headquarters – at the beginning of the twentieth century was dirty by today's standards. People used coal for heating and many streets and paths were not paved, causing considerable amounts of dust, particularly in summer. Flushing toilets existed in wealthy private

1.   From a manual for field doctors in the First World War with hygiene regulations for building a latrine. The canister contained denatured alcohol, which could be obtained easily from distilleries in the conquered territories. The injunction "Wash your hands" was to be strictly followed. "Disinfect your hands" would have been even better. Courtesy of Henrik Eberle.

homes but not in the places where Hitler lived until the 1920s. Faeces accumulated in pits. When the pits became full, the contents had to be shovelled out and collected in drums, which were then taken by horse and cart to sewage farms.[106] The situation was even more extreme at the front, where soldiers had to dig pits quickly for use as latrines.[107] During the two world wars thousands of people died of infectious diseases, particularly cholera, dysentery and typhus. Military experts have surmised that the control of these problems played a decisive role in the outcome.[108] There is thus every reason to believe that Hitler could well have taken to heart the recommendations by army doctors about hand-washing.[109] It can hardly be classified as a 'compulsion' in the psychiatric sense.

The supposition that Hitler had syphilis is also made repeatedly in connection with this alleged compulsive behaviour. One person who spread this rumour was Heinrich Himmler's personal masseur Felix Kersten. He claimed that Himmler divulged to him 'the greatest Reich and state secret', namely that Hitler had contracted syphilis during the First World War with later complications appearing from mid-1942. Hitler's megalomania, his obstinacy, the feared tantrums and trembling hands were all due to syphilis. The diary published by Kersten after the Second World War subsequently turned out to be fake, and Kersten is regarded overall as a 'completely unreliable witness'.[110]

Hitler's personal physician Morell routinely checked for sexually transmitted diseases as part of the regular blood analyses. The finding for 15 January 1940 reads: 'Wassermann-Meinicke turbidity and Kahn reaction negative'. According to the available knowledge at the time, Hitler did not therefore have syphilis.[111] As the Wassermann reaction is not completely reliable, however, it is impossible to fully exclude the possibility.

One indication that Hitler might have suffered from syphilis is the seemingly irrational comments in *Mein Kampf* about the disease, where he states that this 'frightful plague' was a result of prostitution and the 'Jewification of our spiritual life and mammonization of our mating instinct'.[112] In view of these comments, was it not possible to suppose that Hitler had been infected by a Jewish prostitute?[113] In reality, Hitler's comments can also be seen as a polemical opinion in the context of intense public discussion of the subject.

The topic gained relevance in view of the large number of people suffering from syphilis, gonorrhoea and chancre. There are no precise figures but it is estimated that around 0.5 per cent of the population suffered from these diseases and among young people at least 2 per cent.[114] The figure rose during the war and there was a particularly rapid increase in 1919, when doctors recorded over 44,000 new cases per month.[115] Syphilis was a problem of epidemic proportions and was considered incurable until the discovery of Salvarsan (arsphenamine) in 1910. As a result, there was a strong movement in society with dozens of large associations that fought to prevent the spread of venereal diseases. Their aim was to promote and restore good morals through popular science and religious propaganda.[116] Hitler adopted the demands of these groups, effectively linking the socially accepted ideal of a happy, healthy family with anti-Semitic tirades. This is another example of Hitler's propaganda style of attacking the Jews without indicating his influences and points of reference. However, the idea that he might have suffered himself from the disease should be discarded as inapplicable.

## Hitler's Genitalia

In December 2008, there were over 200,000 Google hits for the search item 'Hitler one ball', and Internet users are also reliably informed that Hitler's penis was bitten off by a billy goat. The entertainer Harald Schmidt used these long-standing rumours as material for a sketch that has become a classic on YouTube, in which he jokes that Hitler started the war in order to look for his 'lost bollock'.[117]

New 'facts' came to light in November 2008, discovered by the British tabloid newspaper *The Sun*. The scoop was immediately taken up by *Der Spiegel* and *Bild*, which announced 'How Hitler lost his testicle' and described knowingly how 'he screamed in agony'.[118] According to *Der Spiegel* the 'testicle surgeon' told a Polish priest, who later gave his memos to a Polish amateur historian. According to *Bild* it was not the surgeon but a medical orderly named Johan Jambor. It continued stating 'the attempt to transport Adolf Hitler to a field hospital ended after a few metres – the French began their shelling again'. The medical orderlies are then alleged to have left the seriously wounded Hitler to his fate.

It is unlikely that Hitler, screaming with pain on the battlefield, would ask a medical orderly – in between his calls for help – whether he could still have children, as *Bild* and *Der Spiegel* would have us believe. It is also questionable whether a medical orderly among the craters of no less a major encounter than the Battle of the Somme in 1916, in which there were more than one million killed and wounded on both sides, would recall every individual wounded soldier. Besides, it is unrealistic that a medical orderly could have examined Hitler's scrotum so closely as to be able to determine the precise injury. According to the medical orderly, the wounded soldier's legs were 'full of blood' and it also likely that remnants of clothing were stuck in the wound. However improbable the story sounds, it is still necessary to verify it.

A reliable post-mortem report would provide an answer to this question. It is known that Hitler's body was burnt together with Eva Braun's and the remains buried in a shell crater in the garden of the Reich Chancellery where they were found on 3 May 1945 by members of SMERSH, the Soviet counter-intelligence agency, but then buried again. On 5 May, after the error had been noticed, Soviet soldiers exhumed the 'two incinerated corpses' together with those of two dogs. The bodies were wrapped in blankets and packed in ammunition crates.[119] The subsequent hasty post-mortem was regarded by the Soviet security services as sloppy and for that reason the garden of the Reich Chancellery was excavated again on 30 May 1946 and two fragments of Hitler's left and right parietal bone were discovered. A new forensic analysis was not carried out, however, because the two rival secret services – the KGB (to which SMERSH now belonged) and the NKVD – disputed responsibility.[120]

Regardless of the competence of the Soviet forensic pathologists headed by Dr Faust Shkaravski, it is known that only fragments of the corpse were available. Shkaravski wrote: 'The myocardium is tough and looks like boiled meat.' The penis was burnt and the scrotum 'singed but intact'. 'The left testicle', he continued, 'could not be found in the inguinal canal or in the pelvis.' One possible explanation is that the testicle was lost during the transportation of the body parts. Another is that the post-mortem report was deliberately falsified. This was certainly the case with regard to the cause of death, since Shkaravski had been instructed to prove that Hitler had taken poison like a coward and had not under any circumstances shot himself. The pathologist obediently came to this incorrect conclusion. The historian Lev Bezymenski, who started the myth about Hitler's body and thus indirectly his monorchism in 1968, apologized to his readers in 1995 for the 'deliberate lies' he had spread by order of the KGB.[121]

The answer to the speculation about Hitler's missing testicle, which had already played a certain role in Allied propaganda,[122] can be found in a protocol written by Hitler's personal physician Dr Theodor Morell in the possession of the Nuremberg prosecutor Robert M. W. Kempner.

First of all, it is known that Dr Morell carried out a thorough examination of Hitler in 1936 so as to provide a reliable basis for treatment. In the course of this examination, which also included an anamnesis, or reconstruction of the patient's medical history, Morell noted a scar 'in the middle and on the side' of Hitler's left thigh. The abdominal examination revealed that the cremasteric reflexes were 'detectable' and that there was no indication of an 'inguinal or femoral hernia'.[123] The fact that Morell mentions the absence of an inguinal hernia indicates that he had also examined Hitler's private parts. Regarding the possibility of missing testicles, the fact that the cremasteric reflexes were normal is important, since the cremaster muscle consists of muscle fibre passing along the outside of the sper-

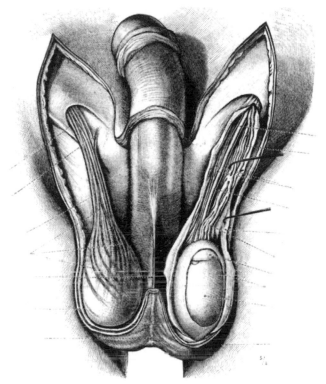

2. This illustration from a 1907 anatomy textbook shows the male reproductive organs. The penis is pointed upwards and the skin and tissue layers have been removed. On the right is the cremaster muscle, which elevates the testis. The muscle is contracted by stroking the inside of the thigh. If the reflex is normal the testis on that side rises. Hitler's personal physician Theodor Morell tested the cremasteric reflex in 1936. Courtesy of Hans-Joachim Neumann.

matic cord and attached to the internal spermatic fascia, which surround the testicles. When the inside of the thigh is lightly stroked the testicles rise.

Another doctor, Dr Eduard Bloch, also confirmed the presence of both testicles. Bloch was the Hitler family doctor, who examined not only Hitler's mother but also Hitler himself. In American exile in 1943, he confirmed that Hitler's genitalia were normal. When the interrogator persisted and asked whether the examination had really extended to the genitalia, Bloch replied: 'Of course. They were completely normal.'[124] One can only agree with the British historian Alan Bullock who, on being asked by a journalist about Hitler's testicles, shrugged his shoulders and replied that it was just a 'one-ball business'.[125]

Another myth needs to be verified in this context regarding the rumour that Hitler's penis was deformed. There are two versions of this often recounted story: that his penis was bitten off, and that he had hypospadias, a congenital defect of the urethra in which the opening is on the underside of the penis and is also often constricted and the foreskin abnormally formed. Those affected generally feel otherwise healthy, although urinating standing up can be difficult if not impossible. Erectile dysfunction can also occur. Morell reports, however, that Hitler had no problems with urination or retention and that the bladder and sphincter tone were normal.[126] Moreover, there is only one single piece of evidence indicating that Hitler might have suffered from this anomaly in the form of a minute by Morell of a conversation of 25 October 1944.[127] The conversation concerned bacterial infections of the urinary system (cystitis) during which Hitler asked about the meaning of hypospadias and spina bifida ('split spine', which Hitler certainly did not suffer from).

Morell's entry for the 10.30 p.m. conversation states verbatim: 'Voice almost better. We talked about the water supply here – it is hard and swarming with bacteria that are not pathogenic but can still upset the metabolism. I said his urine was certainly full of bacteria again. Conversation about hypospadias, spina bifida, cystopyelitis with pathogenic coliform bacteria centred mainly in the prostate. Latter needs to be examined by me soon. Patient prefers to administer nose drops himself.'

In interpreting this entry, it is important to point out that Hitler frequently asked experts for explanations on all kinds of subjects. Reichsbank president Hjalmar Schacht recalls that he would often ask about economics.[128] Hitler's adjutant Fritz Wiedemann also commented on Hitler's sometimes naive questions and desire for more precise information or even instruction.[129] During the table talk, the *Brockhaus* encyclopaedia would also be consulted on occasion if none of those present had an answer. This casual approach to interlocutors and Hitler's non-specific curiosity would disappear to the degree that Hitler no longer trusted the person concerned.[130] Hitler still trusted Morell in 1944, however, and the conclusion that his inquiry about a urethra anomaly was explicitly prompted by a pathological disorder of his own is anything but convincing. It is more likely to have been a comment in a casual conversation.

Curious though it might sound, the story of Hitler's bitten penis is more plausible because it was reported by a contemporary witness whom Hitler did not know personally and who was not obliged after 1945 to justify his involvement with the Nazi dictatorship. On the contrary, this incredible story is related by Dietrich Güstrow, a lawyer who worked from 1933 to 1945 in Berlin as a defence counsel.[131] After 1945, Güstrow continued his career in central Germany. As he was not a member of the NSDAP and was an experienced lawyer he was employed by Merseburg regional council. He escaped from East Germany in the 1950s, however, and subsequently held the position of town clerk of Penne near Hanover.[132] Historians have not to date been able to detect any serious errors in his hugely anti-Communist and anti-Nazi memoirs.[133] His comments as public defence counsel for Eugen Wasner in 1943 are thus credible. Wasner, a former fellow pupil of Hitler and in addition a naive but deeply god-fearing person, had said to battle comrades: 'Oh yeah, Adolf! Even as a kid he was dumb enough to allow a goat to bite off half of his willy . . . He'd made a bet that he could pee into the mouth of a goat . . . I held the goat fast between my legs and Adolf peed into its mouth. As he was doing it, a friend pulled away the stick and the goat jumped up and bit him on the willy. Adi screamed terribly and ran away crying.'

Wasner was naturally denounced and charged. Güstrow requested to the military tribunal that a psychiatric opinion be obtained on the accused since mental illness would make him incompetent (according to section 51 of the Criminal Code) or at least be an extenuating circumstance. The request was refused, however, because Wasner insisted and swore 'by Jesus and Mary' that he was telling the truth.[134]

Even if it is assumed that Güstrow and Wasner were indeed telling the truth, there is still a need to verify whether Hitler's penis was really 'bitten off' and if he himself became 'nutty' as a result, as the dramatist Rolf Hochhuth stubbornly claims.[135] Wasner's story can only have occurred in 1895–6. The penis in boys aged six or seven years is usually around four to six centimetres in length and not particularly prominent. The goat must have had very good aim and Hitler no reflexes for his penis to have been bitten. Besides, it would also invalidate all of the testimony about Hitler's sexual activity. There can thus be no doubt that Wasner was wrong about the consequences of the goat story, even if he himself believed it to be true. Fritz Redlich was quite generous when he rejected the discussion about Hitler's 'genital damage' as 'too unspecific' to link it with the far-reaching speculation about his anti-Semitism.[136]

Ultimately, it must be concluded that all sources appear to indicate that Hitler's genitalia were 'normal', although it should also be pointed out that no reliable primary sources are to hand for the years before 1945. There is no precise description of Hitler's penis and testicles in any medical record, in a mistress's diary, in Morell's minutes or Eva Braun's diary. Speculation about a bitten or deformed penis is nevertheless highly questionable. The spectacular 'findings' may be regarded as a continuation of the Soviet myths dating from 1945. The reasons why individual 'contemporary witnesses' might have made these statements can only be guessed at.

## Gay – Sick, Hitler's 'Homosexuality' According to Sources and Statements

Until 1992 the World Health Organization International Classification of Diseases and Related Health Problems listed homosexuality as a disease.[137] The German legal system prosecuted homosexuals (particularly men) from the mid-nineteenth century, although with varying intensity. The courts have always followed the mood of society, ranging from harsh prosecution of 'unnatural acts' to the relative leniency in the heyday of the Wilhelmine empire, not least because there were avowed homosexuals in the highest government positions. There were general staff officers who dressed in tutus to give cabaret performances in the imperial court, and some of the emperor's closest advisers were said to have homosexual leanings. It was regarded as quite legitimate to enjoy the sight of handsome men in uniform and to perform what were in fact punishable sexual acts.[138] Berlin became the capital of the 'third sex', and before the First World War gays and lesbians who didn't make a show of the fact were able to live practically undisturbed.[139]

During the Age of Reason under Frederick the Great and his famous Round Table, morals were not as strict as people would have liked of their king, who enjoyed conversation with educated and witty men. One picture painted by Antoine Pesne from designs by the king for the evening dinners showed 'young men embracing women (and) mounting billing turtle doves, bucks and rams, goats and sheep'. 'If anyone had suddenly entered, seen this picture and heard us, they would have though that the Seven Sages of Greece were amusing themselves in a brothel.'[140]

In the subsequent intensive medical discussion, fuelled by Sigmund Freud's revolutionary new findings, a relatively clearly defined 'pathology' crystallized, more a 'sexual orientation', because it describes 'arousal and activity in relation to a partner of the same sex'.[141] Section 175 of the Reich Criminal Code of 15 May 1871 made homosexual activity a criminal offence in the German Reich, whereas distinctions had been made in the Wilhelmine era on the basis of class and social status, with the aristocracy and prosperous citizens being hardly touched. During the Weimar Republic public prosecutors and police could also exercise considerable discretion. The stigma nevertheless remained: in the public eye homosexuals were not equated with Greek heroes like Patroclus and Achilles but were seen as 'cowardly faggots in women's clothing'.[142]

Soon after the Nazis came to power, all associations and magazines connected with the homosexual subculture were closed down. It was not until 28 June 1935 that an amendment to Section 175 of the Criminal Code introduced much tougher sanctions. A lexicon from the Nazi era defined homosexuality, in contrast to *Brockhaus*, which in 1908 had described it relatively impartially as a 'contrary sexual sentiment',[143] as a 'pathological' sexual desire for persons of the same sex.[144] Homosexuals were branded as a result as 'deviant' and a 'danger to society'. If a conviction under the more severe Section 175 of the Criminal Code did not achieve the desired effect, victims were sent to concentration camps and in some cases forced to undergo sterilization, the culmination of social stigmatization in connection with homosexuality.[145]

The tougher laws were only introduced after the murder of Ernst Röhm and other members of the SA leadership. Within the NSDAP a different approach had originally prevailed, described explicitly by Hitler in 1931. The military formations of the Party were an 'association of men for a specific political purpose' and not a 'moral institution for the education of young ladies' but rather a 'collection of tough fighters'. The private life of the SA men would only be of interest if it conflicted with the 'main principles' of the Nazi ideology.[146]

According to the historian Anna Maria Sigmund, an expert in Hitler's surroundings in the 1920s and 1930s, Hitler himself regarded homosexuals as 'disgusting creatures'. As a 'cool and pragmatic politician', however, he was willing to make concessions and had therefore tolerated the debauchery, excessive even by today's standards, of the SA leadership.[147]

Whatever place homosexuality might have in an individual's private system of values today,[148] it is nevertheless legitimate to ask whether Hitler's actions could have been influenced by his own homosexuality. It might be discussed, for example, whether Hitler's ability to attract so many men was due to his portrayal of the NSDAP as a sexually charged, homoerotic mass movement. Against this argument is the fact that it was not until after Hitler came to power that the display of virility provoked irrational admiration and enthusiasm – by both sexes.[149] Another possibility to be considered is that Hitler had sexual relations with his closest associates, which would explain the extreme loyalty that was shown to him.[150]

In his book *The Hidden Hitler*, which was published in 2001, the historian Lothar Machtan states that some sources suggested that Hitler might have had a relationship of this nature with his SA head and *Du* friend Ernst Röhm, but he considered it 'improbable'. Above all, he noted, Hitler recognized Röhm's talent for planning and organization. He admired his friend's 'manliness', which he liked to emulate. Rohm taught him 'how to reconcile a self-assured, masculine manner with homosexual tendencies'. Machtan concludes: 'The fact that they were both homosexual, which can hardly have escaped them, would have been conducive to a great sense of attachment.'[151]

Machtan presents further possible or likely sexual partners of Hitler, including:

Rudolf Hess, student and Hitler's secretary with very good connections to academic circles;

Ernst Hanfstaengl, wealthy son of a publisher with very good connections to Munich's cultural smart set and Hitler's chief press officer;[152]

Emil Maurice, head of Hitler's 'stewards', the nucleus of the SA, who had many contacts with 'landsknechts' and Freikorps fighters;

Julius Schreck, founder of 'Stosstrupp Hitler' in 1923 and the SS in 1926, successor to Maurice as Hitler's chauffeur.

Machtan also mentions Hans-Severus Ziegler, chief dramaturge of the German National Theatre in Weimar, as a possible lover of Hitler. Finally he presents numerous police reports about a man speaking in Austrian dialect who is said to have approached young male prostitutes in Munich. In passing he also describes Baldur von Schirach, head of the Hitler Youth, and Joseph Goebbels, Gauleiter of Berlin and propaganda minister, as people with a tendency to homosexuality. The liquidation of the SA leadership in 1934 could thus be interpreted as an act of liberation by Hitler whom, according to Machtan, the *Pariser Tageblatt* had described as a 'prisoner of homosexuals'.[153] Machtan therefore suggests that Hitler could well have made a clean sweep on 30 June and 1 July 1934, eliminating not only Ernst Röhm and the SA leadership but also anyone else who might have known about his homosexuality along with them.

Against this argument is the fact that Hitler, for all the crimes he committed, was not involved in drawing up the death lists in summer

1934. The killing was planned by Goebbels and Göring. Hitler was surprised and really believed that he had been betrayed and that Röhm was planning a coup.[154] The facts that the killing of over 1,000 people was also politically expedient because it eliminated the SA as a military factor and strengthened the position of the regular army was a spin-off effect and possibly even the real reason, although there are no documents to confirm this.

Machtan's book on Hitler's homosexuality provoked intensive discussion. Many reviewers rejected the bold hypothesis. In a ZDF interview, however, Machtan stated that there was an overwhelming abundance of circumstantial and supporting evidence to confirm the hypothesis. Anna Maria Sigmund by contrast says succinctly: 'Books that have claimed that Hitler was homosexual or indulged in deviant sexual practices have proved to be unsound.'[155] Werner Maser worked through the questionable evidence that Hitler was homosexual. Passing over the obvious absurd references to Goebbels or von Schirach, he devoted himself to the biography of Hans Mend, a key witness, who allegedly confirmed Hitler's homosexuality in the First World War. Machtan's most important 'witness' was indeed stationed with Hitler in Flanders during the First World War, but the former comrade-in-arms changed his story several times. He offered the NSDAP a 'heroic' version of Hitler's war experience, to the resistance a negative one. Maser thus describes him as a 'vagrant, troubled rogue' – an assessment that Mend's criminal record indeed suggests: he was convicted on several counts of theft and document forgery and was ultimately imprisoned for various sex crimes against women. He died in Zwickau prison.[156]

In summary, Sigmund states: 'After sober analysis of the material on this sensitive subject and the elimination of gossip, tattle, rumours and manipulated sources, there is little to shed an objective light on Hitler's sex life.' In her view, his sex drive was weak. Ultimately, she concludes, the question of whether Hitler had normal or perverted – and in any case always private – relations with Eva Braun and other women remains 'unanswered and an object of speculation'.[157]

## Heterosexual Hitler – Summary of Research

Hitler's relations with the opposite sex differed from the outset from those of his peers and comrades-in-arms. For years he was tormented by his schoolboy crush on a girl named Stefanie from Linz, while never once having the courage to talk to her, with the result that she had not the slightest idea how much she was 'loved' by a stranger. Kubizek wrote in 1953: 'Thus, Stefanie was two things for him, one part reality, and one part wish and imagination. Be that as it may, Stefanie was the most beautiful . . . and purest dream of his life.'[158]

There is no evidence that Hitler had a French mistress for several years called Charlotte Loboje while stationed on the Western Front. The relationship is even supposed to have produced a son, Jean-Marie Loret. The likeness to Hitler of this alleged son induced Hitler biographer Werner Maser and others to believe Loret's story.[159] This myth has now been disproven. The Belgian journalist Jean-Paul Mulders managed to obtain DNA samples from relatives of Adolf Hitler still living in Austria and the USA and had them examined in a laboratory that normally offers commercial paternity tests. A comparison with genetic material from Jean-Marie Loret, who died in 1985, demonstrated that Loret was not related to the Hitler family and could not therefore have been Adolf Hitler's son.[160]

When Hitler began his career as a politician in the 1920s, there were two groups of women who approached the Führer. The first group included the wives of prominent bankers, publishers and factory owners, all no longer teenagers, who wished to impress Hitler by making large donations of money. The other group consisted of financially insignificant but young and beautiful women. It would appear that Hitler had a weakness for well-built, athletic types.

Even before Eva Braun, Hitler is known to have had long relationships with several women, including his niece Geli Raubal, Magda Goebbels, Leni Riefenstahl, Winifred Wagner, the film actress Renate Müller, Maria (Mizzi) Reiter, daughter of a local politician from Berchtesgaden, Lady Unity Valkyrie Mitford, Inga Ley and Martha Dodd, daughter of the US ambassador. The list makes no claims to completeness and gives little indication of the intimacy of the relationships. Nevertheless, Maria Reiter later had her statement 'that Hitler was a man in every respect' authenticated by a notary.[161] Altogether, however, he never managed to change his basic outlook: for all that he 'loved' women, he feared their possibly damaging influence.

The evidence of Hitler's heterosexuality is thus less spurious than the reasons given for his alleged homosexuality. Eva Braun, his long-time companion and wife of short duration noted in her diary in 1935: 'He needs me only for certain purposes, there is no other possibility. When he says that he likes me, he means it only for the moment.'[162] On 10 May 1935 she wrote: 'As Mrs Hoffmann informed me gently and tactfully, he now has someone else. She is called Valkyrie and looks like one, legs included. But he likes them that size.'[163] Braun is referring to Lady Unity Valkyrie Mitford, sister-in-law of the leader of the British Fascist Party Sir Oswald Mosley.[164] Before Eva Braun, Hitler is known to have had long relationships with other women, including Gretl, the daughter of opera singer Leo Slezak.[165]

Hitler's personal physician Morell, who was not by any means a party to all of Hitler's private life, thought that Hitler was basically sexually potent. It was for that reason that from 1944 he administered the sex hormone testosterone, which had been discovered in 1935, along with hormone preparations prepared by himself (Orchikrin and Prostakrin).[166] The connection with the presence of Eva Braun is evident after Berghof, which Braun managed, became the Führer's headquarters from February to July 1944. From 21 November to 10 December 1944 she also lived with Hitler in the Reich Chancellery.[167] On 19 January 1945 she came back to Berlin, travelled briefly to Berchtesgaden in February and returned – possibly on 7 March – to the bunker underneath the Reich Chancellery.[168]

There can be no doubt that Morell administered the hormones in order to increase Hitler's potency and not merely as a 'general tonic' on account of myasthenia and reduced general health.[169] In the coy language of the time, in which faeces were referred to as 'motion' and genitalia by various misleading names, 'general tonic' meant precisely improving virility.

## 1976: The Jewish Doctor Eduard Bloch as 'Cause' of the Extermination of the Jews

In 1976 the American psychohistorian and professor at Brandeis University Rudolph Binion came out with a spectacular and highly controversial thesis. He believed that he had found the key to Hitler's pathological anti-Semitism, stating that in 1907 the doctor Eduard Bloch had treated Hitler's mother incorrectly for breast cancer, leading to her extremely painful and distressful death. Instead of morphine, which was relatively cheap, Bloch had opted for the expensive 'panacea' iodoform, applied in absurdly high doses to the festering wound where the amputated breast had been.[170]

Subconsciously, Hitler, who sincerely loved his mother, developed a hatred for the Jewish doctor as a result and extended this hatred to the Jews as a whole. Binion regards the fact that Hitler thanked Dr Bloch several times for his selfless attention as part of a complex psychological substitution process.[171]

Other theses by Binion contained in this book about Hitler were just as controversial but did not cause a furore because they were not politically sensitive. One example is the highly speculative suggestion that Hitler's mother was ultimately responsible for her son's criminal development because she breastfed him herself instead of giving him to a wet nurse. This 'breast-mouth incest', he claims, resulted in a very close attachment that made Hitler 'unsuitable for any normal erotic relationship'.[172] This excuse for Hitler, accompanied by his-torically inaccurate comments on the Holocaust, caused a storm of protest, but remained a possible explanation for Hitler's personal-ity.[173] Several psychoanalysts and historians attempted subsequently to verify whether this simple explanation for the Holocaust was plausible.

Some psychiatrists regard Binion's psychoanalytical arguments as sketchy and incorrect.[174] From a historical point of view, it is also misleading to attempt to trace a direct line from Hitler's original intentions to the genocide. Even more importantly, Binion's thesis about an incorrect treatment of Hitler's mother is based on a faulty interpretation of Bloch's notes. As Brigitte Hamann has investigated, Bloch cannot be reproached for the use of iodoform or for his fees. On the contrary, the wealthy family doctor charged Klara Hitler very little for his weeks of intensive treatment.[175] Nor were his qualifica-tions those of a 'poor people's' country doctor, as is occasionally claimed. After leaving school, he studied medicine, biology and philosophy at the University of Prague and completed the clinical semesters at the clinics of the Charles University of Prague while simultaneously performing military service. His doctoral thesis in 1899 was graded 'summa cum laude'. He rejected the position of an assistant at the gynaecology clinic in Dresden because a professor at the University of Prague had offered him an opening. Ultimately, however, Bloch turned his back on this academic career and the promise of tenure because he had established a wide circle of friends during his military service in Linz, fallen in love and wanted to marry. He therefore opened a surgery in Linz and quickly acquired the social standing necessary for him to marry.[176]

There can be no doubt that the thirty-five-year-old was well qualified and was at the height of his career when he treated Hitler's mother in 1907. The attempt to treat the open wounds with iodo-form gauze was by no means the action of an unqualified 'money grabber' but rather a serious endeavour using the medical knowledge available at the time. Iodoform, which is barely used today because of its proven allergic and side effects and the complicated application and intensive smell, has a disinfectant action, stops minor bleeding and alleviates pain, thus making it ideal as a treatment for the patient.[177]

It is probable that Bloch and Hitler were aware that Klara Hitler was likely to die of her disease. But both the doctor and the next of kin were interested in ensuring that she obtained the best possible treatment. According to Brigitte Hamann, the treatment did not place too great a strain on the family's finances. Moreover, there is no indication in the patient records for Klara Hitler that she was given an overdose, as Binion suggests. As Hamann states: 'Nowhere is there any indication of the extent of the iodoform dosage.'[178]

## 1963: Measles as a Pretext

A further monocausal medical explanation for Hitler's politics is the measles. It is interesting to note in this context that after the symptoms have disappeared the patient might still be left with epidemic encephalitic sequelae. A post-encephalitic psycho-syndrome as a later complication of measles could offer an explanation for Hitler's frequent outbursts of rage, which contemporaries described as 'uncontrolled'. Viral encephalitis would also present a plausible explanation for the apparently irrational behaviour of the dictator in his management of the war and also, ultimately, the otherwise inexplicable extermination of the Jews – Hitler was quite simply 'mentally ill'.[179]

This diagnosis was suggested in 1963 by Johann Recktenwald, a neurologist and specialist in depressive diseases. In medical terms, however, the suggestion is absurd. First of all, it is not even certain that Adolf Hitler had the measles, as his brother Edmund had. Second, the sources cited by Recktenwald are highly questionable. He quotes General Guderian, who obtained his information from Max de Crinis, professor of psychiatry and neurology in Berlin.[180] The idea that Hitler was mentally ill was put about not by Guderian, however, but by SD chief Schellenberg. Finally, it should be pointed out that personality changes as a result of measles take place within a few months or years.[181]

From a historical point of view, Recktenwald's remote diagnosis is one of the countless justifying documents that appeared in the 1950s and 1960s suggesting that Nazism also had its 'good sides' but had been 'badly managed'.[182] The thesis of a gradual change in Hitler's personality also includes a further standard argument, that it had been impossible to foresee where the regime was heading.

A study of Recktenwald's own biography will make clear why

he sought to exonerate Hitler in this way. Born in 1882, he studied medicine and qualified as a psychiatrist. During the Nazi regime he headed the provincial clinic and nursing home in Andernach. During the 'euthanasia' action, the killing of the mentally ill in Germany, his clinic was a transit home where people destined to be killed would stay before being transported to the actual killing institutions.[183] After the war Recktenwald was tried before the jury court in Koblenz as an accessory to the murder of patients, crimes against humanity and murder. He was acquitted only because of the lack of documentary evidence.[184]

## Schellenberg's Myths

The recollections of Walter Schellenberg, the last head of the SS Security Service, are also regarded as unreliable. He was born in Saarbrücken in 1910, joined the SS in 1933 while a law student and quickly advanced through the ranks, not least on account of his ability to deliver results. On 9 November 1939, for example, he kidnapped two members of MI6, the British secret service, in the Dutch city of Venlo and presented them publicly and demonstratively as the men behind the attempted assassination of Hitler by Georg Elser.[185] On Himmler's behalf he contacted the Western Allies in 1945. He cooperated with the Allies on a number of other occasions as well, with the result that he was sentenced merely to six years' imprisonment although there was clear evidence that he had been an accessory to the death of millions of people. As he had a severe liver complaint, he was released in 1948. He spent the rest of his days living off advances from British publishing companies, but not one of the spectacular book projects that he promised came to fruition. It was only after his death that his highly revised memoirs were published in English.[186]

As Schellenberg had studied medicine for a short time, he came into contact with Maximilian de Crinis, professor of psychiatry and neurology – probably in Cologne. De Crinis had studied medicine in Graz and Innsbruck and then worked as a junior doctor at the University Neurology Clinic in Graz, rising to become a senior physician there in 1918, before being appointed extraordinary professor in 1924. He was an early supporter of Hitler and joined the NSDAP in 1931. Because of his involvement in a putsch by the Austrian National Socialists during which Federal Chancellor Dollfuss was killed, he fled in 1934 to Germany and became a professor at the University of Cologne in the same year. In 1936 he joined the

SS, taking over several functions, and in 1938 was promoted to Hauptsturmführer. He was summoned to Berlin that year and succeeded Karl Bonhoeffer as professor and director of the Psychiatric Clinic at the Charité hospital.[187] He had close contact with the top SS doctors, including Reichsarzt-SS Ernst-Robert Grawitz and Karl Brandt, Reich Commissioner for Health and Sanitation, who was also one of Hitler's attendant doctors.

Schellenberg described de Crinis as a 'father figure' and painted a very flattering picture of the psychiatry professor, who played a central role in the killing of tens of thousands of patients as part of the 'euthanasia programme'. Schellenberg claims that he was concerned about Hitler's health and sent de Crinis to Himmler to report on the Führer's decline. In April 1945, Himmler is alleged to have said to him while walking in the forest: 'Schellenberg, I don't think we can do anything more with Hitler. Is it possible that de Crinis was right?'[188] There are no witnesses to this conversation because both Himmler and de Crinis committed suicide, nor is there any record of a conversation between Himmler and de Crinis.

De Crinis did not examine Hitler and he could therefore only have made a remote diagnosis on the basis of films or photographs. Moreover, his research is compromised by the way in which Schellenberg announced his sensational findings. He claims that shortly after Heydrich's death he had insight into 'expert opinions' by Hitler's doctors Morell, Brandt and Stumpfegger. And yet none of these doctors wrote 'expert opinions'. Neither attendant doctor Brandt nor Hitler's last doctor Ludwig Stumpfegger wrote documents of this type – not least as they were not informed of Hitler's condition. Stumpfegger entered into Hitler's service only in October 1944. Brandt, who felt that he had been usurped by Morell, did not mention any expert opinions in his comprehensive confession. And Morell wrote only one extensive report on Hitler in 1936. The precise text of this anamnesis is unknown and it is thought that it no longer exists. In brief, there were no expert opinions about Hitler. They were a figment, like many other stories, of Schellenberg's imagination used to assuage the British publishers, who were paying him advances.

He combined these fabrications with a description of Hitler that precisely matched the post-war image. He claimed that Hitler's sense of mission had increased from year to year until it showed all the signs of a pathological compulsion. A nervous paralysis had gradually developed and he now started insulting the Jews more and more and talked about destroying them. Now? Only now? Hitler's physical decline became apparent to observers at the earliest in 1943. And he had spoken of his desire to destroy the Jews in 1919, publicly in 1939 and 1941.

## Cocaine and Dr Giesing's Account

On 22 July 1944, two days after the attempted assassination of Adolf Hitler, Dr Erwin Giesing, an ear, nose and throat specialist, was summoned to the Führer's headquarters from a field hospital near Rastenburg (Kętrzyn) to treat the damage to Hitler's ears. He was dismissed in early October 1944 because he had provoked what now appears to be an absurd dispute among the doctors in the Wolf's Lair.

In 1945 he willingly told the Americans what he knew and believed. He was also quite ready to talk to historians. David Irving, Werner Maser, television – Giesing was happy to tell anyone who wanted to know about Hitler's diseases. He gave the impression of being a calm, reliable and self-assured doctor capable of offering careful guidance to Hitler. This is surprising as there is no record of Hitler ever having recognized or praised Giesing and in any case he would never allow himself to be guided by anyone, let alone a doctor whom he hardly knew.

In his reports, Giesing also gave the impression that he had practically daily access to Hitler's inner circle and that his relationship with Hitler was one of confidence. It is doubtful, however, that Giesing saw Hitler with such frequency, because unlike Morell he did not live in the inner security zone. On the contrary, he had to be summoned from the Karlshof[189] field hospital and could not come and go as he pleased. Although Giesing claims to have been in the Wolf's Lair practically every day, Traudl Junge also has no recollection of him, even saying that she did not know whether she had even heard the name mentioned. Giesing's version is also questionable because Hitler was not a person who sought or allowed close contact. The only exception was Morell, and even then only after 1943 at the earliest, although by that time he had already been Hitler's personal physician for seven years.

Who was Erwin Giesing? He was born in 1907 in Oberhausen in the Ruhrgebiet, studied medicine in Munich before obtaining a post as a junior doctor at the Rudolf Virchow Hospital in Berlin. He obtained his qualification as an ENT specialist in 1936. After joining the NSDAP in 1932 he regularly took part in military exercises and from 1939 served as a senior physician in various field hospitals including the one at Rastenburg (Kętrzyn) in East Prussia.

On his visits to the Führer's Wolf's Lair headquarters, Giesing showed an interest in the tablets that Hitler consumed and even had them analysed. He also claims to have tried out the anti-gas pills and the sulphonamide drug Ultraseptyl on himself to identify possible side effects. He states that he carried out a full physical examination of Hitler on 1 October 1944, even though Hitler rarely allowed such examinations. He also claims to have performed a full neurological examination, revealing that Hitler's neurological status was normal apart from a certain nervous irritability.[190]

The examination on 1 October 1944 is said to have proceeded as follows. The valet Linge called Giesing at his reserve field hospital and summoned him to the Führer's headquarters as Hitler was suffering from terrible pain in his forehead. After Giesing entered Hitler's bedroom, furnished sparsely with a wooden bed, he had a confidential discussion about the causes of jaundice. Hitler had unexpectedly lifted his nightshirt and asked the ENT doctor to examine him. According to Giesing, the examination was one of the longest and most thorough that Hitler had ever allowed. Hitler said: 'Doctor, let's be serious. We mustn't forget the treatment. Take another look at my nose and put the cocaine stuff in it.'

Giesing says that during the cocaine treatment Hitler became increasingly calm and was finally silent. When Giesing asked him how he felt, Hitler did not reply. He suddenly had the idea of putting a merciful end to Hitler with the cocaine: 'At this moment, I didn't want a man like him to exist any more. I realized that this powerful but now unconscious man was completely in my power. I was alone with him. (Linge had left the room.) And as if compelled to do so I dipped a new piece of cotton in the cocaine bottle and covered the mucous membranes once again with cocaine, fully realizing that patient was already suffering from cocaine shock.' Linge had returned in the meantime and Giesing got rid of him again saying: 'The Führer is having his intestinal cramps again; leave him in peace. He will probably want to sleep.' The doctor claims to have returned to Berlin the same evening, not knowing whether Hitler was still alive.

Would Hitler have allowed himself to be examined by an ENT specialist without additional training in internal medicine and neurology? The likelihood is small, because Hitler hated any form of physical closeness and made sure that Morell consulted only qualified specialists. He was unwilling to permit even doctors to come close to him and only Morell was allowed exceptionally to touch intimate parts of his body.

Apart from Giesing's statement, there are no other witnesses of the alleged thorough examination on 1 October 1944. There is no mention of it in Morell's records. Attendant doctor Hanskarl von Hasselbach also later contested that such an examination took place, saying that there was 'no chance' that it could have happened. According to Morell's record for 1 October Hitler was bedridden and extremely weak. And would Hitler, who summoned Morell to him three times on that day, have said nothing about Giesing's examination? This is simply implausible. There was no examination, not least as the ban that Morell imposed on all visitors on 29 September would also have applied to Dr Giesing. At this time no one was allowed to see Hitler without his permission, something that also annoyed the attendant doctors.

A further implausible aspect of Giesing's account is the use of cocaine. Hitler is said to have felt 'relieved' when the cocaine was applied to his mucous membranes before becoming unconscious and later demanding more, like a typical addict.

Did the other doctors know nothing of this cocaine story and its dramatic climax? There is no mention whatsoever in Morell's records. According to Morell, Hitler was administered cocaine in the form of a cocaine-suprarenin solution for conjunctivitis on three occasions, 14 July and 8 October 1944 and 22 March 1945, all at times when Giesing was not serving as an attendant doctor. After 21 August 1944, Morell did not once mention Giesing's cocaine administration, let alone Hitler's loss of consciousness and progressive addiction.

Morell mentions Giesing's name in his records on 27 July, 5 and 18 August and 4 and 5 October, but never in connection with cocaine. It is therefore evident that Giesing deliberately gave false information about Hitler and his health. He recorded these accounts on 12 June 1945 as a prisoner of war in his *Bericht über meine Behandlung bei Hitler* (Report on my treatment of Hitler) for American Field Intelligence Unit No. 4 and in a further report on 11 November 1945.[191]

When Giesing's accounts of 12 June and 11 November 1945 were published, they caused a furore that was reflected in some biographies of Hitler, such as those by John Toland, Ottmar Katz, Werner Maser and David Irving. According to Irving, Giesing, while serving as attendant doctor, kept daily records in a yellow pocket diary that he was able to keep hold of after the collapse.[192] Giesing was tempted to make the statement he did because of the questionnaires prepared by the American interrogation officers, who – as Günther Schenck pointed out – had allowed him to see the protocols and reports of the other doctors. The questions were also leading. Giesing's answers can thus be seen as a means of protecting himself: anyone who thought of putting an end to Hitler's life was bound to be seen in a better light. Under these circumstances, it was inevitable that fact and fiction would get muddled. In March 1947 Giesing was released from military captivity and opened an ENT surgery in Krefeld, where his family lived. He died on 22 May 1977.

Otto Günsche, Hitler's personal adjutant and an SS-Sturmbannführer, said this about Giesing: 'Dr Giesing's statements can be ignored. He said things that weren't true, and in many cases he lied . . . (I) cannot imagine that he examined the Führer . . . without Morell in areas that are not part of an ENT doctor's speciality.'[193]

# — 3 —

# HITLER'S DOCTORS:
# PERSONAL PHYSICIAN MORELL
# AND OTHERS

## Medical Treatment before 1934

In view of the myths and legends surrounding Adolf Hitler's supposed
diseases, it is worthwhile first of all to look at the doctors who treated
him, when and why. Dr Erwin Giesing's account shows that not every
person who treated Hitler sometime or other had a real insight into
his entire medical history. First of all, it is necessary to decide which
doctors actually or probably treated him.

Adolf Hitler was born in Braunau am Inn in 1889. He moved in
1895 to the tiny village of Hafeld (today part of the 1,000-strong
community of Fischlham) in Upper Austria. In 1897, Alois Hitler sold
the small farm and moved with the family to the slightly larger market
town of Lambach, before purchasing a small house in Leonding, at
the time a small town of 4,000 inhabitants. It was there that Hitler
attended the fourth- and fifth-year primary school classes.

Nothing is known of the doctors who might have treated Hitler for
childhood diseases. We do not know whether Hitler's brothers and
sisters who died in childhood were treated by a doctor. There were
probably doctors in the border town of Braunau and no doubt in
Leonding as well. Child mortality was nevertheless high and Hitler's
family was affected by it like any other family. Sister Ida died in 1888,
brothers Gustav and Otto in 1887 and Edmund in 1900, the last
named, according to his official death certificate, of measles.[1] Hitler's
mother Klara sold the house in Leonding in 1905 and moved with her
son Adolf, her sister Johanna ('Hanni') and her daughter Paula (born
1896) to a rented apartment in Linz. She was treated for breast cancer
by Eduard Bloch, a practising Jew and well respected doctor in Linz.
Bloch, who also treated Adolf Hitler for various minor complaints,

provided information about his patients after emigrating to the USA. This information by the family doctor has never been questioned to date and may be regarded as reliable, not least because it also contains the medical record of Hitler's mother.

By contrast, nothing is known of Hitler's time in Vienna and Munich. It has not been possible to determine whether the vagrant Bohemian ever visited a doctor. Hitler's medical record from the First World War has disappeared, possibly destroyed. There is an official record of the fact that he was injured on 9 November 1923 on the march to the Feldherrnhalle. His bodyguard Ulrich Graf was hit by several bullets, and a fellow collaborator in the attempted putsch, who stood in front of Hitler to protect him, was shot in the head. Max Erwin von Scheubner-Richter, who was marching next to Hitler, was hit in the heart and pulled Hitler, whom he had linked arms with, to the ground, causing him to injure his left shoulder. It is not known whether he broke the top of his upper arm; he is more likely to have dislocated it.[2] The emergency treatment was carried out by Walter Schultze, a war volunteer and Freikorps combatant, who had been able to continue his medical studies in 1917 after having been wounded. He obtained his doctorate in 1919 at the University of Munich and later gained a further qualification as a specialist. In 1929 he was one of the founder members of the National Socialist German Doctors' League. In 1933 he was appointed honorary professor at the University of Munich. Although he was not tenured, he held the post of Reichsdozentenführer (head of the professors in the Reich) from 1935. He was involved in the 1940s in the killing of mentally ill children.[3]

At all events, Hitler's injury in 1923 did not leave any permanent damage. A report of 8 January 1924 by senior medical officer Dr Joseph Brinsteiner, prison doctor in Landsberg am Lech, considered this possibility but concluded: 'His capacity to act is not impaired.' His assessment was altogether favourable: Hitler had 'successfully taken the populist idea of a Greater Germany to a large public'. Brinsteiner described Hitler as a 'fascinating personality' with 'infectious oratory' whose 'mental activity did not have pathological influences'. He was not 'burdened' as a result of his origins or education, and the 'temporary pathological depression' that had existed 'for a short time' after the failed putsch 'gave no indication of a pathological disposition'.[4]

This report by a medical officer remained the only source of information about Hitler's health until 1932, when he consulted the ENT specialist Karl-Friedrich Dermietzel in Berlin during an election tour. It is not possible to determine how he came into contact with Dermietzel, and there is no information in the files. Dermietzel originally had his surgery in Berlin-Tempelhof, and it is possible that Hitler consulted him for acute hoarseness because the stadium and Tempelhofer Feld public park were frequently used by the SA for rallies. If Hitler had had a problem with his voice, Dermietzel's surgery would have been the closest.[5] A handwritten curriculum vitae confirms that Dermietzel joined the NSDAP in April 1932, in other words after treating Hitler. He became a member of the SS in June 1932.[6]

Who was this doctor about whom next to nothing is known?[7] Dermietzel was born in Lunow, Brandenburg, in 1899. He served in the war from 1915 as an officer cadet and lieutenant and was wounded several times. He was discharged from the army in 1919, studied medicine and qualified as a specialist. Shortly after the Nazis came to power, Dermietzel took over a surgery in Tauentzienstrasse close to Hitler's dentist Johannes Blaschke. In 1935 he became the doctor in charge of the ENT department of Westend Hospital in Berlin, where a number of SS doctors held leading positions at the time.

In April 1933 he had already been appointed head of the SS Medical Office and in 1937 he became commander of the Medical Department of the SS-Verfügungstruppe (special combat forces). He organized the training of medical officers within the future Waffen-SS, laying the foundations for the exemplary Waffen-SS medical service. On the way, he had a number of conflicts of authority with Reichsarzt-SS Ernst-Robert Grawitz. Dermietzel had himself transferred to a fighting unit. In 1944 he became chief medical officer of the 2nd SS Tank Corps and was promoted to SS-Brigadeführer and Generalmajor (brigadier) in the Waffen-SS. He was taken prisoner by the Americans with the rest of the decimated 2nd Tank Corps near Vienna in 1945. Dermietzel was not prosecuted, although he had also been responsible between April 1936 and July 1937 for the medical departments of the SS guard units and for medical care in the concentration camps.[8]

While Hitler's examination in 1932 is documented, the claim that Hitler suffered in 1929 from stress, painful spasms and gastrointestinal cramps is based on hearsay. His adjutant Wilhelm Brückner recommended Ballistol, a typical soldier's remedy. Originally developed as a universal oil for the German army for care of weapons and leather, etc., this oil–alcohol mixture soon became an all-purpose home remedy. Neo-Ballistol for human consumption was until recently indicated for gastric pain, heartburn, intestinal pain, flatulence, etc. It is still used for external application to treat wounds and also for sunburn. The laxative effect is unquestioned, while headaches and nausea are known side effects caused by the methyl-1-butanol contained in it.[9]

It is also known that Hitler's health deteriorated in mid-1933. At Christmas 1934, Ernst-Robert Grawitz, then doctor in charge of the Internal Medicine Department of Berlin-Westend Municipal Hospital, treated him for 'headache, diplopia (double vision), vertigo, tinnitus'. Grawitz diagnosed symptoms of poisoning, after which Hitler stopped taking Neo-Ballistol.[10] At the same time Hitler's gastrointestinal problems became worse and he now complained of pain, eructation, flatulence and constipation. In 1935 Grawitz prescribed 'anti-gas pills' (see chapter on Hitler's pharmacy), a treatment that Morell continued.[11] It was probably for this reason that a major examination was conducted by the SS doctors working at Westend Hospital under Ernst-Robert Grawitz. The records of this examination have disappeared. In retrospect, Grawitz's medical competence might also be questioned.

Grawitz was born in 1899 in Berlin. His father was a professor of medicine and he himself took his high school leaving certificate in 1917 before participating in the First World War. He studied medicine in Berlin from 1919 and wrote his doctoral thesis on 'A case of gonococcal sepsis'. He then worked as a junior doctor at Westend Hospital before opening a practice as a specialist in internal medicine in 1929. As a student he belonged to the Freikorps units that took part in the Kapp putsch. He joined the SS in 1931. He was appointed chief medical officer in 1933 in recognition of his active participation in the Nazi movement, and he quickly rose within the SS to become Reichsarzt. In 1938 he was appointed managing director of the German Red Cross. He was indirectly involved in the killing of mentally ill patients, as it was he who seconded SS doctors for the killing centres. He personally coordinated the medical experiments in the concentration camps and regularly reported on them to Himmler. He avoided prosecution for his crimes by committing suicide.[12]

The examination carried out at Westend Hospital in 1935 was inconclusive. Attendant doctor Brandt recommended that a university hospital be consulted, but Hitler declined. He preferred an experienced and discreet expert who would take his complaints seriously and could be consulted without causing a stir. It would appear that his photographer Heinrich Hoffmann recommended Theodor Morell, who had a successful surgery on the Kurfürstendamm with many prominent patients.

# Hitler's Personal Physician and Attendant Doctors

## Personal Physician Theodor Morell (1886–1948)

Revisionists like the British historian David Irving seek to absolve Hitler of the crimes committed by the Nazis. 'How sick was Hitler really?' asked Irving in 1980 naively before going on to state that Hitler's personal physician Theodor Morell had treated him incorrectly and put him in a 'euphoric trance-like state', with the result that Hitler could not be held responsible for his actions.[13] The facts do not in any way bear out this claim.

There were others who doubted Morell's competence and many dismissed him after 1945 as a bungler and charlatan – an assessment that former patients and also Hitler's secretary Traudl Junge[14] and adjutant Otto Günsche[15] energetically refuted. Nevertheless, Morell was remembered for the most part as a 'negative figure', as the doctor Ernst Günther Schenck put it.[16] Even the Hitler biographer Werner Maser believed that after taking Pervitin and caffeine Hitler 'took decisions or made statements that were outside his rational control'.[17]

Joachim C. Fest, whose studies were based on Maser's research, wrote that Hitler took medicines 'literally in quantity' and 'resorted to stronger drugs at shorter intervals', but he mentioned no names. He was more specific about the last years of the war: 'After Stalingrad he took a drug against depressive moods every other day.' This latter assertion is not substantiated by Morell's records. According to Fest, Hitler's physical decline was due to Morell's treatment, whose drugs produced 'euphorias' in the Führer. It is not clear from Fest's description whether Hitler was addicted to the methamphetamine Pervitin – no doubt the journalist and *FAZ* publisher was unwilling to make such a categorical statement.[18]

The rumour about Hitler's drug dependence would not go away, however, and even in 2006 Bernd Freytag von Loringhoven, Keitel's adjutant and later a general in the German army, wrote that Morell prescribed 'injections of glucose and other tonics'. He would 'personally administer such stimulants . . . Hitler insisted on these medicaments, which apparently had a toxic effect on his health.'[19] General Heinz Guderian also rejected Morell, having seen 'what this fat, unappetizing charlatan had done to Hitler'.[20] Hans-Dietrich Röhrs, deputy Reichsgesundheitsführer (Reich Health Leader) and SS divisional medical officer, was even more scathing. He worked as a general practitioner in Hamburg in the 1960s, and in 1966 published a book about Hitler's health in which he accused Morell of putting

Hitler into 'euphoric states' with his 'power therapy' and of 'slowly poisoning him' as a result. The stimulant Pervitin had destroyed the 'enlightened performance' of this 'gifted politician'[21] and caused psychological changes leading to far-reaching 'miscalculations'. Röhrs also reproached Morell for having the 'hygiene habits of a pig', called him a 'pest' and one of the 'greatest war profiteers in the Third Reich'.[22]

Even Hanskarl von Hasselbach, the reserved attendant doctor and colleague of Morell, commented that Hitler's choice of personal physician showed a 'lack of understanding of human nature' because he had regarded Morell as an 'unusually competent doctor and scientist'.[23]

Who was this 'grey eminence', who was sometimes even thought to exert a Rasputin-like influence in Hitler's 'court'? Morell's ancestors were Huguenots, who fled France for Germany to escape religious persecution and settled in Neu-Isenburg near Frankfurt am Main. His father, Karl Morell, was a teacher, and Morell himself was born on 22 July 1886 in Trais-Münzenberg, Oberhessen, and baptized Theodor (Theo) Karl Ludwig Gilbert.[24] His mother, Elise Morell née Häuser, came from a prosperous farming family in Hesse. There was something of a tradition of teaching in the family, since not only Morell's father but also his grandfather and older brother Adolf exercised this profession. The father at least naturally assumed that Theo would keep up this family tradition. He did in fact attend a preparatory school when he was fourteen and then went on to a teacher training college and taught for a year in 1905 in Bretzenheim near Mainz. He decided that year, however, to obtain his *Abitur* (university entrance qualification), because he was not satisfied with what he had achieved to date. In 1907 he enrolled to study medicine at his local university in Giessen, but transferred after a semester to Heidelberg. After a brief period at the École de Médecine in Grenoble, mainly to find out where his family, Diex, came from, he returned to Heidelberg, where he passed his first medical examination with the grade 'very good' on 26 July 1909. At the end of that year Morell went to Paris, where he stayed until summer 1910, making an initial acquaintanceship with bacteriology at the Institut Pasteur and attending lectures by the Nobel Prize winner Ilya Mechnikov. On his return to Heidelberg, he soon felt the attraction of Munich, where he passed the examination for doctors of medicine on 10 May 1912 and then worked for a year as a junior doctor in Bad Kreuznach. At the end of that year he received his licence to practise medicine and was awarded his doctorate in August of the same year.

Between 1912 and 1914 Morell went to sea as a ship's doctor and saw something of the world. He sailed on ships belonging to the renowned Norddeutsche Lloyd and voyaged as far as the coast of East Africa. He later undertook expeditions inside the countries to conduct medical studies and find out about the traditions and customs of other peoples and countries. Through his voyages and expeditions he gained an insight into a type of medicine that had little in common with classical Western medicine.[25] Traudl Junge recalled in 2001 that Morell was an experienced, able and good-natured doctor who, as a former ship's doctor, sought to apply the 'Far Eastern holistic approach to medicine' even at home. He was a doctor 'with heart and soul', she said looking back.

On his return, Morell had a small medical practice in Dietzenbach until 1915 before being conscripted to the Western Front as a battalion medical officer. He spent some months in field hospitals on account of a chronic kidney complaint and was discharged as unfit for duty in 1918. He moved to Berlin where he opened a practice for electrotherapy and diuretic disorders (the old name for urology) in Bayreuther Strasse near Wittenbergplatz.[26] On 7 August 1919 he married Johanna ('Hanni') Möller at Berlin-Charlottenburg registry office. She came from a wealthy family and Morell was thus able to equip his practice with the latest medical technology. During the 1920s Morell became a well-known and fashionable doctor. If the German Crown Prince, important industrialists and theatre and film actors sought his medical advice he must have had a good reputation – long before the Third Reich. After 1933 his patients included generals and high-ranking politicians like Göring, Goebbels, von Ribbentrop and Speer. His prominence also led to the award of honorary titles from other countries. According to his own statement, he could have been court doctor to the Shah of Persia, or personal physician to the King of Romania.[27]

In 1935 Morell moved to the Kurfürstendamm where he practised as a 'dermatologist and venereologist', although this is no longer documented. From here his career continued to prosper, taking him to Wilhelmstrasse, the Führer's headquarters and ultimately to an American internment camp. Hitler quickly came to trust Morell, who had been recommended to him by Hoffmann in May 1936 when Hitler had been suffering from acute pain. It is possible that Morell took time to explain his holistic approach and the Mutaflor treatment that he often used.[28] The treatment worked, and Hitler was sincerely grateful to the doctor. He said later in a private circle: 'He saved my life. I was so miserable at the end of 1936 that I could hardly walk.

I was treated wrongly at the time . . . I had eczema on both legs and had to bandage them the whole time so that I couldn't wear boots. Then Morell came and made me healthy again.' The statement was right about the eczema but there can be no question of Morell having saved Hitler's life. The chronically recurrent gastrointestinal spasms were not life-threatening and were not therefore taken seriously by Ernst-Robert Grawitz and the SS doctors.

From 1937 Hitler placed his health care in Morell's hands. Over the next few years Morell kept Hitler on form – certainly by replacing his intestinal flora but also through regular injections of his own Vitamultin, a preparation containing glucose and vitamins. It is understandable that Morell should have felt flattered to be asked by Hitler to be his personal physician, and many other doctors would have felt the same. He took up this position at a time when there was no war in sight and the genocide of the Jews had not yet begun. Moreover, Morell was completely apolitical, even if he had joined the NSDAP in 1933. He would have done so, like many others, for purely pragmatic reasons: because of his dark complexion he was often thought to be Jewish, apparently losing patients for that reason. After he joined the Party, his waiting room began to fill up again. There is probably some truth in the claim by Hitler's attendant doctor Karl Brandt, who used his position to acquire high political office, that Morell 'for all his slyness . . . was too stupid for political reasoning'.[29] The fact that he was envied by many people including the attendant doctors for his position with Hitler should not be forgotten when interpreting statements like this. Freiburg professor Alfred Nissle, for example, expressed his disappointment that Morell and not he had the privilege of experiencing 'events of global historical significance in the Führer's headquarters'.[30]

Morell was also much in demand among general staff officers and Reich government officials.[31] He had a good relationship with Albert Speer, for example, who had visited him on Hitler's recommendation in his Kurfürstendamm office for a stomach complaint. Morell, who prescribed Mutaflor – which Speer remembered as 'Multiflor'[32] – addressed Speer familiarly in his letters as 'My dear Speer', and the armaments minister occasionally referred to Morell as 'My dear professor'.[33] Speer knew that Hitler would never have accepted a quack and he therefore assumed that Morell had the necessary qualifications and experience as a doctor.

Morell also enjoyed a good reputation with some foreign statesmen and diplomats. The Romanian head of state Marshal Ion Antonescu, the Finnish marshal Gustav von Mannerheim and the Japanese ambassador general Hiroshi Oshima were among Morell's patients. The president of Czechoslovakia Emil Hacha suffered a collapse while visiting the Reich Chancellery on 14 March 1939, the day on which Hitler unceremoniously demanded Hacha's agreement to the occupation of his country. Morell gave him a glucose injection. Hacha, who is said to have been treated until 1944 by Morell with Septoiod, Prostakrin and Vitamultin-Ca, was a recipient of Morell's Vitamultin preparations, as was Vojtech Tuka, the Slovakian prime minister by the grace of Hitler.[34] Vitamultin was dispensed at Morell's instigation by Engel-Apotheke at Mohrenstrasse 63/64 in the government district of Berlin.

As personal physician Morell received a high but not exceptional salary of around RM 60,000 per year. This was supplemented by the income from his private practice, which he continued with the aid of two assistant doctors.[35] He also enjoyed various privileges and successfully exploited his closeness to Hitler for financial gain. He had shares in several pharmaceutical companies in Germany and the conquered territories and saw that the drugs produced by him were used in the Wehrmacht, the German Labour Front and the SS. Hitler himself ensured that Morell received the first electron microscope made by Siemens in autumn 1944. It could not be used, however, before the end of the war.[36]

On 26 February, Speer sent the following telegram to Morell following an award that had been given to him by Hitler: 'Sincere congratulations on the award by the Führer of the Knight's Cross of the Cross of Military Valour. I wish you many years of success and above all assistance to the Führer. I would be particularly grateful if I could occasionally take up some of your spare time away from your other important tasks for me.'[37]

Morell kept up with the latest findings by reading medical journals, but he nevertheless overestimated his status in the world of science. The penicillin research he arranged in his pharmaceutical companies and institutes produced nothing of value. According to Schenck, he managed ten scientific articles and was mentioned in six others – a modest tally for the years of research.[38]

But what about his main task, looking after Hitler's health? Until August 1941 Hitler rarely required medical attention, but after that time Morell was in action continuously in the various Führer headquarters. Hitler's modesty, which some have occasionally described as pathological, and his dread of physical contact made it difficult for Morell to carry out regular checkups. During the Eastern campaign he refused to allow Morell any diagnostic measures such as X-rays or gastrointestinal examinations. Morell's records show how difficult Hitler, referred to as 'F.' for Führer, was as a patient. On 13 August 1941 he noted: 'F. refused to be examined, said everything was OK.' And on 27 September 1944: 'In the evening commented to F. that he looked yellow and asked if I could examine him, but was refused.' On 16 November 1944 he was once again roundly rejected: 'When I suggested a trip to Berlin and an X-ray there F. became very irritated with me, more so than he has been in the whole of the last eight years.'[39]

In other respects, by contrast, Hitler was quite cooperative. When his digestive problems became unbearable he would even eat gruel and stoically drink infusions made of apple peel or caraway. He happily agreed to undergo leeching to 'cleanse' his blood and reduce his high blood pressure. He also permitted blood letting. He frequently requested camomile or calomel enemas, believing that they were 'cleansing'.[40] He was particularly keen on poultices.[41]

Morell repeatedly recommended walks, but Hitler was a reluctant patient in this regard, except during his early sojourns on the Obersalzberg when public appearances helped to increase his popularity. Later, when walks in the complete isolation of his headquarters in East Prussia were useful only to his health but not to his reputation, it was difficult to persuade him at all. Morell frequently urged Hitler to leave the bunker and go for walks in the East Prussian forests. The dictator was only willing to take his Alsatian Blondi for the occasional walk. Morell noted on 1 October 1944: 'New bunker unsuitable for him . . . too little oxygen in spite of ventilation system.' Hitler promised thereupon 'to take more walks'. Morell wrote in his diary: '"You say that but then you don't," I argued.'[42]

It is clear that by acceding to Hitler's whims and wishes, Morell's reputation as a doctor suffered. Each of the doctors in Hitler's headquarters had a fixed idea of how the Führer should be treated, and Morell's colleagues naturally questioned his competence as a result. On the other hand, Morell could not speak about his patient's wishes and desires because the other resentful doctors surrounding Hitler would quickly have accused him of violating doctor–patient confidentiality. It cannot be said that Morell acted irresponsibly. He respected the maximum daily drug dosages and rarely exceeded them – in spite of what the attendant doctors might have thought. Morell also consulted with other specialists such as the professors at the Charité Hospital in Berlin.[43]

Former attendant doctor Hanskarl von Hasselbach, who made no secret of his antipathy to Morell, was honest enough to admit after 1945 that it was difficult if not impossible to examine Hitler at all. He also admitted that he did not understand Morell's treatment methods because he had not been informed of the diagnoses. He was also critical of Morell on account of his manner, which he found repulsive. Morell's ill-kempt look and lack of hygiene offended everybody. Traudl Junge confirmed that his appearance left a lot to be desired and that he disgusted a lot of people in the Wolf's Lair on account of his manners, particularly the enormous amounts he ate and the noises he made while doing so.[44] After eating he would also regularly fall asleep and snore loudly. Von Hasselbach and Eva Braun both complained to Hitler about Morell's lack of personal hygiene and body odour. Hitler was apparently unconcerned and interested only in his ability as a doctor: 'I don't employ Morell for his fragrance but to look after my health.'[45]

Another episode illustrates the particular relationship of trust between Hitler and Morell. On 3 July 1943, he told Hitler that he had 'always been careful to handle everything under the strictest secrecy, using assumed names, etc.' and had therefore made no mention of Hitler's cardiovascular situation. In his records Morell added: 'F. said I am quite right and that this is no concern of Z[abel – producer of dietary food in 1943] – I alone am his doctor.' During this discussion Hitler mentioned 'how he longs to have pea and bean soups and suchlike but doesn't dare to because of flatulence'. Morell reassured him and said that eventually he would be able to eat other dishes. Hitler, who was alone in his room, invited Morell to dine with him. They started talking about private concerns. Morell told him that he was forgoing breakfast in an effort to lose weight, as he was twenty pounds overweight. 'The F. was very concerned and insisted that I don't overdo it or I might do myself harm.'

Hitler expressed his particular gratitude to Morell on 8 November 1944: 'I'm not an ungrateful person, my dear doctor. If we both survive the war, you will see how generously I will reward you!'[46]

Morell was in better health himself after being treated in his own practice in early 1944 and was extremely busy at this time. Some of those close to him interpreted his business activities to mean that he intended to resign his position as personal physician and to devote himself exclusively to his private research laboratories at Hradisko Monastery in Olomouc (Olmütz) and Bayrisch Gmain. Contrary to appearances, by 1944 Morell no longer felt up to working as personal physician for health reasons. He never spoke of this with Hitler. He considered a 'full replacement' for himself, not just a successor. He regarded Professor Erwin Becher from Frankfurt am Main as a suitable candidate, but he died in October 1944. Even if Morell had succeeded in putting his plans into practice, however, the assassination attempt on Hitler on 20 July 1944 changed everything, because he now became indispensable.

Morell, who by now was repeatedly falling ill again, was not dismissed as personal physician until 21 April 1945. The diary entry consisted of five letters: 'Entlg' (Dismissal). Hitler recommended to Morell that he take off his uniform, put on civilian clothing and return to his practice on the Kurfürstendamm, which must have sounded like a mockery to the doctor. Was Hitler not aware that the practice on the Kurfürstendamm was a ruin? Morell flew with a Condor to Munich at 2 a.m. on 22 April. Hitler's pilot Hans Baur, who had been a friend of Morell's for years, had made available one of the last aeroplanes, enabling Morell and others to leave the Führer's bunker in Berlin. An American reporter discovered Morell in May 1945 in a hospital in southern Bavaria and conducted an interview with him. A few days later he was arrested by the US military police.[47]

After the collapse of the Third Reich, Morell was severely ill with his old kidney complaint and cardiac insufficiency. He was also confused following a stroke and was released by the Americans on 30 June 1947 as unfit to be kept in prison and transferred to a local clinic at Alpenhof in Tegernsee, where he died on 26 May 1948. Entry no. 116 in the register of birth, deaths and marriages of Tegernsee registry office gives the cause of death as 'cardiovascular insufficiency'.[48] After the fall of the Third Reich Morell's health was too poor for him to be interrogated and for that reason information about Hitler, which would no doubt have been very revealing, was unavailable. His wife Johanna was questioned, but her information was limited since her husband's close contact with Hitler had for the most part taken place in the forests of East Prussia, far from Schwanenwerder, the Morells' Berlin home.[49]

Morell's greed and business acumen in connection with his pharmaceutical empire and research institutes are undeniable and were detrimental to his reputation as a doctor. His position was no doubt full of temptations that he was not strong enough to resist. After 1945 Morell was also accused of having treated Hitler incorrectly for years and of undermining his health. This is not true, as is revealed by Morell's own detailed records from 1941 to 1945, which have the hallmark of a conscientious general practitioner.

## Hitler's Attendant Doctors

Apart from his personal physician, Hitler also had other doctors, qualified surgeons, who worked as attendant doctors in the Führer's headquarters. Their main task was to provide initial medical treatment, in the case of a traffic accident or possible assassination attempt on Hitler or his entourage. They included Karl Brandt and Hanskarl von Hasselbach, later replaced by Ludwig Stumpfegger, Himmler's long-standing attendant doctor.

## Karl Brandt (1904–1948)

Karl Brandt was born the son of a police officer in Mulhouse, Alsace, on 8 January 1904.[50] He was expelled from Alsace in 1919 after Germany lost the war. He graduated from high school in Dresden in 1922 and studied medicine in Jena, Freiburg, Munich and Berlin from 1922 to 1928. Brandt, who knew the Alsatian evangelical theologian and doctor Albert Schweitzer, intended to work as his assistant in the tropical hospital founded by him in Lambaréné on the west coast of Africa. The plan fell through and after three years as a junior doctor under Professor Georg Magnus in the Surgical Department of the Bergmannsheil Hospital in Bochum he became senior surgeon in the 2nd Surgical University Clinic in Ziegelstrasse, Berlin, which was headed by Professor Magnus. Under his old boss he headed the polyclinic and became Hitler's attendant surgeon in 1934. On 17 March of that year he married the German backstroke swimming champion Anni Rehborn in Munich. They had a son in October 1935. Anni Rehborn had known Hitler since 1925.

After seeing Hitler in the early 1930s in Essen, Brandt joined the NSDAP on 1 March 1932. He had applied in 1932 for membership of the National Socialist Doctors' League and was accepted on 17 December of that year, giving his NSDAP membership number as 1009617.[51]

By chance Brandt was the first doctor on the spot when Hitler's chief adjutant, later SA Obergruppenführer Wilhelm Brückner, had an accident while driving to Reit im Winkel and needed surgery at Traunstein hospital.[52] This was the start of his rapid rise in the Third Reich, in which he achieved the rank of SS-Gruppenführer and Generalleutnant in the Waffen-SS. A year after the accident he accompanied Hitler, through Brückner's intercession, on a trip to Italy and in 1934 he became Hitler's attendant surgeon.

At the end of October 1939, Hitler signed an instruction on the Berghof, which he backdated to 1 September, the day on which war broke out. Those chiefly involved in the drafting of the instruction were Philipp Bouhler, head of the Führer's chancellery, Reich Health Leader Leonardo Conti and Professor Maximilian de Crinis, head of the Charité Neurology Clinic. The authorization issued by Hitler was tantamount to an order to kill: 'Reichsleiter Bouhler and Dr. med. Brandt are commissioned on their own responsibility to extend the authority of specifically named doctors so that mental patients who are considered incurable may be granted a merciful death after critical assessment of their medical condition.'[53]

If Brandt's position as Hitler's attendant doctor had until then been of no consequence, this instruction meant that from this time at the latest he was directly involved in the Nazi crimes. According to him, Hitler believed that 40 to 50 per cent of the patients in mental asylums should be 'removed'. He then demanded a 'completely unbureaucratic solution to the problem'.[54] In compliance with Hitler's wish, Brandt and Bouhler very quickly established an effective killing machinery to which 70,000 people fell victim and whose technology – for example the newly developed gas chambers – made possible the subsequent murder of millions of Jews.[55]

Through a decree by Hitler on 28 July 1942, Brandt was appointed General Commissioner for Health and Sanitation with the task of reducing tensions between military and civilian health authorities, a task that he did not succeed in performing. In 1943 he was promoted again to head of the medical supply authority and coordinator of medical research. On 25 August 1944 he also became Reich Commissioner for Health and Sanitation, a rank equivalent to that of the head of a supreme Reich authority (*Oberste Reichsbehörde*).[56]

Brandt's career came to an abrupt end when he was accused of high treason shortly before the end of the war. To protect his wife and son from the approaching front, he took them to Bad Liebenstein in Thuringia – a dangerous undertaking, which led to his arrest on 16 April 1945 on Hitler's personal command. He was accused of defeatism – lack of belief in the final victory – and high treason. Hitler signed the death warrant of his former attendant doctor and General Commissioner. The execution was stayed through Speer's intervention with Himmler, and after Hitler's death Speer managed to prevail on Dönitz to have Brandt released.[57]

Karl Brandt was charged in 1946 in the Nuremberg Doctors' Trial and sentenced to death for the murder of mentally ill patients and his involvement in medical experiments. In a personal interview with the Nuremberg prison psychologist he clearly indicated that he stood by his position in spite of the sentencing. He said that as a German doctor he saw the 'state as an individual' to which he was 'primarily committed' and continued: 'We do not therefore hesitate to destroy a collection of, for example, a trillion cells in the form of a number of individual persons if we believe that they are harmful to the organism as a whole – the state – or if we believe that the state will prosper without them.'[58]

## Hanskarl von Hasselbach (1903–1981)

Von Hasselbach was Hitler's second attendant surgeon from 1935. He obtained the position thanks to Karl Brandt, who like him had worked under Professor Georg Magnus in Berlin. He joined the NSDAP and SA early on, in 1932.[59] A year later he joined the SS. At the start of the war he was a medical officer with the rank of SS-Hauptsturmführer and was stationed on several occasions in the various Führer headquarters. After April 1943 he was a surgeon in the Wolf's Lair, Hitler's headquarters in East Prussia.

Von Hasselbach was awarded the title of extraordinary professor on Hitler's fifty-fourth birthday on 20 April 1943. This was a standard promotion; it did not reflect any special protection by Hitler but was rather the result of a solid academic career.

Born in Berlin on 2 November 1903, von Hasselbach completed his schooling in 1921 in Hirschberg (now Jelenia Góra), Silesia, and studied medicine in Breslau (now Wroclaw), Rostock, Munich and Freiburg. He received his medical licence in 1927 and completed a doctorate at the University of Freiburg with a thesis on fibroma of the neck. He worked subsequently in Bergmannsheil Hospital in Bochum, an accident hospital, before being employed as a junior doctor at the Charité Hospital in Berlin.[60] While working in Hitler's entourage, von Hasselbach's academic development suffered, and it was not until 1938 that he habilitated with a paper on endangiitis obliterans, constriction of the veins and arteries of the hands and feet, and surgical remedies.[61]

Von Hasselbach was given leave of absence from his lecturing commitments at the University of Berlin. The doctors' dispute in autumn 1944 led to his dismissal as an attendant doctor, after which he worked in a field hospital on the Western Front.

During his American captivity and as a witness at the Nuremberg trials, von Hasselbach was regarded as an upstanding person who stood by his opinions, even if they differed from other people's. The military tribunal described him as the most honest and credible defendant, and the one who had been least 'corrupted' by Hitler.[62]

After being liberated from American captivity, von Hasselbach was head of the Surgical Department of the Bodelschwinghsche Anstalten in Bethel near Bielefeld. He died on 21 December 1981 near Munich.

*Ludwig Stumpfegger (1910–1945)*

Brandt's successor was the orthopaedist Dr Ludwig Stumpfegger, a liegeman of Himmler, whose attendant doctor and *Du* friend he had been for many years previously. Fifty years later, Himmler's secretary Gretel Grothmann still recalled the doctor very well: 'He had the best reputation among the adjutants and secretaries (and) was a tall, handsome and fantastic man.'[63] The 1.90 metre former German fistball champion[64] and ski instructor must indeed have cut a very imposing figure.

He was born in Munich on 11 July 1910 as the son of a post office clerk and attended schools in Landshut and Rosenheim before studying medicine at the University of Munich. He took the state examination in 1935 and received his licence in 1936. In the same year he was employed as a junior surgeon at the SS sanatorium in Hohenlychen north of Berlin.[65]

Stumpfegger joined the SS as a student on 2 June 1933 (no. 83668) and became a member of the NSDAP in 1935 (no. 3616119).[66] In the SS he underwent military training and joined the medical service. He was also rapidly promoted to head of an SS medical company (*Sanitätssturm*) at Hohenlychen. In 1938 he completed a three-month training course in an army machine gun unit. After his discharge as a reserve non-commissioned officer he was immediately enlisted in the *Führerreserve* section of the SS-*Verfügungstruppe*, forerunner of the Waffen-SS. According to an assessment by one of his superiors, he was 'extremely ambitious, highly assiduous, deliberate but also highly consistent'. In 1939 he became the personal assistant of Himmler's friend Karl Gebhardt, who was not only medical director in Hohenlychen but as 'SS consultant surgeon' was increasingly involved with war wounded and their treatment and thus gradually consigned his function as Himmler's attendant doctor to Stumpfegger. It is not known whether Hitler became acquainted with the young doctor at this time, or whether he already knew him from earlier. It is possible that the first contact took place in 1936 when Stumpfegger was working as a medical consultant to the German Olympic team.

Stumpfegger must have had a close relationship at least to Himmler, as can be seen from a letter signed by the Reichsführer-SS and Minister of the Interior of the German Reich of 2 September 1944: 'SS-Obersturmbannführer Waffen-SS Dr Ludwig Stumpfegger acts on my behalf and has full authority. All military and civilian offices are to provide him with information. His orders are to be obeyed.'[67] It has not been determined to date where and to what extent Stumpfegger availed himself of this licence to act, however.

61

From May 1942, he performed military service with the SS-Leibstandarte 'Adolf Hitler', which he left again after being slightly wounded. As a highly career-oriented doctor, he worked towards his habilitation and assisted Gebhardt with his human experiments at Ravensbrück concentration camp. This cruel series of experiments, which lasted two years, was prompted by the attack on Reinhard Heydrich on 27 May 1942 in Prague. After being injured by a hand grenade, he appeared to be recovering following an operation, but sepsis set in and Heydrich died on 4 June.[68] Gebhardt, Stumpfegger, the second assistant Ernst Fischer and the assisting camp doctors Gerhard Schiedlausky, Rudolf Rosenthal and Herta Oberheuser infected the legs of women inmates with mixed bacterial cultures. Various treatments, surgical and medical including the use of sulphonamides, were then attempted. Some of the women bled to death, some died from the infections, and the others were left with lifelong sequelae.

At the same time Stumpfegger started experimenting on the transplanting of muscles, tendons and bones. As the writer Freya Klier reconstructed in 1994 on the basis of eyewitness accounts, under anaesthetic women inmates had pieces of bone removed from the ridge of the tibia and transplanted elsewhere. Other experiments called for their tibia to be broken and reassembled or for tendons to be transplanted.[69]

Stumpfegger summed up his findings in a paper entitled 'Free autoplastic bone transplantation in reconstructive surgery of the limbs'. Neither the paper itself nor the letters sent by Stumpfegger to accompany the numerous reprints give any indication that he carried out his experiments on concentration camp inmates.[70] In autumn 1944 he received his habilitation from the Medical Faculty of the University of Berlin.

Stumpfegger was appointed as Hitler's attendant doctor after the dismissal of von Hasselbach and Brandt on 9 October 1944. He had close contacts not only with the doctors in Hohenlychen and Reichsarzt-SS Grawitz but also with SS-Obersturmführer Dr. med. Bruno Weber, head of the Waffen-SS and Police Hygiene and Bacteriology Institute in Auschwitz. Weber was particularly interested in infectious diseases. He used flesh from murdered inmates to breed his bacterial cultures. The experiments he carried out on humans were almost always fatal.[71]

On 24 October 1944, Stumpfegger asked Weber to complete an experiment he had started in Ravensbrück. He had read in old medical papers that the oriental cockroach (*Blatta orientalis*) was effective

Der Reichsführer-ᛋᛋ
Oberbefehlshaber Westmarken

2. Sept. 1944

ᛋᛋ-Obersturmbannführer der Waffen-ᛋᛋ
Dr. Ludwig S t u m p f e g g e r
handelt in meinem Auftrag und hat alle
Vollmacht.

Ihm ist von jeder militärischen und
zivilen Stelle Auskunft zu geben.
Seinen B efehlen ist zu gehorchen.

(Siegel)          gez.: H. Himmler

20 Sep 1944

3. This authorization of 2 September 1944 by Himmler for his long-standing
attendant physician Ludwig Stumpfegger is an astonishing demonstration of
trust. The copy was placed in his personal file.

in treating dropsy. As he was no longer working in Ravensbrück, he asked Weber to verify the diuretic properties of cockroaches. A few weeks later Weber sent the results of his findings to the Führer headquarters indicating that the ground cockroaches did indeed have a diuretic effect. Stumpfegger immediately suggested that further studies be carried out in Hohenlychen and the Robert Bosch Hospital in Stuttgart. In January 1945, only fourteen days before Auschwitz was liberated, Stumpfegger drew Weber's attention to a study on streptococci, but no experiments on the subject were carried out.

On 20 April 1945, Hitler promoted his attendant doctor to SS-Standartenführer and colonel in the Security Police. These promotions were recorded in his personnel file. After Morell's dismissal, Hitler had himself treated by Stumpfegger, but they did not become really close – the cyanide capsules had long been distributed.

On 30 April 1945, Stumpfegger witnessed the incineration of Hitler's body. He died along with Martin Bormann on 2 May 1945 during an attempt to break out of the bunker under the Reich Chancellery. It is possible that they committed suicide.

*Hugo Blaschke (1881–1959)*
Hugo Johannes Blaschke, born the son of a master carpenter on 14 November 1881 in Neustadt, western Prussia, attended primary and secondary school in Berlin. In 1900 he performed voluntary military service and was discharged as a reserve non-commissioned officer.[72] His father forced him to obtain commercial training in Berlin, Geneva and Paris. He was not happy with this choice, however, and opted to study dentistry. As this discipline was not recognized in Germany as an academic subject in its own right, however, he completed his training abroad, studying from 1907 to 1911 at the University of Pennsylvania in Philadelphia and later specializing in maxillofacial surgery in London. In 1911 joined the practice of the Imperial Court Dentist, which he later took over.[73] During the First World War he was initially an instructor in Frankfurt/Oder before working as a dentist in the Frankfurt garrison hospital. He was transferred in May 1915 to the Dentistry Unit of the Third Army Corps. He opened his own practice in 1919, shortly after the end of the war, at Kurfürstendamm 213, Berlin.[74]

Blaschke was very well qualified as a dentist although he did not himself publish any scientific articles. From around 1930 he became Hermann Göring's personal dentist.[75] It is no longer possible to determine when Blaschke treated Hitler for the first time. Various dates have been mentioned; Blaschke himself states that it was at the end of 1933. He had been summoned to Hitler, who was suffering from acute toothache, by chance. The next morning he received a call stating that the pain had disappeared. From then on Blaschke stood high in Hitler's favour. He states that Hitler was a 'model patient' who faithfully followed the instructions on dental hygiene given to him. He remained Hitler's dentist until 20 April 1945. It was Blaschke's dental technicians who had made the crowns and bridges that helped to identify Hitler's skull in 1945.

Although Blaschke described himself in the interrogations after 1945 as a non-political specialist, he rose rapidly in the ranks of the NSDAP and SS, probably under the protection of Göring and Hitler. He joined the NSDAP on 1 February 1931 (membership no. 452082) and a month later he became a member of the SA. In 1932 he was awarded the rank of Sturmbannführer. Blaschke, who also treated Goebbels, Himmler, Bormann and Ley, was admitted to the SS in 1935. In the same year he became director of the Dental Health Department in the staff of Reichsführer-SS Heinrich Himmler.

He was described as 'confident and soldierly' in appearance with a 'very reliable and dignified' character. In 1943 Reichsarzt Grawitz called Blaschke 'a fanatical National Socialist'. Within the SS he developed a dental service for the rapidly growing troop, which – according to Grawitz – was 'new territory ... in practical and organizational terms, at least for Germany'.

This inevitably meant that Blaschke neglected his private practice, which brought him into financial difficulties. In January 1941 Grawitz therefore consulted Oswald Pohl, head of the SS Head Office, to arrange payment for Blaschke's activities in the SS. He claimed that Blaschke's services were required at least on a part-time basis for the development of dental care and ongoing treatment within the SS. He should not abandon the practice of dentistry altogether, however, because he was the personal dentist of the Führer, Reichsführer, Göring and others and needed to keep up his practical skills. He was ultimately promoted to SS-Oberführer in the SS Medical Service and received a monthly salary of RM 2,500.

As the dentist responsible for the SS Medical Service, Blaschke also took custody of the dental gold from 'deceased inmates in protective custody', as a letter from the Head Office for Administration and Economic Affairs put it. By October 1942 he had acquired a reserve of over 50 kg of dental gold, sufficient for treatments for 'the next five years', as a clerk from section A noted. For 'security and practical reasons' it was 'not possible' to collect more gold for the treatment of SS members, wrote the clerk deputizing for the head of section A, and for that reason 'dental gold' from 'natural deaths' in the concentration camps should from now on be 'delivered to the Reichsbank against a receipt'.[76] In January 2009, 50 kg of gold would have been worth around one million euros. At the time the gold extracted from the teeth of Jewish victims was valued at RM 200,000.

The files with details of the gold deliveries were destroyed.[77] Until August 1942, the whereabouts of the valuables taken from the murdered Jews cannot therefore be reconstructed. Neither the SS mobile units nor the commandants of the extermination camps were willing to hand over the precious metals to the civilian authorities. Within the SS the responsibility was also unclear, and there were a very large number of 'irregularities'. It was not until August 1942 that the Head Office for Administration and Economic Affairs was made responsible, and section A opened an account at the Reichsbank for the delivery of gold and other precious metals.[78]

The Head Office for Administration and Economic Affairs made no complaint about the gold reserve. Blaschke's position as the personal dentist to Hitler, Himmler and Göring apparently made him untouchable. On 31 August 1944 he was awarded the rank of Dentist in Charge in the Staff of the Reichsführer-SS and on 9 November 1944 he was promoted to SS-Brigadeführer and Generalmajor in the Waffen-SS. Hitler had personally awarded Blaschke the title of professor on 5 June 1943.

Shortly before the end of the war, Blaschke fled to the Alpine Fortress in Bavaria. During his internment in Bad Gastein, he helped to identify Hitler's teeth. Fedor Bruck, who took over Blaschke's abandoned practice on Kurfürstendamm, gave the names of technicians Käthe Heusermann and Felix Echtermann to the NKGB as witnesses who could possibly identify Hitler's teeth.[79] Heusermann, who was arrested by the NKGB, eventually found X-ray photographs of Hitler's teeth in the bunker, for which crowns had been made in 1945.[80]

Blaschke himself was later interned in Nuremberg, where he was required as a witness to identify various Nazis. He was not charged and was only asked in passing about the whereabouts of the Jewish dental gold. He claims that it was a 'special action' about which he had known nothing.[81] Nor did anyone ask him whether Hitler's gold teeth came from Jewish victims. The likelihood is very high, however. Blaschke had the dental gold at his disposal and also ran his own dental laboratory in which bridges and crowns were made. The senior SS dentist was classified as a 'follower' (*Mitläufer*) and released in 1948. He opened a dental practice in Nuremberg and died in 1959 at the age of 78 years.

SS-Wirtschafts-Verwaltungshauptamt

Berlin, 8. Oktober 1942

Chef A/Fr/B.

Tgb.Nr. 899/42 geh.

## Geheim

GEHEIM !

Betr.: Zahngold.

An den
Reichsführer-SS,
Berlin

Reichsführer !

Das von verstorbenen Schutzhäftlingen stammende
Zahn-Bruchgold wird auf Ihren Befehl an das Sanitätsamt
abgeliefert. Dort wird es für Zahnbehandlungszwecke
unserer Männer verwendet.

SS-Oberführer Blaschke verfügt bereits über einen
Bestand von über 50 kg Gold; das ist der voraussicht-
liche Edelmetallbedarf für die nächsten 5 Jahre.

Mehr Gold für diesen Zweck zu sammeln, halte ich sowohl
aus Sicherheitsgründen als auch im Interesse der Ver-
wertung nicht für angängig.

Ich bitte um Bestätigung, dass das künftig aus den
normalen Abgängen der K.L. anfallende Zahn-Bruchgold
an die Reichsbank gegen Anerkennung abgeliefert werden
darf.

Heil Hitler!

I.V.

Frank

SS-Brigadeführer
und Generalmajor der Waffen-SS.

4. Letter of complaint of 8 October 1942 to Reichsführer-SS Heinrich Himmler from the SS Economic and Administrative Head Office (WVHA). The dental gold from 'deceased' inmates had previously been made available to the Health Office. Hugo Blaschke, Senior SS Dentist, now had 50 kg, which would be sufficient for the coming five years. The clerk requested that in future the gold be sent to the Reichsbank 'to be disposed of'.

67

*Erwin Giesing (1907–1977)*
The ear, nose and throat specialist Erwin Giesing treated Hitler's ear-drum injuries and sinusitis following the assassination attempt on 20 July 1944. After 1945 he acted frequently as an eyewitness. A short biography can be found in the section 'Giesing's story'.

## The Specialists

*Carl Otto von Eicken (1873–1960)*
Carl Otto von Eicken was born on 30 December 1873 in Mülheim an der Ruhr. He studied medicine in Kiel, Geneva, Munich, Berlin and Heidelberg and following his prize-winning dissertation on the disinfection of infected wounds he started training for two years as a surgeon in 1899 in Heidelberg under Vinzenz Czerny before transferring as a junior surgeon to Gustav Killian in Freiburg.[82] Under Killian's supervision he completed a habilitation thesis in 1903 on the clinical assessment of methods for the direct examination of the respiratory tract and oesophagus. Seven years later he was summoned to Giessen. In 1922 he was appointed as Killian's successor at the Friedrich Wilhelm University of Berlin, where he amalgamated the first and second ear, nose and throat clinics at Charité into a single clinic, whose director he became in 1926.

Together with Killian, von Eicken developed new examination methods by laryngo-bronchoscopy and oesophagoscopy.[83] The International ENT Congress took place in Berlin in 1936 under von Eicken's presidency, which was a great scientific success for him. He chaired the different panels with great competence in several languages.[84] In 1940 his *Atlas der Hals-, Nasen- und Ohrenkrankheiten* was published, a collection of typical syndromes with topographical, diagnostic and therapeutic commentaries, which became a standard work.

Von Eicken, now a general practitioner, did not join any political party but was appointed by Hitler on 18 August 1942 as a member of the Scientific Senate of the Army Medical Corps and received the Goethe Medal for Art and Science from him in 1944.[85]

The first contact with Hitler took place in 1935 following an attack of hoarseness early in the year. Hitler was worried and lived in fear that he could lose his voice. As he was aware of the fate of Emperor Frederick III, who had died in 1888, he was also tormented by the idea that he might have laryngeal cancer.[86] On 15 May 1935, van Eicken therefore presented himself at the old Reich Chancellery and examined Hitler, discovering a polyp on the right vocal cord that needed to be removed. He performed the operation on 23 May in the Chancellor's apartment assisted by a nurse Maria, who was the only person allowed by Hitler.[87] Von Eicken advised his patient to protect his voice for four weeks, which Hitler extended until early August, giving rise to fresh rumours about his health. It finally became evident at the 1935 Reich Party Rally that Hitler's voice had completely recovered as it boomed from the wireless transmitters with its usual force.

Von Eicken was not to see Hitler again for another nine years. In October and November 1944 he had to travel to the Wolf's Lair to conduct a maxillary antral lavage on account of shadows seen in X-ray photographs of the sinuses. On this occasion he once again found a polyp on the vocal cord, which according to Morell's notes had a diameter of 2 mm. As Hitler and his entourage were obliged to leave the Wolf's Lair quickly on account of the advancing Soviet troops, von Eicken visited the Reich Chancellery on 22 November to remove the polyp.[88] He also brought relief by cleaning out the tonsils and irrigating the left maxillary sinus.[89]

On 30 December 1944, von Eicken examined Hitler again, flying specially from Berlin to the Eagle's Nest headquarters in the Taunus. He was satisfied with the results of his examination and according to Morell remarked that he was 'surprised at the good general health of the patient', who seemed to him to be 'strong and confident'.[90]

In the last months of the war, von Eicken operated in the basement of Charité and in the Sauerbruch surgical bunker. The 'tall, gaunt and elderly man', as a Russian interpreter described him, gained the respect of the Russian authorities on account of his devotion to duty. The investigating NKGB officers were impressed by the fact that von Eicken had also treated a Bulgarian student, indicating that he seemed not to have any racial prejudices.[91] Von Eicken remained in office after 1945 and became a member of the German Academy of Sciences in Berlin.[92] He retired at the age of seventy-seven and left East Berlin, dying in Heilbronn in 1960.

*Walter Löhlein (1882–1954)*
Hitler's ophthalmologist Walter Löhlein was born on 1 May 1882 in Berlin. He studied medicine in Bonn and elsewhere. In 1910 he obtained his habilitation in ophthalmology at the University of Greifswald. He was appointed extraordinary professor there in 1914 and taught from 1918 onwards at the University of Dorpat (Tartu, Estonia), which had been recently founded by the Germans. During the revolution and civil war, however, he lost his position

69

and returned to Germany. In 1921 he became an ordinary professor and clinic director at the University of Jena. In 1932 he moved to Freiburg and in 1934 to the University of Berlin, where he replaced a professor who had retired for reasons of age. Historians who have studied the history of the University of Berlin believe that it was not a politically motivated appointment.[93] Löhlein did not join the NSDAP until 1940.

He studied innovative methods of corneal transplantation and wrote the definitive manual on what was a new surgical method at the time. He was also interested in the heritability of certain eye diseases such as glaucoma. It was this interest in hereditary diseases that led to his appointment as an expert witness in the hereditary health trials. These trials often ended with the sterilization of the defendants to prevent their genes from being passed down.[94]

The Soviet cultural officers who studied the University of Berlin in 1945 classified Löhlein, in spite of his NSDAP membership, as 'non-incriminated' and confirmed his appointment as director of the ophthalmology clinic at Charité. When the Soviet-dominated denazification committees conducted a new review in 1948 and demanded a statement on his activities in the hereditary health courts, Löhlein, by then sixty-seven years old, submitted his resignation in 1949.[95] He taught thereafter as an honorary professor at the newly founded Free University of West Berlin and died in Essen on 14 September 1954.

*Alfred Nissle (1874–1965)*
Born on 30 December 1874 in Cöpernick (now Berlin), Alfred Nissle studied medicine in Berlin and Freiburg where he sat his final examinations and submitted a doctoral thesis on diseases of the sphenoidal sinus. After working as a junior doctor at the University of Berlin, he decided to specialize in hygiene. He worked at the Hygiene Institute of the University of Munich, habilitating in 1912 at the University of Königsberg (now Kaliningrad) in hygiene and bacteriology. He was appointed director of the Medical Research Office for Infectious Diseases in Baden in 1915, which also came with the title of extraordinary professor at the University of Freiburg.[96] His research focused on the therapeutic use of coliform bacteria. In 1917 he had isolated a viable bacterial strain of Escherichia coli from the intestine of a non-commissioned officer on the Balkan front who, unlike his colleagues, was not suffering from diarrhoea. He believed that 'his' strain of coliform bacteria could remove 'dysbacteria', i.e. the colonization of the intestine with 'degenerate' coliform bacteria.[97]

The drug developed by him was named Mutaflor. He had the name registered and the product was marketed by Handelsgesellschaft Deutscher Apotheker (HAGEDA). His commercialization of Mutaflor elicited mixed reactions from his colleagues.[98] It is still included in the Rote Liste (German index of medicines) and in 1939 was recommended for over twenty indications.[99]

Morell was a supporter of Nissle's dysbacteria theory, which he had learned about under Nobel Prize winner Ilya Ilyich Mechnikov at the Institut Pasteur in Paris.[100] It can no longer be determined precisely when Morell and Nissle met for the first time. Their correspondence in 1941 was friendly and very intense, which would suggest that they had communicated prior to that time. The relationship came to an end in 1944 after Morell opted for a preparation developed by himself with dead bacterial cultures.[101] Until this time, Nissle frequently spoke on the telephone with Morell to report on the results of examinations and the analysis of the stool of 'patient A.'.

In political terms, Nissle described himself as an extreme right-wing populist. He was the first member of staff of the University of Freiburg to offer lectures, from 1920 onwards, in genetic biology, eugenics (including important chapters on racial theory) and their importance for demographic policy. In 1922 he published a clearly right-wing but not anti-Semitic brochure on 'guidelines and proposals for the rebuilding of the strength and performance of our people'.[102] In the summer term of 1933 he was given an official teaching assignment, and his lectures, which had hitherto been optional, now became compulsory. He himself was thought to be unsuited to teach 'courses reflecting the National Socialist ideology', and the lectures were therefore delivered by an external lecturer.[103]

After his retirement, Nissle founded his own private research institute in 1938, which he directed until his death in 1965. He was awarded a start-up subsidy of RM 70,000 on Hitler's personal instructions. It is almost certain that Morell suggested this financing to Hitler, but Hitler himself was a firm believer in Mutaflor as it relieved his irritable bowel syndrome and, in his opinion, was responsible for the almost complete disappearance of his eczema.

*Arthur Weber (1879–1975)*
Unlike Brandt and Blaschke, who frequently spent time in the Führer headquarters and had important positions in the SS, the cardiologist Arthur Ernst Weber[104] must be regarded as a non-political expert. He was born on 3 August 1879 in Fechenheim near Frankfurt am Main and studied medicine in Marburg, Leipzig and Greifswald. He worked as a junior doctor in several university clinics including

71

Heidelberg and Kiel. In 1909 he habilitated with a thesis for the Department of Internal Medicine on the treatment of severe anaemia with human blood transfusions.[105] In 1914 he became director of the Medical Research Department of the Bäderkundliche Anstalt in Bad Nauheim on the eastern edge of the Taunus. This institute was part of the University of Giessen enabling Weber to continue to remain in close contact with academic researchers.

Bad Nauheim, a spa resort, had been modernized a few years previously at great cost. The grand duke of Hessen-Darmstadt, a small state with just over one million inhabitants, regarded science and medicine as economic factors. The thermal brine discovered in the mid-nineteenth century was said to have a positive effect on cardio-vascular complaints. As a result, the spa developed not only into a fashionable resort for the aristocracy and wealth of old Europe but also into a centre of medical research.

Weber himself was interested in electocardiography, an examination method that had first been developed around 1910,[106] and quickly took responsibility for medical training in this new diagnostic method. He had been extraordinary professor at the University of Giessen since 1914, and in 1926 he took over as medical director of what was then called a spa facility but which today would be regarded as a clinic specializing in cardiovascular complaints. He managed to acquire considerable state subsidies for the development of the University Department of Balneology, as it was called, and by 1929 its facilities and equipment put it on a par with leading private clinics and research institutes.[107]

Weber presented his first comprehensive work on electrocardiography in 1926. It was reprinted four times with revisions until 1948.[108] He also published several articles on the diagnosis of myocardial infarction and the distinction between infarction and coronary insufficiency. He retired as medical director in 1944 at the age of sixty-five and as a lecturer at the University of Giessen in 1950. In 1927 he had been one of the co-founders of the Deutsche Gesellschaft für Kreislaufforschung (German Cardiac Society) and in 1958 he was one of the founders of a society for studying and combating heart disease.

Weber was therefore regarded as *the* expert in cardiovascular diseases and it is understandable that Morell would consult with him to interpret Hitler's ECGs. The confidential tone of the correspondence would appear to indicate that Morell frequently consulted with him on patients or requested his expert opinion. It is unclear whether Weber knew whose ECGs he was evaluating, not least as Morell's accompanying letter referred only to a 'member of the Foreign Ministry'.[109]

## Hitler's Doctors: Summary

Hitler's dentist Hugo Blaschke managed the dental gold from Jewish victims, his last attendant doctor Ludwig Stumpfegger was involved in human experiments and received reports on the latest research results from Auschwitz. His predecessor Karl Brandt was responsible for the killing of tens of thousands of mentally sick patients. Karl Gebhardt and Ernst-Robert Grawitz, thought to be Hitler's doctors in 1935, later carried out medically unnecessary and in some cases fatal operations on healthy Polish concentration camp inmates at the SS hospital at Hohenlychen. Both Gebhardt and Grawitz ordered further human experiments in concentration camps.[110]

It is not surprising in retrospect that some of Hitler's doctors participated in Nazi crimes. They were close to the dictator and had extensive authority, which they exercised in Hitler's spirit. However, the examples of specialists like von Eicken and Löhlein or attendant doctor Hanskarl von Hasselbach also demonstrate that the doctors had other alternatives. Although close to Hitler, they did not use this familiarity for personal gain or to obtain power.

Theodor Morell's behaviour lies somewhere between. He used his position as personal physician for monetary gain but was not interested in furthering his own status politically. He was glad to accept honours and enjoyed being a focus of attention. He respected his patient, who made increasing demands on him, and considered Hitler's actions to be correct. As such, he regarded it as his task to ensure that Hitler remained capable of performing. This was one reason why he consulted a number of top specialists when he deemed it necessary. The microbiologist Alfred Nissle, the cardiologist Arthur Weber and the Charité professors were among the best in their respective fields. Morell's decisions on which drugs to prescribe and what diet to order for 'patient A.' will be discussed in the following chapter.

73

# — 4 —

# HITLER'S MEDICINE CHEST: THE DRUGS AND THEIR EFFECTS

## The Drugs

The records kept by personal physician Morell indicate that Hitler was prescribed a considerable number of drugs, even if most of them in retrospect prove to have been harmless.[1] As Hitler had no intention of changing his lifestyle and Morell could not find the energy to contradict him, an impressive number of preparations were prescribed over the years. There is no question that some of them were indicated and necessary; but at the same time there is also no doubt that many were superfluous and had no effect. The extent to which they had a stimulating or narcotic effect will also be discussed here.

During the years of his rule, Hitler took an almost pedantic interest in leading what he regarded as a healthy lifestyle. While he avoided alcohol almost completely and had an aversion to nicotine, the meagre, low-calorie diet he ordained for himself might not, however, have been completely safe in view of his chronic digestive problems. Hitler himself regarded his vegetarian diet as healthy but allowed that others did not follow his example. He commented to his dentist Professor Hugo Blaschke: 'You can see, doctor, how little my instructive influence has on those around me. I am the leader and yet I'm the only vegetarian, non-smoker and non-drinker.' Hitler was referring to the hedonism of some of those surrounding him. He forgot to add that he was continuously complaining about it.[2] In contrast to his lifestyle otherwise, his medicine chest was full to overflowing with painkillers, tranquillizers and sleeping pills, as well as pills to help with digestion and a number of vitamin and hormone preparations.

Morell supplied Hitler with drugs from 1936 onwards and did indeed achieve some remarkable medical results in a relative short time. His adjuvant 'medicinal nutrition' was designed primarily to maintain Hitler's performance and if possible to improve it. For years he injected what he described as a medicinal 'basic therapy' consisting essentially of a 10 or 20 per cent glucose solution, Vitamultin and the metabolic stimulant Tonophosphan. It was intended to cure both physical and mental exhaustion. This basic medication or adjuvant medicinal nutrition was administered by intravenous or intramuscular injection. This was perhaps one of the reasons why Göring described Morell as 'Reich Minister of Injections'. Morell's notes reveal, however, that Hitler appears to have had no objection to these injections and regarded them as genuine medication. He did not seem to take oral medication seriously and consumed sleeping pills and painkillers without compunction. Morell frequently modified or extended this basic programme. He combined his preparations skilfully, believing for example that glucose with added vitamins and hormones would have a generally fortifying effect and increase his patient's wellbeing, if only for a short time.

Hitler's surgical attendant doctors Brandt and Hasselbach, who did not have a close insight into Morell's treatment, expressed not unjustified reservations on several occasions about the 'mysterious avalanche of injections and pills' administered by the 'miracle doctor', claiming that frequent injections of glucose produced a feeling of euphoria and a real energy boost, an assertion that is open, however, to question. The 10 to 20 per cent glucose solution used by Morell will scarcely have improved Hitler's caloric intake. Morell refused to use higher concentrations, however, on account of possible side effects (disruption to the flow of fluid from blood to tissues). Even if he administered some 350 glucose injections in four years, it would be wrong to classify glucose as an addictive drug.

We have calculated that Hitler received a total of eighty-two drugs in the form of injection or through oral administration. David Irving, Ernst Günther Schenck and Ian Kershaw put the number at ninety over the five years of war. Joachim C. Fest, by contrast, speaks of a mere twenty-eight that Morell recalled on interrogation and named in the Morell protocol of 1945. Hans Bankl, based on Werner Maser's account, cites thirty different preparations that Hitler is said to have taken between 1936 and 1945.[3]

The composition of the pharmaceutical preparations, their administration and dosage were reconstructed on the basis of the seventh edition of the GEHE Codex of 1937 and the *Rote Liste* of 1939 and 1949.[4] This double verification was necessary because GEHE was the reference for pharmacists, while doctors based their prescriptions

# GEHES
# CODEX

der pharmazeutischen und organotherapeutischen Spezialpräparate(ein-
schließlich der Sera, Impfstoffe, Kos-
metica, Reinigungs-, Desinfektions-
und Schädlingsbekämpfungsmittel),
umfassend deutsche und zahlreiche
ausländische Erzeugnisse

mit kurzen Bemerkungen über die Zu-
sammensetzung, Anwendung und Dosie-
rungsweise nebst Angabe der Hersteller

Bearbeitet von der Wissenschaftlichen Abteilung der
GEHE A.-G., Chem. Fabriken, Dresden-N. 6

**Siebente,** neu gestaltete Auflage

1938 : 149
1937

SCHWARZECK-VERLAG G.M.B.H., DRESDEN-N. 6

5 and 6.    In the first half of the twentieth century many drugs were still
dispensed by pharmacies according to their own formulations. The preparations
made by the pharmaceutical industry were registered in a list called the GEHE
Codex. (The pharmaceutical wholesaler, which was founded in Dresden, is now
called Celesio AG and operates some 7,000 pharmacies throughout Europe.)
Drugs approved by the Reich Health Department were contained in the Red
List [Rote Liste]. This list is still published, although drug approval is now the
responsibility of the European Union. Courtesy of Hans-Joachim Neumann.

# PREISVERZEICHNIS
## deutscher pharmazeutischer
## Spezialpräparate

### 3. Auflage

# *Rote Liste*
## *1939*

Herausgegeben

von der

### Fachgruppe Pharmazeutische Erzeugnisse
der Wirtschaftsgruppe Chemische Industrie

### Berlin 1939

Courtesy of Hans-Joachim Neumann.

on the *Rote Liste*. Not all of the drugs prescribed for Hitler are to be found in these reference works. A large number of Morell's drugs came from his own pharmaceutical empire and were developed between 1943 and 1944, which meant that they could no longer be authorized.[5]

Some of the drugs might have been questionable, and it is possible that the Reich Health Department would not have authorized them. One conclusion that might be inferred from this is that 'patient A' may have been used by Morell as a guinea pig. This is unlikely to have been the case, however. Morell took over several pharmaceutical companies but they all had regular development departments and bodies that subjected every drug to thorough testing. Besides, Morell would have been too afraid of possible reprisals to try out drugs that had not been adequately tested.[6]

Around twenty preparations came from Morell's pharmaceutical factories. They included Vitamultin, made in Olomouc, in various forms, the sulphonamide Ultraseptyl developed in Budapest and manufactured in the Kosolup dye factory, Trocken-Coli-Hamma, also made by Morell himself – as an alternative to Mutaflor, the coli-bacteria preparation developed by the bacteriologist Alfred Nissle from Freiburg – and finally various hormone preparations and organ extracts.

There are several questions that are consistently raised. Did Morell know the activity spectrum of all of the drugs he prescribed for Hitler? Did he know that some batches of the Vitamultin tablets contained or could have contained the stimulant Pervitin? Or was it even perhaps at his instigation? Did he know about the strychnine in the harmless-seeming anti-gas pills, which Hitler often took in amounts in excess of the recommended daily dosage?

These questions will be addressed here in a systematic and alphabetic overview. This is what Hitler's 'medicine chest' looked like.

## Laxatives

*Laxatives (including enemas)* that Hitler took and administered himself were available over the counter in some cases, or by prescription only in others. They included Boxberger pills, Leo pills, calomel, Mitilax, Obstinol, Relaxol, castor oil, Yatren pills and camomile and were designed as treatment for his frequent constipation. The cause of constipation is slow intestinal transit as a result of a low-fibre diet and lack of movement, both of which applied to Hitler.

78

Evacuation can also be stimulated by massaging the abdominal wall, which Morell frequently proposed but which Hitler resolutely refused. Laxatives work in different ways, either as stool softeners, lubricants or peristaltic stimulants, or bulk-producing agents. The stool softeners include paraffin oil in the form of Mitilax or Obstinol. The latter is a mixture of two questionable laxatives, namely viscous paraffin and phenolphthalein.[7] The bulk-producing agents include wheat bran and linseed, or saline agents like Glauber's salt, Epsom salt, Carlsbad salt and Boxberger pills. These contained saline Kissinger salt and were also prescribed for constipation. The maximum recommended daily dose of one to two pills was occasionally increased by Morell to four or even nine.

On Morell's recommendation Hitler also reluctantly drank Karlsbad mineral water. The castor oil prescribed by Morell was an excessive measure that causes complete evacuation and is used before diagnostic, endoscopic and surgical interventions in the gastrointestinal tract. Hyperosmotic agents like castor oil increase water retention in the colon and act by reversing the flow of water back into the colon or by osmotic water retention in the intestinal lumen. Hitler preferred to administer enemas containing camomile on his own and for that purpose Morell provided him on 1 October 1944 with an enema syringe.

## Preparations

*Anti-Gas Pillen*, Dr. Köster & Co., Berlin-Wilmersdorf, a digestive used by Hitler for hyperacidity, meteorism (distension of the abdomen) and constipation, contained extract of deadly nightshade (*Atropa belladonna*) and also the plant toxin strychnine, a poisonous nitrogen compound found in the seeds of the *Strychnos nux-vomica* tree.[8] With some interruptions, Hitler took anti-gas pills for flatulence before every meal until October 1944. It was not Morell who prescribed these pills but SS Reich doctor and internal medicine specialist Dr Ernst-Robert Grawitz, who had recommended them to Hitler as early as 1935. As Hitler found the effect agreeable, Morell continued the treatment. After the assassination attempt on 20 July 1944 the anti-gas pills were the object of a hefty dispute ending in the dismissal of some of Hitler's attendant doctors, who attributed his jaundiced coloration in September 1944 to a strychnine overdose.[9] Hitler's close companion Martin Bormann had the anti-gas pills analysed by SS-Gruppenführer Dr Carl Blumenreuter from the Main Medical

Supply Department of the Waffen-SS, who found only small and non-toxic traces of strychnine and belladonna in the pills. Morell became more careful and had the possible side effects of other preparations examined by Blumenreuter. All of them proved to be safe according to the knowledge available at the time.[10]

*Brom-Nervacit* containing pyramidon, sodium diethyl barbiturate and 4 per cent potassium bromide was prescribed by Morell as a sedative. It was also supposed to help Hitler sleep and make him less agitated. To prevent bromine hypersensitivity it was initially pre-scribed only once every two months. Hitler subsequently took one to two tablespoonfuls per day, the maximum recommended daily dose being three to four tablespoonfuls.

*Calomel powder* was a laxative containing mercury that Morell rec-ommended for enemas, which were administered between 1941 and 1944, on some occasions by Hitler himself.

Following the suspicion of coronary sclerosis expressed in 1941 by cardiology professor Arthur Weber from Bad Nauheim, Morell treated Hitler with strophanthin and Cardiazol, occasionally alternating with Protophanta, which also contained strophanthin.

*Cardiazol*, Knoll AG, Ludwigshafen (pentylenetetrazol) was avail-able in ampoule, tablet, solution and powder form. It also came as a coated tablet combined with quinine (made from the bark of cinchona trees, an antipyretic used mainly to treat malaria and toxic in high doses). It was used as an analeptic (stimulant) in acute car-diovascular insufficiency. Morell prescribed Cardiazol from 1941 for Hitler's cardiovascular debility, which manifested itself in the form of recurrent ankle oedema. The treatment was interrupted as long as there were no symptoms. Morell proscribed both liquid Cardiazol and Cardiazol-Ephedrin in a recommended daily dosage of fifteen to twenty drops three times a day, the maximum daily dosage advised by the manufacturers for the liquid being four times twenty drops. As Morell knew that Cardiazol was regarded as a stimulant, he prescribed it with caution.

*Castor oil* was prescribed by Morell for stubborn constipation.

*Chineurin*, a quinine-containing cold remedy in capsule form made by Hamma GmbH Olomouc was prescribed by Morell instead of the sulphonamide Ultraseptyl, especially when Hitler was incubating a cold.

*Cocaine solution*, 10 per cent, was used by ENT specialist Dr Erwin Giesing, according to his own statement from 21 August 1944, to reduce pain caused by a suspected pansinusitis and with adrenalin to reduce the swelling of Hitler's nasal mucosa.[11] Giesing claims to have treated Hitler with cocaine until 1 October. He applied it with a brush on a daily basis and according to Giesing Hitler was well on the way to becoming addicted. Mention has already been made of Giesing's notorious unreliability as a witness. Hitler's incipient cocaine addiction clearly belongs to the myriad myths surrounding the dictator. Morell's records mention cocaine only three times and there is nothing about application with a brush, which also puts the frequency claimed by Giesing into question.

*Coramine* (pyridine-b-carbonic acid diethylamide) had a similar action to Cardiazol. Morell prescribed it with interruptions as a circulatory and respiratory stimulant and for oedema. He exercised the same caution as with Cardiazol, because Coramine was also regarded as a stimulant.

*Cortiron*, a drug made by Schering-Werke (deoxycortisone acetate) for diseases of the liver and gallbladder, was allegedly administered on just one occasion to treat myasthenia. As a single administration would have had no effect, Morell's claim might be questioned.

*Dolantin drops*, which contain the opioid pethidine hydrochloride and has a morphine-like action on the central and peripheral nervous systems, was made by Bayer. It was (and is) subject to the Narcotics Act (addictiveness and respiratory depression). Hitler took the opioid analgesic from 1941 to 1944 as required to treat severe pain.

*Enterofagos ampoules* from Morell's pharmaceutical empire, a polyvalent bacterial preparation made from typhus, paratyphoid fever, enteritis, dysentery and coli strains, were prescribed in 1942 and 1943 for gastrointestinal complaints before Morell's Trocken-Coli-Hamma preparation was available.

*Esdesan cum Nitro* from Pharmarium GmbH, Berlin, a preparation made of valerian, mistletoe, papaverine, strophanthin, chloral hydrate and nitroglycerine, was given to Hitler by Morell on

17 December 1942 as an emergency remedy for angina pectoris attacks. Hitler never needed it as the heart attacks in summer 1941 did not recur.

*Eubasin* (sulphapyridine), a sulphonamide from Nordmark-Werke, Hamburg, was administered to protect against infection. Its main indication was septic diseases and pneumonia, which Hitler never had as an adult. It was also indicated for festering skin and mucous conditions. Morell was reluctant to administer Eubasin for the severe pain caused by the intramuscular injections. As Hitler had chronic problems with his intestinal flora and Eubasin was supposed to have an effect on coliform bacteria, Morell also used this sulphonamide instead of Ultraseptyl, which Hitler's stomach had difficulty tolerating. Morell mostly used Ultraseptyl, however, a sulphonamide with questionable side effects, which he later manufactured himself. Hitler occasionally received up to six injections a day. He was also alleged to have taken one or two Ultraseptyl tablets per day, particularly for catarrhal inflammations of the upper respiratory passage and for angina, despite the fact that his stomach rebelled against the tablets.

*Euflat*, a combined preparation from Südmedica, made from the medicinal plant angelica, papaverine (a non-addictive spasmolytic opium alkaloid acting mainly on the gastrointestinal tract), aloe, pancreas and gallbladder extract, together with coffee charcoal, recommended particularly for excessive abdominal gas. Morell used Euflat from 1939 to 1944 in doses of one or two tablets per day to encourage digestion and to prevent meteorism.

*Eukodal* (dihydroxycodeinone chlorohydrate) from Merck, Darmstadt, was a synthetic morphine derivative subject to the Narcotic Prescription Regulation. It was used increasingly as an analgesic and spasmolytic. It came in ampoules (0.005, 0.01, 0.02 and 0.1 g) and tablets (0.005 g). Thanks to its strong analgesic and spasmolytic effect, Morell could achieve relief with a single intravenous injection. He used it as a potent spontaneous synthetic spasmolytic in 1943 and 1944.

*Eupaverin*, another Merck product (1-(3,4)-methylenedioxybenzyl-3-methyl-6,7-methylenedioxyisoquinoline) was an even stronger spasmolytic than papaverine but was less toxic. It came in ampoule and tablet form. Morell injected it as indicated for abdominal cramps and colic, increasingly with Eukodal, administered by intramuscular injection and for the first time intravenously on 17 October 1943. The increase in Eukodal injections, noted meticulously by Morell, is interesting. While Hitler received this morphine derivative for spasms four times in 1943, he was given nineteen injections in 1944, an indication that his spasms increased significantly in the penultimate war year.

*Gallestol*, a preparation from Efeka, Hanover, containing senna leaves was prescribed by Morell in 1944 for diseases of the liver and gallbladder and also as a digestive agent.[12]

*Glucose* in 10 or 20 per cent solution from HAGEDA and other manufacturers was injected by Morell from 1937 onwards. Apart from its properties as a general tonic he sought to improve Hitler's calorie intake. He frequently administered it every two or three days with strophanthin, adding a multivitamin preparation from 1943 until February 1945. The glucose injections formed the main pillar of Morell's basic medicinal programme.

*Glyconorm* (organ extract with nicotinamide, vitamin $B_1$ and C) was recommended for vitamin $B_1$ and C deficiency, fat absorption disorders and neuritis. According to Morell, he injected it intermittently from 1938 to 1940 to relieve Hitler's digestive problems. This claim is incorrect: Hitler received Glyconorm until 1944. It was made by Nordmark-Werke, Hamburg, and came in the form of ampoules and Glyconorm beans. Alongside glucose, Vitamultin and Tonphosphan, it was also part of Morell's basic medicinal arsenal.

*Harmine*, an alkaloid hydrochloride obtained from harmal and made by Merck, was taken by Hitler for the first time on 15 April 1945 for the 'abnormal shaking palsy', as Morell described Hitler's Parkinson's disease. Harmine was indicated for epidemic encephalitis and hypokinetic states. Morell was unable to administer injections himself in April 1945 because of his own tremor and was replaced by Dr Ludwig Stumpfegger, Hitler's surgical attendant doctor. It was not possible for Morell to determine whether harmine helped Hitler's tremor, because he was dismissed as personal physician six days after the start of treatment.

*Homatropine POS eye drops* were used when examining Hitler's eyes to dilate the pupils.

*Homoseran* from the Anhaltisches Serum-Institut, Dessau and Berlin, a preparation made from retroplacental blood, basically consisting of ovarian and pituitary hormones, vitamins and other restoratives, was injected by Morell for the first time from 7 to 15 November 1944 (series of five injections) to treat Hitler's tremor. It was indicated for septic diseases, epidemic encephalitis and climacteric complaints and was also said to strengthen resistance and combat depression. Based on his experience with the drug, Hitler requested a further course of treatment with Homoseran, which Morell commenced in December 1944.

*Intelan*, a multivitamin preparation from Ankermann, consisted of the active ingredients of cod liver oil, vitamin A, $B_{12}$, $D_2$ and glucose. Morell used it mostly to strengthen resistance, combat infections and arouse appetite and to treat Hitler's chronic fatigue. He employed it therapeutically like Vitamultin with two tablets a day. According to Morell, Hitler was treated with Intelan for three years, from 1942 to 1944.

*Leber Hamma* was a liver extract from Morell's own production with which he treated Hitler from 1943 to strengthen his resistance. In spite of the reported side effects, it was approved by the Reich Health Department on 3 January 1944.

*Luizym*, a standardized digestive enzyme preparation from Luitpold-Werk, Munich, containing cellulose, hemicelluloses, amylase, proteases and esterases, was used for digestive orders, particularly after gas-forming food. Morell prescribed one to two tablets or coated tablets after meals. He sought to compensate for nutritional deficiencies on account of Hitler's vegetarian diet and also to combat meteorism.

*Mutaflor*, a coliform bacteria preparation developed by Professor Alfred Nissle, director of the Bacteriological Research Institute in Freiburg, came in enteric-coated yellow and red capsules and was designed to suppress and replace degenerated pathogenic intestinal flora. It was indicated for colitis, diarrhoea, meteorism and chronic constipation and is still on the *Rote Liste* for irritable bowel syndrome. Its activity spectrum goes far beyond treatment of abnormal bacterial flora. Nissle also recommended its use for eczema, gastric and duodenal ulcers, migraine and depression and even cancer of the colon. According to Morell, not to mention Nissle, Mutaflor was something of a medicinal miracle weapon. He used it as a means of repopulating Hitler's intestinal tract with physiological flora.

Nissle had a dubious reputation among practitioners of traditional medicine, particularly clinicians, but this does not seem to have bothered Morell. He started prescribing Mutaflor in 1936 for Hitler's digestion problems, which he believed to be the result of abnormal intestinal flora and also the cause of his eczema.[13] The eczema, which had hitherto proved resistant to therapy, cleared up within six months, although Mutaflor did not improve the irritable bowel syndrome as much as Morell would have liked.

*Nateina*, a Spanish preparation marketed in Germany by HAGEDA, consisted of vitamin A, B, C, D and calcium phosphate and was administered orally to treat haemophilia and all kinds of haemorrhagic diathesis. Morell prescribed it for Hitler as a haemostatic to treat the heavily bleeding middle-ear injuries following the assassination attempt on 20 July 1944. It is unclear why David Irving should describe it as a 'mysterious haemostatic' as it was listed in both the GEHE Codex and the *Rote Liste*.[14] And it was not Dr Giesing who used Nateina to stop the bleeding in Hitler's middle ear, as Irving suggests but Morell, before Giesing was even consulted. The two doctors appear to have disagreed later on Nateina's utility. Giesing asked for a 10 per cent cocaine adrenaline solution, which Morell reluctantly obtained for him.[15]

*Nitroglycerine* was given by Morell to Hitler on 17 December 1942 with the Esdesan drops for emergencies after Weber's ECG had indicated the possibility of ischaemia of the coronary arteries and hence the danger of angina pectoris attacks. Hitler never used it.

*Omnadin*, a mixture of proteins, lipoids and animal fats made by Behring-Werke, Leverkusen, was administered to Hitler by his personal physician for colds, angina and incipient infections. It was generally assumed that Omnadin mobilized the body's defences by way of non-specific stimulation and it was therefore regarded as an alterative agent. Morell even preferred Omnadin to Ultraseptyl as it was non-toxic. It was occasionally combined with a Vitamultin preparation.

*Optalidon* (isobutylallyl barbituric acid, dimethyl aminophenazone and caffeine) was an effective painkiller and tranquillizer made by Sandoz, Nuremberg. Hitler took it mainly for headaches. His doctor recommended a dosage of one to two tablets per day as required. When taken regularly, the barbiturate component needs to be monitored. If Hitler took only one or two tablets per day, however, this warning is not so important, since the pharmacopoeia indicated a maximum daily dose of six tablets or two suppositories.

*Orchikrin*, an extract of seminal vesicles and the prostate of young bulls, like Prostakrin, was a Hamma product and could therefore have been used by Hitler only after 1943 for exhaustion, fatigue and depression. Morell claims to have injected it only 'now and then', usually when he was together with Eva Braun. It was administered by intramuscular injection.[16]

*Penicillin-Hamma*, prepared in the form of a powder by Morell's head chemist Dr Kurt Mulli, was used for ten days after the assassination attempt on 20 July 1944 to treat the skin injuries on Hitler's right hand. It had practically no antibiotic effect.[17]

*Pervitin* (methamphetamine hydrochloride) has a strong stimulating effect on the central nervous system.[18] There are no records of Morell having requested narcotics. Apart from the fact that such records might have been destroyed, this can also be explained by Morell's practice of ordering the corresponding products by telephone and having them delivered by couriers, thereby avoiding the need for a prescription.

*Phanodorm* (cyclohexenyl-ethyl barbituric acid), one of Hitler's preferred sleeping potions in tablet form, contained barbituric acid as its sole active ingredient. It was indicated for insomnia of various origins. Hitler occasionally took a further Phanodorm tablet in the early hours of the morning if he had not managed to sleep during the night despite having taken a tablet before retiring.

*Progynon-B oleosum* (benzoic acid ester of dihydrofollicle hormone dissolved in oil) made by Schering-Kahlbaum AG was administered by intramuscular injection in 1937, 1938 and 1944 to improve blood circulation in the gastric mucosa and to relieve gastrointestinal spasms. According to Morell's diagnosis, Hitler suffered in 1937 and 1938 from gastroduodenitis, an inflammation of the stomach and duodenum.

*Prostakrin*, like Orchikrin an extract of seminal vesicles and prostate, was administered in 1943 twice daily by intramuscular injection to

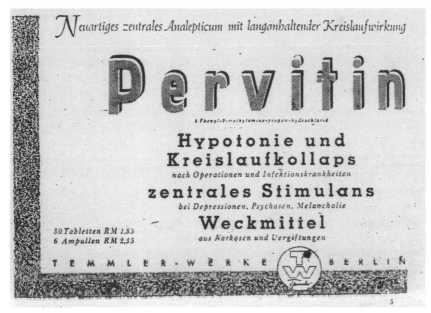

7. Pervitin, developed in 1938, was a powerful psychostimulant that after 1941 was obtainable only by prescription. Courtesy of Henrik Eberle.

combat Hitler's depressive moods. Like Orchikrin, Prostakrin was one of Morell's Hamma products from Olomouc. The indications for the two products were identical.

*Prostophanta*, a combined injection consisting of strophanthin, glucose, vitamin B complex and nicotinic acid, was administered by intravenous injection between 1942 and 1944 in alternation with strophanthin. It was also a Hamma product from Olomouc.

*Scophedal S.E.E.*, a combined preparation from Merck consisting of scopolamine, Eukodal and ephedrine and subject to the provisions of the Narcotics Prescription Regulation, was injected by Morell occasionally as a sedative, for example at 2 a.m. on 3 October 1944. S.E.E. was identical to Scophedal.

*Septoiod*, a concentrated aqueous solution with 3 per cent iodine, was used for respiratory infections. Morell also hoped that it would retard the progress of Hitler's coronary sclerosis. Between 1941 and 1944 he administered 10 cc intravenous injections. Morell also used

Septoid instead of Ultraseptyl because it was less toxic. It was made by Chemische Fabriken Dr. J. Wiernik & Co., Berlin.

*Strophanthin*, a glycoside found in *Strophanthus gratus* made by Boehringer & Söhne GmbH, Mannheim, was injected intravenously by Morell as a heart tonic to treat Hitler's incipient coronary sclerosis in several three-week cycles from 1941 to April 1945. It was administered with 10 cc of a 20 per cent glucose solution so as to lower the strophanthin concentration.

*Sympathol* (p-methylaminoethanol phenol tartrate), a circulation and heart tonic from Boehringer with an action similar to adrenaline available in ampoule or tablet form and as a solution, was taken by Hitler from 1942 in a dose of up to ten drops per day.

*Tempidorm tablets or suppositories* from Palm Schorndorf containing barbituric acid, like Phanodorm, were taken by Hitler as an alternative to Phanodorm from 1943 to 1945. They had a two-phase action with delayed absorption. Apart from Phanodorm and Tempidorm, Morell also gave Hitler phenobarbital, Luminal (not verified), and Luminaletten to help him sleep. The barbiturate-containing drugs Profundol and Quadro-Nox, indicated for sleep disorders of all aetiologies, were also occasionally administered.

Morell's figures on Hitler's sedative intake are not reliable. He frequently noted: 'no sedative' or 'night without sedatives', which would appear to indicate that otherwise Hitler always took sleeping pills. Morell also frequently wrote 'sedative' without further details. Finally, Hitler also took sleeping pills outside of Morell's influence.[19]

*Testoviron* from Schering, a testosterone propionate in oily solution, was injected by Morell in 1943 and 1944. It was recommended as a simple hormone therapy to increase sexual potency. It is possible that Morell hoped to improve Hitler's diminished general health and to fortify him rather than increasing his sexual potency. He noted thirteen intramuscular Testoviron injections in May, four in September and three in October. Morell's figures on the composition of the hormone injections are unclear – deliberately or not. It is known that testosterone deficiency in elderly men leads to erectile dysfunctions and osteoporosis. Long-term therapy, which Morell certainly believed that Hitler needed, normally improves the general health. There also appears to be a direct correlation with the presence of Eva

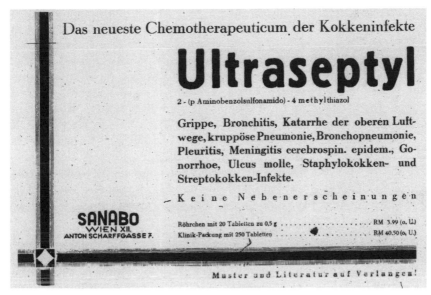

Das neueste Chemotherapeuticum der Kokkeninfekte

# Ultraseptyl

2 - (p Aminobenzolsulfonamido) - 4 methylthiazol

Grippe, Bronchitis, Katarrhe der oberen Luft-
wege, kruppöse Pneumonie, Bronchopneumonie,
Pleuritis, Meningitis cerebrospin. epidem., Go-
norrhoe, Ulcus molle, Staphylokokken- und
Streptokokken-Infekte.

Keine Nebenerscheinungen

**SANABO**
WIEN XII.
ANTON SCHARFFGASSE 7.

Röhrchen mit 20 Tabletten zu 0,5 g . . . . . . . . . . . . . . . . . . . . . RM 3.99 (o. U.)
Klinik-Packung mit 250 Tabletten . . . . . . . . . . . . . . . . RM 40.50 (o. U.)

Muster und Literatur auf Verlangen!

8. Morell's standard medication Ultraseptyl was advertised in the Munich
Medizinische Wochenschrift as the latest chemotherapeutic drug. Clinicians had
reservations about the sulphonamide contained in it because of its diverse side
effects. Courtesy of Henrik Eberle.

Braun with Hitler at the Berghof and the Reich Chancellery in Berlin,
since Hitler's long-standing mistress lived close to him from 1944
onwards (with interruptions).

*Tonophosphan* (sodium salt of dimethyl-amino-methyl-phenyl-phos-
phinic acid), a strong nerve and metabolic tonic made by Hoechst
and Bayer, available in ampoules or as tablets, was administered by
Morell by intramuscular injection from 1941 to 1944 to strengthen
Hitler's muscles. It was part of Morell's basic therapy programme
and was administered as frequently as Vitamultin.

*Ultraseptyl* (sulphomethylthiazole), the sulphonamide mentioned
earlier from Morell's pharmaceutical empire, was taken after meals with
fruit juice or water. The application and dosage have been described.

*Veritol* (b-(p-oxyphenyl)-isopropylmethylamine) is basically a blood-
pressure stimulant. It is also used in ophthalmology in the form of eye
drops for mydriasis (pupil dilation), as required by Hitler from March
1944 prior to eye examinations.

*Vitamultin-Calcium*, a multivitamin preparation containing vitamins A, B complex, C, D, E, K and P, was administered by Morell from 1938 to 1944 every two days without appreciable interruptions. Manufactured in huge quantities by Morell's pharmaceutical empire, Vitamultin formed one of the pillars of Hitler's basic medication along with Tonophosphan. It was available in ampoules and various tablet forms (Vitamultin-Calcium, Vitamultin forte, Vitamultin tablets). The Vitamultin tablets were the 'deluxe Vitamultin', whose ingredients were a closely guarded secret.[20] In 1942–3 the production of Vitamultin according to the original formulations of Nordmark, Hamburg, the original manufacturer, was transferred indirectly to Morell's Hamma GmbH in Olomouc and Hamburg. It was modified and reformulated by Morell's research laboratory, however, before going into production.[21]

*Yatren*, an odourless powder made of 7-iodo-8-oxyquinoline-5-sulphonic acid and sodium bicarbonate, was made by Bayer and prescribed by Morell along with Calomel in August 1941 for diarrhoea. Yatren pills were indicated above all to treat amoebic dysentery and all infectious intestinal diseases.[22] Hitler suffered from diarrhoea in his headquarters in East Prussia in summer 1941, but probably not amoebic dysentery, which occurs under unhygienic conditions in warm countries. It was probably bacterial dysentery, for which Yatren is not indicated. When Morell attempted to change the treatment, Hitler refused, saying that he was happy with Yatren.[23]

## Summary of Medical Preparations by Type

### Sedatives and soporifics
Brom-Nervacit, Luminaletten, Phanodorm, Tempidorm, Luminal (unverified), Profundol, Quadro-Nox

### Analgesics
Optalidon, Dolantin, Eukodal, Scophedal (all except Optalidon subject to the Narcotic Prescription Regulation)

### Cardiovascular agents
Sympathol, Strophanthin, Strophantose, Prostophanta, Septoid, Cardiazol, Coramin, Esdesan cum Nitro, nitroglycerine (the last two never used)

*Digestives*
Tonophosphan, Mutaflor, Enterofagos ampoules, Trocken-Coli-Hamma, Glyconorm, Luizym, Euflat, Anti-Gas Pillen, Acidol-Pepsin, Enzynorm, Gallestol

*Spasmolytics*
Eupaverin, Eukodal, Dolantin (the last two mainly as painkillers)

*Haemostatics*
Sangostop, Nateina, Thrombovit, Koagovit, Suprarenin (for local haemostasis)

*Antibacterial and flu agents*
Ultraseptyl, Eubasin, Tibatin, Omnadin, Septoiod (also used by Morell to treat Hitler's coronary sclerosis), Chineurin, Cortiron, Penicillin-Hamma

*Vitamins*
Intelan, Vitamultin-Calcium, Vitamultin forte, Vitamultin tablets (might have contained Pervitin), Cantan, Betabion, Benerva forte

*Hormones*
Cortiron (used to combat infectious diseases), Prostakrin, Orchikrin, Progynon, Testoviron, progesterone

*Stimulants*
Caffeine, Pervitin (not continuously), Cardiazol, Coramin (the latter two used by Morell to stimulate circulation and respiration)

*Eye drops*
Homatropine, Veritol

*Anti-tussives*
Codeine, Pyrenol

*Agents for shaking palsy (not explicitly Parkinson's disease)*
Homburg 680, Homoseran, harmine

*Fortifying agents*
Glucose, Glycovarin

It must be concluded that in spite of the fluctuating quantities Hitler's drug intake was unusually high. On 15 and 18 October 1944, for example, he received no fewer than eight different drugs, injections and tablets from his personal physician.[24]

Morell was not miserly in his choice of remedies. On the contrary, he treated his patients with several different drugs at the same time. Hitler's attendant doctors rightly pointed to the drug interactions, although it must be said that the attention to side effects was not as great as it is today.

Morell's 'basic therapy' was also polypharmacological. It consisted of a frequently varied and amended basic programme.[25] It should be borne in mind that Hitler was a difficult patient who, for all the therapeutic measures offered by Morell, only really believed in injections as an effective remedy.

To determine whether Hitler was ill, we needed to open his medicine chest, because its contents provide information about diseases requiring drug treatment. The range of drugs was so extensive, however, that it gives little indication of specific diseases. As the number of remedies was extraordinarily high, the layperson might be inclined to conclude that Hitler was seriously ill, requiring many drugs to keep him alive. In reality, Hitler was casual in his approach to many of the tablets he took. The Cola-Dallmann drops, which were still in circulation in the 1950s and which he liked to suck, are a typical example. He only regarded injections as real medicinal therapy.

Hitler clearly had diseases that needed medicinal treatment. His chronic gastrointestinal spasms could be treated only with spasmolytics. Cardiovascular agents were prescribed only after the ECG findings from Professor Weber. He ended up taking painkillers and sleeping potions on a regular basis and also acquired them on his own. The excessive supply of pills, tablets and injections by Morell does not prove that Hitler was ill but rather demonstrate that Morell was in awe of his patient A. In that regard, it would not be completely wrong to accuse him of irresponsibility as a doctor.

The common assumption that Hitler was an addict is not borne out by the fact that he frequently took a large number of mostly harmless remedies that in some cases even cancelled one another out.[26]

## Addictive Behaviour

Was Hitler addicted to drugs that removed inhibitions and controlled his destructive programme? Were they the reason for his behaviour?

Did the genocide of the Jews have something to do with addictive drugs? Did Hitler issue the senseless and futile command not to retreat from Stalingrad under the influence of these substances? Was he capable of getting through the daily military briefings in the last years of the war unassisted? Even if we need to ask these questions, it should be pointed out at the outset that his fanatical aims – the annihilation of the Jews and the destruction of his main ideological enemy, the Bolshevik Soviet Union – were already detailed in his book *Mein Kampf*.[27] But was Hitler already under the influence of drugs at this early stage? Was his ideology the result of dependence on stimulants? We shall attempt in the following section to study this question and reach a conclusion.

In the extensive writings, both the numerous autobiographies by persons in Hitler's immediate circle and studies by serious historians, various substances are cited to which Hitler was supposedly addicted. They include barbiturate-containing sedatives, the plant toxin strychnine, the morphine derivative Eukodal, the narcotic cocaine, and the stimulant Pervitin. Other wonder drugs or witches' remedies (*Hexenmittel*) are also mentioned in passing by a number of authors.

There is even speculation that Hitler was the most addicted of all the Nazi leaders and that his 'dealer' Morell kept him going by injecting 'huge amounts of Pervitin, cocaine, Eukodal, strychnine, belladonna, Testoviron, caffeine preparations and the heart stimulants Cardiazol and Coramin'. Of these, the only ones of relevance are Pervitin, Eukodal and cocaine, and to a lesser extent Cardiazol and Coramin, both of which were administered in low doses, because Morell was aware that they were regarded as stimulants.

## Barbiturate Alcohol Profile

All hypnotic barbiturates (a basic ingredient of many sedatives)[28] create physical dependence similar to that of alcohol – hence the concept of a 'barbiturate alcohol sedative profile'.[29] There was no danger of Hitler becoming dependent on alcohol because he drank only on 'special occasions', and then only a glass. According to Traudl Junge, Hitler preferred *Trockenbeerenauslese*, a very sweet wine normally served with desserts.[30] Heinz Linge, Hitler's personal ordinance officer, told the NKVD interrogating officers that after the Battle of Stalingrad Hitler occasionally drank a glass of slivovitz, but not on a regular basis.[31]

According to Morell's daily records, Hitler took various sedative substances during the war years, all of which contained barbiturates and which, in the appropriate dosage, were capable of inducing physical dependence. Between 1941 and 1945 Morell prescribed Phanodorm, Tempidorm, Brom-Nervacit, Profundol, Luminal (unverified) and Quadro-Nox (see Chapter 4). The details regarding quantities are less reliable because Hitler also took these substances without being expressly advised to do so. On 3 November 1944, for example, Morell noted that Hitler had told him that 'he took Brom-Nervacit when it was bad'.[32] Our conclusions are not therefore definitive and can only describe the likely tendency.

Morell gave Hitler Phanodorm and Brom-Nervacit six times in a month in 1941. In 1944 he prescribed them a further nine times in the whole year. If the annual intake from 1941 had extended over the entire year, Hitler would have received barbiturate-containing sedatives a total of seventy-two times. There is nothing in Morell's notes to suggest that this was the case.

Tempidorm was prescribed for the first time on 19 April 1943, after Morell had noted for 2 April that Hitler had taken a strong sedative.[33] Was this the Luminal searched for in vain in Morell's notes? In the last few months of the Nazi regime Morell prescribed a sedative four times: Euminal, which Hitler apparently didn't take, on 25 January, Brom-Nervacit on 10 February, Luminaletten on 26 February, and Tempidorm on 2 April. These small amounts would not be worth mentioning were it not for Morell's written comments that raise questions about his own claims. On 22 January 1945, he wrote: 'Sleep without sedatives'; on 19 March, by contrast, he wrote: 'slept badly despite sedatives', although there is no mention of sedatives in the entry for the previous day. Most interesting is Morell's entry for 18 April: 'Sleep possible at present only with Tempidorm.' In other words, Hitler was unable to sleep in the last weeks of his government without this substance. It can therefore be assumed that Tempidorm was taken on other occasions besides 2 April.

According to the current German Narcotics Act, one reason why barbiturates are included in the list of commercialized and prescribable narcotics is that they can lead to dependence. The abrupt termination of chronic barbiturate intake can cause withdrawal symptoms such as insomnia, agitation and increased anxiety. In severe cases it can produce confusion, seizures, tremors and psychotic states.[34]

If Morell's records are to be believed, the quantity of barbiturates consumed by Hitler is so small that he is not likely to have been dependent or suffered withdrawal. The problem of abrupt discontinuation is also irrelevant, as the substances were not taken over a long period. Even if Morell's comments such as 'no sedatives' mean that otherwise Hitler could not sleep without them, which according to Morell's records was probably the case after 18 April 1945,[35] or if he forgot to make an entry, the fact remains that Hitler was not dependent on barbiturates.

## Pervitin ('Speed')

Methamphetamine (Pervitin) was brought onto the market in 1938 by Temmler-Werke, Berlin, as a stimulant. Of all the putative addictive substances used by Hitler, it is the one on which the greatest speculation centres. Pervitin abuse brings about a short-term boost in energy and performance but frequent intake leads to psychological and physical dependence. There is also a decrease over time in the effect, with the result that increasing quantities are required.[36]

Many members of the Nazi elite were dependent on stimulants and addictive substances. Göring was a morphine addict and had already acquired cocaine for himself as a fighter pilot during the First World War. After Hitler's attempted putsch in 1923, Göring was treated with morphine for his abdominal injury and remained addicted to it until 1945. Goebbels noted in his diary following the recurrence of renal colic on 13 April 1943: 'For this hour I had to endure intolerable pain, and Professor Morell gave me a strong morphine injection, which brought some relief.'[37] Morell, who was later suspected of being a drug addict himself, treated practically all of the leading Nazis. There is no evidence in Goebbels' diaries or elsewhere that he encouraged his patients' addictions, however.

Pervitin was used extensively during the Second World War, particularly in the Polish and French campaigns. It was nicknamed 'tank chocolate' and 'Stuka tablets' and was used to make tank drivers, bomber pilots and U-boat crews less anxious and to increase their performance. The Wehrmacht is said to have been supplied with around 35 million tablets between April and June 1940. Chocolates containing Pervitin were even sold. Heinrich Böll wrote to his parents from the front asking them to send him Pervitin, which he continued to rely on even after the war.[38] Pervitin was used in enormous quantities in the Wehrmacht and armaments industry until the uncontrolled consumption was brought to an end.

Free access to the drug was prohibited in 1941 by Dr Leonardo Conti, Reich Health Leader and State Secretary in the Ministry of the Interior. He made it subject to prescription, bringing about a considerable decline in consumption in this way. The substances contained in Pervitin are known today by various names – crystal meth, speed, yaba, ice, and many others – and the purer crystalline form is particularly potent when smoked. This trend can also be traced back to the chemical laboratories of the Third Reich.[39] In 1988, Pervitin, which was already listed in the Narcotics Act, was withdrawn from the market in West Germany. According to the East German pharmacopoeia, Pervitin ampoules and tablets could still be prescribed in the GDR in 1988.

In a selection of fifteen biographies and pathographies of Hitler by historians, doctors, jurists and journalists, five authors suggest that Hitler was addicted to Pervitin. Seven believe that he might have been but cannot be certain. These books clearly talk about stimulants but not specifically about Pervitin. Only four authors remain of the opinion that Hitler was not addicted.

The most radical version is by Leonhard and Renate Heston, who blame Morell for Hitler's supposed addiction. They cite his rapid physical and mental decline after 1944 as evidence. In 2007 the American psychiatrist Leonhard Heston reiterated his 1979 view and wrote that Morell increased the morning methamphetamine injection 'from 2 to 4 to 10 cc's'.[40] By contrast, following an extensive study of source material, Ellen Gibbels came to the conclusion in 1990 that Hitler was not addicted to Pervitin.[41]

Eyewitnesses saw it differently. Hitler's secretary Christa Schroeder recalls: 'Hitler became increasingly dependent on these substances.' She was referring to Vitamultin and mentioned in particular the stimulant injections.[42] In Traudl Junge's opinion as well, 'Hitler was completely dependent on Morell.'[43] The only person able to give material evidence, however, was Ernst Günther Schenck, who had the ingredients of the Vitamultin tablets determined more or less illegally.[44]

Historians tend to be vague on the subject.[45] Werner Maser and Ian Kershaw avoid the issue, although Kershaw says 'that Hitler was ... drugged on opiates ... or dependent on cocaine ... can be discounted'. He continues: 'Whether Hitler took amphetamines ... is uncertain. That he was dependent on them ... cannot be proved; nor that his behaviour was affected by them.'[46]

It is known that Hitler took Vitamultin tablets, which might or might not have contained Pervitin. The composition of the tablets was discussed as the need arose in nocturnal telephone calls by Morell to his head chemist Dr Kurt Mulli. On 3 August 1944, for example,

Morell noted: '1 a.m. telephone call to Mulli.' It is certain that the batches contained caffeine and some also Pervitin. This is the conclusion reached by Schenck, who had the contents of the coded tablets examined by the Institute for Military Medicine.[47] The Vitamultin tablets, wrapped in gold or silver paper, were made in Mulli's laboratory with the marking 'S.F.' or 'S.R.K.' (special preparation for the Führer or Reich Chancellery) and delivered by courier from the Hamma factories in Olomouc or Hamburg to the Wolf's Lair or the Reich Chancellery.

In his book about Hitler, Schenck wrote that Morell's notes did not provide any clinical indication of a chronic Pervitin intoxication or dependence and was of the opinion that Morell did not supply Hitler regularly with this stimulant. His comment that Hitler took Vitamultin tablets in large quantities on a daily basis appears strangely contradictory.[48]

According to Morell's records from 1941 to 1945, Hitler received three Vitamultin tablets on 9 August 1941, whereas there is no mention of them at all in 1942. The following year Vitamultin is mentioned only once: on 19 July, when Hitler flew to visit Mussolini in Treviso, Morell decided that it would be wise to prepare Hitler for the meeting with drugs, although there is nothing in his notes to indicate how many tablets he administered. It is highly likely that he took some because during the meeting Hitler was so euphoric and verbose that Mussolini was barely able to get a word in edgeways. On 4 May 1944, Morell recommended that Hitler take four to six Vitamultin tablets with meals. This comment is contradicted by an entry on 27 October, in which he advised Hitler to take two Vitamultin tablets three times a day. Why did he make a special mention on this day, when Hitler had apparently been taking the drug since May? If he had suggested a new dosage on 27 October, the note would have been understandable. In either case, the dose was six tablets per day.[49]

Handwritten notes on the menu for the last three months of 1944 indicate that Hitler drank Vitamultin tea at breakfast. There is no mention for the main meal. Oral Vitamultin was available in tablets, pastilles, coated tablets and drops, and in this way the tea could be 'enriched' with Vitamultin as required. In front of the word Vitamultin is the number of pastilles or coated tablets to be added to the tea. The tablets were wrapped in gold or silver paper and thus identifiable as such, at least for those who knew about them.

## Vitamultin – Pervitin?

At this point we owe our readers an explanation of Morell's idio-syncratic abbreviations and way of writing. Sometimes he wrote 'Vitamultin-Täfelchen' (tablets) with a hyphen and sometimes as one word, giving the possibility for different abbreviations.

On 9 August 1941 he wrote: 'For today Yatren 3×3 pills, 1 Intelan, 3 Vitam. tablets', whereas on 19 July 1943 he has merely 'Vitamin-Täfelchen', which on 4 May 1944 became '4–6 Vitam[ultin] t[äfelchen]'. On 15 October Morell suggested one tablet three times per day, but Hitler apparently took only two. Morell noted on 27 October 1944: 'Pointing out the need for more vitamins to increase resistance, the patient should take 3×2 Vitam.t. per day'. Irving transcribed Morell's 'Vitam.t' as 'Vitamulin A'. He might just have misread it, but it could also have been deliberate to underpin the thesis that the Führer was a drug addict and no longer responsible for his actions.

Morell is alleged to have given Hitler an injection in the morning to get him fit for the day.[50] Leonhard Heston disputes this justifica-tion by Morell, saying that at the time the only two 'stimulants' in Germany were caffeine and Pervitin, with the result that Morell would have had difficulty achieving a stimulant effect with vitamins alone or with Vitamultin, without Pervitin, not to mention the fact that Hitler tended not to fall asleep properly – if he managed to sleep at all – until the early morning.

Nordmark-Werke in Hamburg and Morell's Hamma-Werke man-ufactured five different drugs under the name Vitamultin, but there was no Vitamultin A. For this reason, Irving's transcription must be questioned. There is a vitamin A preparation (retinol palmitate), but it contains no other vitamins except in some cases α-tocopherol, i.e. vitamin E.[51] According to Heston, Morell must have added Pervitin to the harmless vitamin mix, because no one perked up so much as Hitler after his injection.[52]

To improve the flavour of Vitamultin tablets, later special versions had added cocoa or cocoa butter, which was not to the taste of Hitler or Morell. According to Morell's entry for 27 October 1944, Hitler feared that the cocoa would cause constipation and that the daily dose of six tablets was therefore too high. Morell reduced the dose to 2×2 tablets.[53]

The abbreviation 'Vitam.t.' referred to the Vitamultin tablets. Hitler evidently wished to reduce his intake of these tablets, which does not sound consistent with an addiction. The intake of this

Pervitin-containing 'chocolate' was not mentioned again in Morell's records.

According to Irving, Morell wrote the name of the stimulant Pervitin only once in his records, on 19 December 1944, without using the description Vitamultin-Täfelchen: 'Pervitin on request because of current pressure of work'. As Pervitin is not mentioned anywhere else in Morell's records, this is also no indication of dependence on Hitler's part. Besides, the entry on 19 December 1944 also raises the question of why Morell mentioned it explicitly on that date and at no other time before or afterwards. One possible explanation is that he administered it on that day by injection: Pervitin was available as a 1 cc ampoule for intramuscular, subcutaneous or intravenous injection. The interpretation 'Pervit.-I.' is also questionable. There is no dot on the i, there is also one hyphen too many, and the t at the end of Pervit could just as well be a d. A more likely interpretation would be 'Perand-I.', standing for Peranderen, a testosterone prospionate approved in 1937.[54]

Morell entered all of the injections of Eukodal, a morphine derivative. Did he make an exception with Pervitin, because it had a 'whip like' effect on the organism[55] and it was therefore better to refrain from making any written reference to it? If so, why did he enter the Vitamultin tablets at all?

There is no indication that Hitler was able to conduct his daily briefings only because he took Pervitin or that his insane ideas – the holding of Stalingrad at all costs and the final offensive in the Ardennes – were hatched under the influence of this substance. Even today it is commonly believed that Hitler's mind was altered by drugs. The internationally renowned historian Leonhard Heston goes as far as to suggest that Hitler's tremor was not a symptom of Parkinson's disease but of chronic Pervitin dependence, a likelihood that can be excluded.[56]

For the sake of completeness, a word might be mentioned of the witches' remedies (German: Hexenmittel) or wonder drugs known to the Greeks and Romans that Morell is alleged to have used.[57] Today there are seminars on Hexenmittel in homeopathy, which were used by sorceresses in prehistoric times as remedies.[58] This all sounds highly mystical and esoteric, and the Hexenmittel are surrounded by an aura of magic.

None of this formed part of Hitler's medicinal therapy. Even Hitler's deputy attendant physician von Hasselbach used the term only as a disparaging description of Morell's method of treatment. The vast majority of the substances prescribed by Morell were listed in the German pharmacopoeias. A few came from Austria or Hungary and some were made by Morell's pharmaceutical empire. *Hexenmittel*, by contrast, have enchanted or harmful powers and are surrounded by a magical mystique. Their composition and effect are not known. None of this applied to the substances in Hitler's medicine chest, whose contents can still be analysed today.

## Strychnine

Toxic doses of strychnine (rat poison) are described in the textbook on toxic plants by Luth Roth and others as causing acute intoxication, spasms and death. Its effect is similar to that of tetanus.[59] In low doses it has a slight stimulating effect; in high doses it is paralyzing. It is generally agreed that the amount of strychnine in the anti-gas pills was small.

Strychnine is discussed here in Chapter 4 in connection with Hitler's anti-gas pills. It is also mentioned in connection with the dispute in early autumn 1944, when the attendant physicians led by Giesing incorrectly diagnosed Hitler's jaundice and gastrointestinal cramps as strychnine poisoning. Because of Hitler's jaundiced appearance, the anti-gas pills were analysed by order, among others, of Reichsleiter Bormann. According to the report made by Schenck for Irving in 1969, 120 anti-gas pills contained 0.035 g strychnine, making 0.00029 g per pill.[60] Hitler himself had informed Morell by phone on 13 October 1944 that R.l. [Reichsleiter] Bormann had had the anti-gas pills examined by Gruppenf[ührer] Dr Blumenreuter and that the pills were completely harmless. The manufacturer Dr. Köster & Co. recommended a daily dose of two to four pills three times a day. Based on a frequent or regular intake of sixteen pills a day, Hitler received 0.0046 g strychnine per day, much less than half the maximum daily dose of 0.01 g.

The ear, nose and throat specialist Giesing almost certainly overestimated the toxicity of strychnine. On the contrary, it was even recommended as an analeptic. In 1940 Hans Eppinger wrote of strychnine: 'The excellent effect of strychnine appears to have remained unknown for so long because in the past humans have received only subliminal amounts . . . I [can] recommend strychnine as the optimum peripheral cardiovascular agent.'[61] Eppinger gave his patients a daily dose of up to 0.048 g, almost five times the approved maximum daily dose of 0.01 g. According to the toxicological analysis by SS Head Pharmacist Carl Blumenreuter, the strychnine content of the anti-gas pills was so small that a person could take as many as forty pills a day without intoxication.[62]

Blumenreuter's readings were higher than the level recommended in the GEHE Codex and this could have been one of the reasons for Giesing's overestimation. GEHE is an official German pharmacopoeia and the data in it were more reliable than those of a single laboratory assay.[63]

It is therefore evident that Hitler's jaundice was not caused by the anti-gas pills. The assertion by the attendant doctors was rejected not only because Hitler always supported Morell but also and above all because the strychnine content of his pills was too low to cause damage to the liver parenchyma.[64]

According to the reference work on poisonous plants at the time, an intake of just 0.02 g strychnine can cause intoxication symptoms.[65] Spasms can occur with 0.015 g, and 0.1 to 0.3 g can be fatal. Death can be caused by an intake of as little as 0.03 g.

Giesing was certainly wrong in claiming that one pill had the strychnine content of 120 pills. Had his claim been correct, the dose would indeed have been toxic according to the GEHE Codex, although not Schenck's report for Irving. It can be said that even the increase to sixteen pills a day was not harmful and that while strychnine is toxic it is not addictive, so that Hitler could not therefore have been dependent. Hitler's jaundice must have had a cause other than strychnine. In retrospect, Morell's diagnosis of cholestasis (bile retention) is more likely than strychnine intoxication, a hypothesis formulated by Hitler's attendant physicians on the basis of incorrect assumptions.

## Eukodal

Eukodal (dihydroxycodeinone chlorohydrate), which was listed in the Narcotics Prescription Regulation from 1929 onwards, is worth discussing in terms of addiction because it was not only a fast-acting opioid analgesic but as a synthetic morphine derivative also increased the subjective feeling of wellbeing. Morphine is the main alkaloid in opium. Morphine-type addiction results in both psychological and physical dependence.[66] As Hitler's spasms increased in 1943 and 1944 he received a number of intravenous Eupaverin and Eukodal injections, and it is possible that these led to euphoria and a loss of inhibition. Morell's records for 1944 include Eukodal – the word is even underlined – but there is no mention of injections of this spasmolytic painkiller in 1941, 1942 and 1945, while Morell cites four occasions when he administered Eukodal injections in 1943, and as many as nineteen in 1944. The main form of administration in 1943 was intramuscular, but starting on 17 October and then throughout 1944 it was administered intravenously. Morell combined the Eukodal injections with the spasmolytic Eupaverin.[67]

It is unclear whether Hitler also had the Eukodal injections administered on account of their euphoric and stimulating effect as indication of an addiction. Morell's entry for 30 October 1944 reveals that this was probably not the case: 'Summoned to pat. without delay and instructed to bring Eupaverin.' Hitler said to him: 'What good fortune it is that we have this Eupaverin.'[68] He did not remind Morell not to forget the Eukodal but ordered him to bring the spasmolytic Eupaverin. Eukodal was not used by Hitler except when medically indicated.

In the dying days of the Third Reich, Hitler described Göring disparagingly as a morphine addict, which he would certainly not have done if he had been one himself. Hitler's irritability and tantrums, particularly during the military briefings in the face of Germany's imminent defeat, were not withdrawal symptoms. Hitler was not addicted to the morphine derivative Eukodal.

Production of Eukodal ceased in 1990 and since 1998 it has been available in the form of Oxycodon. Other trade names of this opioid analgesic are Oxygesic, Percodan, Percocet, Tylox and OxyContin, known among drug users as hillbilly heroin. Oxycodon has a morphine-like effect that is ten to twelve times as strong as that of the opiate derivative codeine. It has a high potential for misuse and is a dangerous addictive substance. One Oxygesic tablet contains eight to sixteen times the dose of the old Eukodal tablets.[69]

## Cocaine

Cocaine-type addiction also causes both psychological and physical dependence.[70] Cocaine is a psychotropic plant and chemical substance with addictive potential and is listed in the German Narcotics Act as a highly addictive drug that causes loss of inhibition and euphoria. It is also used as a local anaesthetic, however, and was part of the standard issue of army medical officers. Doctors on the front appreciated the painkilling and numbing effect of cocaine and regarded its addiction potential as a secondary consideration. It was with this in mind that in August 1944 ear, nose and throat specialist

Erwin Giesing ordered a 10 per cent cocaine solution from Engel-Apotheke in Berlin with a view to applying it to Hitler's nasal mucosa as treatment for sinusitis.[71] It is not surprising that Morell makes no mention of this treatment in his diaries. Cocaine is listed three times in his records, on all occasions in the form of eye drops. There is no mention whatsoever of Giesing's treatment.

Giesing's subsequent assertion that Hitler was addicted to cocaine does not stand up to scrutiny. Had he been, he would have requested another doctor, with Morell as the most likely candidate, to continue the nasal treatment after Giesing's dismissal as an attendant physician. This was not the case. It is also worth pointing out that a single application of cocaine as an analgesic is not sufficient to cause dependence. Even if Giesing did use cocaine on Hitler as he claims, it does not necessarily mean that it would have caused an addiction.

# — 5 —

# HITLER'S MEDICAL HISTORY

## Acute Illnesses

### Pulmonary Diseases in Hitler's Childhood and Adolescence

Hitler's medical history as a child and adolescent can be summarized briefly. He does not appear to have suffered any serious illnesses either as a child or during his years in Vienna and Munich. The effects of the gas attacks during the First World War have been discussed elsewhere. Hitler appears to have been healthy, although several of his close relatives died unusually early.[1] When he was eleven years old, his elder brother Edmund succumbed to measles and two years later his father died of a stroke.[2] The most painful loss came in 1907 with his mother's death of breast cancer.[3] Of her nine brothers and sisters, seven died as children; only Klara and her sisters Johanna and Theresia survived the nineteenth century.[4]

In view of this experience, Hitler was also concerned about the prospect of an early death. His mother had died at the age of forty-seven, and when he reached that age in 1936, his companions were mystified, as they had to put up with his gloomy thoughts of an early death. Albert Speer reported that from the end of 1937 Hitler would occasionally conclude discussion about his gigantic building projects with the words: 'I don't know how long I am going to live . . . Perhaps most of the buildings will be finished only when I am no longer here.'[5] He was assailed at this time by fears of death and after the ECG of 14 August 1941 commented on occasion that he had only two or three years to live.[6]

Hitler's first documented illness was scarlet fever in February/March 1897. A report from the single-class primary school at Fischlham near Lambach to the district school board states that:

104

'Adolf Hitler is suffering from scarlet fever',[7] a dreaded disease, from which he recovered quickly, however. Some people claim that he had his tonsils removed as a child.[8] According to David Irving, Hitler had the normal childhood illnesses.[9] He also claims that Hitler had had his tonsils removed. In this case, however, his research was incomplete as a more careful study of Morell's diaries, which were available at the time, would have revealed.[10]

According to Morell's initial examination in 1936, Hitler could have suffered as a child from chronic angina of the tonsillar crypts, which Morell inferred from the unevenness and scars on his patient's tonsils.[11] There are also a number of indications in Morell's notes that Hitler's tonsils were not removed.[12] Dr Eduard Bloch, the Hitler family doctor in Linz, recalled later that he had occasionally treated the young Hitler, who was conspicuously sallow and frail, for colds[13] and tonsillitis.[14] It is a myth that Hitler had his tonsils removed as a child.[15]

The doctor could not recall any serious illness. The desire voiced by Hitler's father – as expressed by Hitler in *Mein Kampf* – that his son pursue a career in the civil service was strongly resisted by the latter, who wanted to be an artist, but under no circumstances a civil servant. 'Then suddenly an illness came to my help and ... decided my future ... As a result of my *serious lung ailment*, a physician advised my mother in most urgent terms never to send me into an office. My attendance at the Realschule had furthermore to be interrupted for a year ... Concerned over my illness, my mother finally consented to take me out of the Realschule and let me attend the Academy.'[16]

Instead of going to school in autumn 1905 he was allowed to convalesce with relatives in the country. This visit to the Waldviertel was intended to strengthen the patient, but he apparently fell ill while with his relatives and was taken to hospital. Dr Karl Keiss from Weitra in the Waldviertel suspected pulmonary phthisis, which 'did not look very hopeful. Against expectations, however, he recovered relatively quickly.'[17] It is no longer possible to determine whether Hitler was sent to the country by his mother because he was ill or whether he became ill while he was there. At all events, he was removed from school, work and his normal surroundings.

When Dr Bloch entered Hitler's life he found no signs of a pulmonary disease. According to Bloch's papers, he treated Hitler for minor ailments. There is no question of him having had a 'serious lung ailment',[18] and Bloch also vehemently refuted this idea. It seems likely, however, that Hitler did suffer from some kind of acute respiratory illness. [19] It might have been acute bronchitis or a chronic obstructive respiratory disease. Pneumonia cannot be excluded either, and pulmonary tuberculosis could be considered as a possibility, although it would not have cleared up as quickly as Hitler's 'lung ailment' appears to have done. The most likely diagnosis is influenza or a general infection, which Hitler inflated into a 'serious lung ailment'.[20] Kubizek also notes that the young Hitler was prone to respiratory infections: 'His health was, in fact, rather poor, which he was the first to regret. He had to take special care of himself during the foggy and damp winters which prevailed in Linz. He . . . coughed a lot. In short, he had weak lungs.'[21]

Hitler's 'serious lung ailment' helped him out a second time. In autumn 1908 he went to Vienna, the big city, where he could disappear even more easily than in Linz. In this way he avoided being called up for military service. In May 1913 he went to Munich, where he lived as a 'stateless person' with Josef Popp, a tailor. On 18 January 1914, however, his self-imposed exile was interrupted by a visit from an officer of the criminal police, who presented him with a summons to register for military service in Linz. He duly appeared before the Austrian consulate in Munich on 19 January 1914. In a written plea he informed the consular official that he suffered from a recurrent chronic illness – the old 'serious lung ailment'. The medical took place as a result not in Linz but in Salzburg, where he was found to be 'too weak' for military service. Thus his 'severe lung ailment' gained him exemption from joining the army.[22]

## First World War

Six months later, Hitler volunteered paradoxically for the Second Bavarian Reserve Infantry Regiment No. 16, where he served for four years without being sick for a single day – except for his war injuries – and with no respiratory problems. On 5 October 1916 he was wounded in the left thigh by a shell explosion during the Battle of the Somme, but was discharged from the Beelitz Reserve Hospital near Potsdam on 1 December, although he did not return to his regiment at the front in Flanders until early March 1917. The injured left leg subsequently gave him trouble, despite the fact that the scar was pale and non-irritant and the bone had not been damaged.[23]

On 14 October 1918 he was partially blinded during a mustard gas attack and was treated in the neurology and psychiatry department of the reserve hospital in Pasewalk. Apart from colds with nasal catarrh, coughing, hoarseness and occasional inflamed tonsils, Hitler had no acute diseases worth mentioning during his youth. He was healthy even before the war. The only striking note was a pathological fear of infection that made him avoid people with flu-like symptoms, who were not allowed to approach him because of his manifest dread of viruses and bacteria. He was never to lose this fear, even during the Second World War.[24]

## Recurrent Hoarseness and Polyps

In the years of his political ascent, Hitler literally talked his way to power. During election campaigns, as in 1932, he held up to ten speeches a day in different places.[25] He was already fanatical by nature and would talk himself into a frenzy, paying no attention to the strain this put on his voice. Traudl Junge, his last secretary, reported in 1997 that he would start dictating slowly and sitting down. As he continued, however, he would stand up and pace up and down, and his voice would get louder until he ended up shouting. It was the same at the Reich party rallies and other public events, at which Hitler strained his voice to the extreme. It was inevitable that his voice would ultimately become hoarse as a result.

He was treated on this account for the first time in 1932 by the doctor Karl-Friedrich Dermietzel in Berlin. There is no indication from his file whether he was a competent ear, nose and throat special ist, but the records show that in the examination in early April 1932 he could not identify the causes of Hitler's hoarseness. Suspecting that he was straining his voice, the doctor recommended speech therapy. Hitler accepted this advice and on 6 April 1932 consulted Paul Devrient, a celebrated tenor, who was recognized by his colleagues as an excellent voice trainer.[26]

In 1935 Hitler's voice was once again so hoarse that a 'singing teacher' offered to give him speech therapy. Cough remedies and scarves knitted by admirers were also sent to the Reich Chancellery.[27] Hitler's suspicion that he had cancer came to the attention of the daughter of the United States ambassador, who was acquainted with several high-ranking Nazi politicians.[28] As a Soviet agent, she natu- rally passed on this information. In this way the rumour that Hitler was dying of cancer also reached the ears of Stalin.[29]

It was not until Hitler was examined by Professor Carl Otto von Eicken, director of the Ear, Nose and Throat Clinic at Charité Hospital in Berlin that a confirmed diagnosis was obtained. The examination, performed in Hitler's service apartment in the Reich Chancellery, revealed a change in the vocal cords due to a polyp.

The operation by von Eicken to remove the polyp also took place in Hitler's apartment. The specimen was submitted to Professor Robert Rössle, director of the Pathological Institute at Charité, for microscopic analysis, which confirmed that the biopsy sample taken from the patient 'Adolf Müller' was benign.[30]

Another change in the vocal cords was noted nine years later, although by this time Hitler gave very few speeches and strained his voice only during the briefings. Professor von Eicken was summoned to the headquarters on 20 September 1944 for consultation on the vocal cord findings. As the hoarseness was increasing, Morell had asked von Eicken to examine Hitler on 17 November 1944 in the Wolf's Lair. Morell noted in his diary: 'sm. pol[yp] (approx. 2 mm) on r[ight] vocal cord'.[31] Hitler was operated on by the ENT specialist in the Reich Chancellery in Berlin on 22 November 1944.[32]

Rössle confirmed the benignity of the specimen and informed von Eicken of his findings on 25 November 1944: 'Diagnosis: early stage singer's node. Assessment: not a genuine tumour but a swelling of the mucosal lining . . . caused by inflammation and shock to the vocal cord.'[33] With proper speech therapy this recurrence could possibly have been avoided.

### Dysentery and Hitler's Alleged Leadership Crisis In 1941

Hitler's health suffered in high summer 1941 when he experienced a bout of dysentery in the last week of July and two weeks in August. He was severely incapacitated by stomach cramps, diarrhoea, nausea and vomiting, joint pain and occasionally fever and chills. When they gained knowledge of this attack of dysentery, the generals referred to it as an 'indisposition'.[34] General Franz Halder, the Army Chief of General Staff, noted on 8 August 1941 in his daily journal (war diary): 'In spite of his indisposition the Führer gave precise instructions as to how the air force (Eighth Fighter Corps and Air Fleet I) are to be used.' [35] Goebbels, who visited the Wolf's Lair on 18 August, wrote in his diary: 'The Führer has unfortunately been somewhat ill in the last few days. He has had an attack of dysentery.'[36] On account of the dysentery and associated gastrointestinal spasms, Morell had sent stool samples of 'Pat. A.' to Nissle, who replied with a four-page letter, mentioning his 'wonder drug' Mutaflor (see Chapter 4), which not only regulated and repopulated the intestinal flora but was also an all-purpose medicine.[37]

During a meeting with the Romanian Marshal Ion Antonescu on 6 August in Berdichev, Ukraine, Hitler suffered from headache, a troublesome noise in his left ear and diarrhoea, which made him appear tired and sick.[38] After 7 August Morell kept a detailed record of Hitler's health.[39] Apart from the dysentery, he noted a tremor in the left arm and heard for the first time about the buzzing in the ear, which Hitler claimed had been troubling him for years.

The dysentery began to clear up in mid-August. According to Morell's records, it was probably bacterial dysentery caused by the Shigella genus. There are two possible courses and according to Morell, Hitler had the milder form, similar to infectious gastroenteritis. Fever, vomiting and tenesmus (painful straining during bowel movement or urination) and sudden onset are the typical symptoms of this form of dysentery. Dysentery itself has a large number of possible causes and, in the marshy headquarters in East Prussia, pathogens could have been transferred in water, milk or contaminated food, or through dirt or smear infections, however meticulously Hitler and his entourage observed basic hygiene principles. Hitler was probably not the only person affected because, according to Nicolaus von Below, members of the general staff also suffered from this disease in summer 1941, even if Morell makes no mention of it.[40]

Because of his ill health, Hitler's normal confidence was apparently compromised so much that he did not have the strength to resist the insistent demands made by the army leadership.[41] There is no question of a leadership crisis in August 1941, however, since against the wishes of the army high command Hitler changed the strategy for the advance and ordered that the assault on Moscow by Army Group Centre be stopped, as he believed that Moscow could be more easily captured by a pincer movement by Army Groups North and South. At the same time, prompted by economic considerations, he urged that the advance in Ukraine be speeded up.

The gradual disempowerment of the army high command by the Supreme Commander of the Wehrmacht had already started in late September 1939, and the resistance in summer 1941 was therefore relatively easy to overcome. Hitler increasingly determined, together with the army high command, which operations the army should carry out. He sought a military decision on the two flanks, while the army high command sought to advance in the centre.[42] Hitler's decision was later harshly criticized, and the view was expressed that the war against the Soviet Union could have been won if Hitler had followed the advice of the generals. The most important theatre was not in the south but around Moscow. The ensuing loss of time is claimed to have been decisive for the course of the war.[43]

It is now clear that it was not the Third Reich that lost the war at this time but the Soviet Union that won it. It was not the change in the marching orders but the reaction by the opposition. The Soviet leadership managed within a few weeks to achieve what no one had thought possible, namely the reorganization of its military command structure. Moreover, immense reserves were mobilized in a very short time. It was the successful counter-offensive by the Red Army in December 1941 that stopped the German campaign. The Soviet Union achieved this first victory after a series of disastrous defeats with heavy loss of life, but even if it had been defeated at Moscow, the army was prepared to continue the fight.[44] Hitler's dysentery and the non-existent leadership crisis had nothing to do with the course of the war.

### Autumn 1944: Jaundice and the Doctors' Dispute

Hitler was the only person to remain practically unscathed by the assassination attempt on 20 July 1944, while others lost their lives or were severely injured. Stauffenberg's bomb did nevertheless cause some minor injury. Countless small wood splinters had to be removed from Hitler's legs, and his right ear began to bleed. A balance test also indicated that the inner ear had been damaged, with the result that Hitler subsequently had a tendency to lean to the right when he walked. He also complained of a taste of blood in his mouth. The problems with both ears increased with time: the right ear became deaf and he had difficulty hearing with the left ear. As a consequence, a consultation with an ear, nose and throat specialist was called for.

As Professor von Eicken was not available, Professor Brandt summoned the most readily accessible specialist from Berlin, Oberstabstarzt Dr Erwin Giesing from the Karlshof Reserve Hospital near Rastenburg, who examined Hitler on 22 July. He proposed that the eardrum injury be treated by cauterizing with astringent Hexaminkron solution to form granules that would close the perforations in the eardrum. Dr Giesing treated Hitler for around two months and wrote two controversial reports after the war during his interrogation as an attendant physician.[45]

Hitler demanded a booster dose of sulphonamide with Ultraseptyl to prevent a possible inflammation of the middle ear. Giesing refused. It was Hitler's belief that 'Morell has such a good drug, called Ultraseptyl, it's helped me a lot in the past.' When von Eicken examined Hitler on 18 August, he recommended treatment with the more effective and less toxic Tibatin, which Morell rejected saying: 'Not possible, the Führer is intolerant to other drugs, he only tolerates Ultraseptyl.'

110

Hitler's pathological susceptibility to infections has already been discussed. Because of the tremor in his hand he now had to be shaved, something he was quite averse to because the knife at his throat made him feel uneasy. On 17 August he caught a severe infection from his personal hairdresser August Wollenhaupt. He said reproachfully: 'The man has had a cold for five days and didn't mention it to me.' From experience both he and Morell were aware that inflammations of the nose, throat and upper respiratory tract were very difficult and never took fewer than six weeks to heal. Hitler was annoyed about the infection. He had a feeling of pressure in his head, particularly around the forehead. Professor von Eicken noted on 18 August: 'Consultation: both eardrums healthy . . . uncertainty only when walking in the dark. General health much better than on 23 July.' Giesing considered that Hitler's new complaint was probably due to frontal sinusitis or pansinusitis. He took over the treatment and ordered a 10 per cent cocaine solution from the Engel-Apotheke in Berlin to relieve Hitler's headaches. Morell would like to have prevented the order but because the patient was Hitler he had to accept Giesing's suggestion regardless. On 21 August Giesing started the application of cocaine to the nasal mucosa. Hitler immediately felt relief and could think more clearly and requested two or three applications a day as a consequence. Morell made no mention of this treatment.[46]

According to Giesing, who continued the cocaine treatment until 1 October, Hitler fainted for ninety seconds on 12 September. He had a blackout and his pulse was racing and weak. When he came round he spoke incoherently. Giesing claims to have wanted to discontinue the cocaine treatment, but Hitler allegedly insisted that it be kept up. According to Giesing, Hitler fainted again on 14 and 16 September. As soon as the cocaine wore off, Hitler's headache returned with undiminished intensity. Dr Giesing and the other doctors therefore advised Hitler to have an X-ray taken of his skull without delay. After a good deal of persuasion, he finally agreed and after the SS had carefully checked the premises for explosives he was X-rayed on 19 September in the Karlshof Reserve Hospital near Rastenburg.[47]

The following day, Dr Giesing was struck by an unusual redness in Hitler's face, and he informed the deputy attendant surgeon, Professor von Hasselbach, of his observations. Morell also appears to have noticed this change, but none of the doctors could explain the cause. When Professor von Eicken came to the Wolf's Lair on 22 September to treat the inflamed left maxillary sinus he confirmed the observations made by the attendant physicians and found an inexplicable photosensitivity in addition. Giesing also told von Eicken that

Hitler's voice was noticeably husky and that 'the Führer's hoarseness' had already lasted three weeks. On 27 September Morell entered in his diary after visiting Hitler: 'At 9 p.m. this evening I commented to the Führer that he was looking a bit yellow. I wanted to examine him: refused.' Dr Giesing believed that Hitler was suffering from jaundice, which Morell vehemently disputed.[48]

The next day Morell once again injected Eukodal and Eupaverin because Hitler was suffering severe colic immediately after eating lunch. Morell also noted on 28 September: 'Face yellow, no fever' and urine 'brown as beer'. At fifteen minutes past midnight Hitler had the same symptoms as the previous evening, prompting Morell to repeat the injections he had administered in the late afternoon; in other words giving the patient the morphine derivative for the second time that day. On 29 September he ordered Hitler to rest in bed and prohibited all visits. This meant that the attendant physicians could not see him either – including Giesing, whom Hitler supposedly expected every day for the cocaine treatment.[49]

Giesing believed that all of Hitler's health problems were due to his unusually high drug intake. When he was at the Wolf's Lair in August for the cocaine treatment, he noticed by chance that Hitler's breakfast tray contained a whole saucer full of pills and tablets that he could not identify. He was particularly struck by the small black globules, the anti-gas pills. Giesing read their composition and was shocked to discover that they contained two potent neurotoxins (atropine and strychnine) (see Chapter 4). According to SS-Sturmbannführer Heinz Linge, Hitler's valet from 1939 onwards, he took 'terrifying quantities' of these pills every day. Giesing was outraged that Morell simply allowed Hitler to take as much strychnine as he wanted. He thought it possible that all of Hitler's problems were symptoms of poisoning. When he met Hitler by chance outdoors, he noticed that his skin and eyes were yellow.

This realization and his suspicion that Morell might have been acting negligently began to worry Giesing increasingly. Who could he confide in? Not Morell, who was his 'main suspect'. As Hitler supported his personal physician, he could not tell him either. If Giesing was to prevent any further damage, however, he had to confront Morell. Going through the proper channels, he therefore consulted Professor Brandt, the senior attendant physician, along with von Hasselbach, who declared spontaneously 'that must be one of Morell's many witches' remedies!', and left it to Brandt to decide what to do. The situation then took the course Giesing had hoped for.[50]

Hitler was really ill at the end of September and Morell treated him at this time with castor oil and hot camomile tea enemas, unsweetened camomile infusions and gruel soup. For his tender liver and gallbladder region he applied wet poultices and a heating pad or, as he wrote on 30 September, 'heating pad on wet stomach-liver poultice'. After the doctors at headquarters had informed Brandt about Hitler's jaundice, the chief attendant physician set off immediately from Berlin, obtained an 'illicit' urine sample from Hitler on 3 October and had it tested for strychnine, as Giesing attributed Hitler's yellow colour to that substance. Hitler's 'official' urine samples, including the last one on 30 November, were normal.[51] On 30 September Morell suggested an X-ray of the stomach, intestines and gallbladder, not least to exclude the possibility of gallstones. As so often, the suggestion was ignored.

On the same day, Brandt arranged a meeting with Morell, which the latter carefully noted: 'Brandt said the Führer had been swallowing sixteen anti-gas pills every day, which contained so much strychnine that it came perilously close to the maximum dose; he claimed that the present illness and all the previous ones were a chronic case of strychnine poisoning. In his (Brandt's) opinion the Führer was getting better now because during the last five days in which he had been confined to bed the Führer had stopped consuming the anti-gas pills . . . He said the tremor could also be attributed to this cause . . . I've got all I need (said Brandt) to prove this was a clear case of strychnine poisoning.' Morell also noted how Brandt had obtained the information, having made a comment in the presence of Dr Raimund von Ondarza, Göring's personal physician, about icterus with bile reflux.[52]

After ten days Hitler's apparent jaundice had practically disappeared. Icterus (jaundice) is caused by increased levels of bilirubin (haemoglobin by-product) in the blood, leading to absorption in the skin. Hitler's jaundice could have had several causes. The attendant physicians believed that the liver parenchyma had been damaged by strychnine and that Hitler was suffering from drug-induced or intrahepatic jaundice. Morell diagnosed obstructive jaundice as a result of a mechanical blockage to the bile flow. This occurs through inflammation of the bile ducts in connection with gallstones or a tumour and results in bile reflux. Morell therefore excluded the possibility of strychnine poisoning. It is also worth considering the possibility of type A viral hepatitis, which can occasionally result in a protracted two-peak course of up to six months. The 0.1 to 1 per cent risk of hepatic damage can increase by a factor of thirty to sixty.[53]

Strychnine poisoning as a result of excessive intake of anti-gas pills, as the attendant physicians accused Morell of having brought about, could not have been the cause of Hitler's jaundice, however, because the strychnine content of the anti-gas pills was small, as the survey of Hitler's medicine chest has shown. Moreover, strychnine poisoning normally causes tetanus-like spasms and even death by asphyxiation through the involvement of the respiratory muscles. As Hitler had been taking the anti-gas pills since 1935 and the maximum daily dose increased after Stalingrad, he would long have had symptoms of poisoning.[54]

In the event, Morell's diagnosis was probably correct. On 3 October, for example, he noted that the jaundice had been caused by the pyloroduodenum with bile reflux. Hitler had long suffered from gastrointestinal spasms, and the severe digestive problems following his illness obliged Morell to inject spasmolytics with increased frequency. The suspicion voiced by Schenck that Hitler was suffering from viral hepatitis can probably be discounted since hepatitis takes four to eight weeks to clear up, whereas Hitler was healthy again after ten days. The jaundice was thus most probably the result of bile reflux, as Morell suggested.

Morell's diagnosis is also likely to have been correct in the light of the change in the way he described Hitler's chronic gastrointestinal problems. He had generally spoken of 'spasms', but after 28 September 1944 he wrote 'severe colic pain'. In theory, Hitler could also have had gallstones, which are often asymptomatic (silent gallstones) and produce colic (gallstone attack) only following an obstruction or inflammation of the bile ducts. The symptoms include a feeling of fullness in the upper abdomen, sometimes with meteorism, nausea and vomiting, and jaundice. Hitler lost three kilograms during this time and was so poorly that he did not contest Morell's instruction that he be confined to bed.[55]

The vexing strychnine story had considerable consequences for Hitler's doctors. Hitler was furious that they had dared to confront Morell. During the attack Morell himself certainly felt uneasy because the outcome was unclear, however blameless he felt, not least because he did not know how many anti-gas pills Hitler was taking every day. Hitler backed Morell to the hilt, however, and said to him on 3 October: 'Just let these gentlemen come and try telling me that! . . . What is this stupid bunch after?' As Morell took his leave after his regular consultation, Hitler said: 'Doctor, I am so happy to see you every morning!'

Hitler had boundless confidence in his personal physician. When Hitler had a submandibular swelling at this time and Giesing was

DER SEKRETÄR DES FÜHRERS
REICHSLEITER MARTIN BORMANN

FÜHRERHAUPTQUARTIER  10.Oktober 44
ANSCHRIFT FÜR POSTSENDUNGEN
MÜNCHEN 33, FÜHRERBAU

Bo/Ur.

An den
Reichspressechef
Herrn Reichsleiter Dr. Dietrich

Führerhauptquartier

Sehr verehrter Herr Dr. Dietrich!

Wegen seiner Tätigkeit als Reichskommissar schied Professor
Dr. B r a n d t mit Wirkung vom 10.10.44 als Begleitarzt
des Führers aus, desgleichen Professor Dr. von H a s s e l-
b a c h, der ihn längere Zeit als Begleitarzt vertrat.

Der Führer ernannte mit Wirkung vom 10.10.44 zum Begleitarzt
den SS-Obersturmbannführer Dr. S t u m p f e g g e r.

Heil Hitler!
Ihr

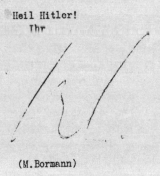

(M.Bormann)

43.  October 1944: The doctors' dispute in the Führer headquarters led
to the dismissal of long-standing attendant physicians Karl Brandt and
Hanskarl von Hasselbach. They were replaced by Himmler's attendant
physician Ludwig Stumpfegger.

once again called in on 4 October, Hitler is said to have asked him:
'Doctor, where did you get the story of the anti-gas pills from? You
have given Morell a huge fright. He looks quite pale and distraught
... But I put his mind at rest.' Hitler's dentist, Professor Blaschke,
was also summoned on 4 October, as swellings of this type are often

odontogenetic (caused by the teeth). Blaschke was unable to identify the cause either, however. Morell believed that Giesing had scratched the mucosa with his fingernail while examining Hitler, causing an inflammation in the mouth. The swelling subsided and by 12 October was completely gone. Hitler's tonsils remained red until 18 October.[56]

After this wearisome pill story, the days of Brandt and von Hasselbach as attendant physicians were numbered. Brandt had hoped finally to bring about Morell's downfall. But it did not work out that way and on 8 October Morell was able to note with satisfaction in his pocket diary that the Führer had informed him that Dr von Hasselbach had been sent back and that Brandt would henceforth only perform his duties as commissary general for the health service in Berlin. The new attendant surgeon was a young doctor by the name of Stumpfegger, who for some time had attended Reichsführer-SS Himmler.

Brandt and von Hasselbach were dismissed on 9 October. An hour later it was the turn of Giesing, who had started the dispute. Martin Bormann told him not to take it so seriously and assured him: 'We have nothing against you. On the contrary the Führer has only the highest praise for you.'[57] On 10 October 1944 Bormann sent a letter to Reich Press Chief Dr Otto Dietrich to notify him of the changes in the attendant physicians.[58] On 13 October, Hitler summed up the affair, saying to Morell: 'So the pills only harmed them!'[59] On 8 November, Hitler brought up the subject again: 'That these idiots [the attendant physicians] didn't consider what they would have done to *me* ... [They] surely ... knew that you [me] had saved my life ... several times in the last eight years. And how had I been before that? All of the doctors who were brought to me had failed.' Morell replied: 'My Führer, if a normal doctor had treated you since then, you would have been away from work for so long that the Reich would have collapsed. I *had* to give you high-dosed emergency treatment and *had* to go to the limits of what was allowed, although I was criticized by many colleagues for it, but I accept the responsibility because if you had been out of action for a long time in the present situation Germany would have gone to pieces.' Hitler appeared to be so moved by his doctor's concern, not only about his health but also about the fate of the Reich that he said: 'My dear doctor, I am content and happy to have you.'[60]

## October 1944: Hitler's Tonsillitis

Hitler's tonsils, which not only remained red but were also once again acutely inflamed, were treated by Morell alone. The acute condition proved stubborn, however. Morell noted the need to 'dab tonsils

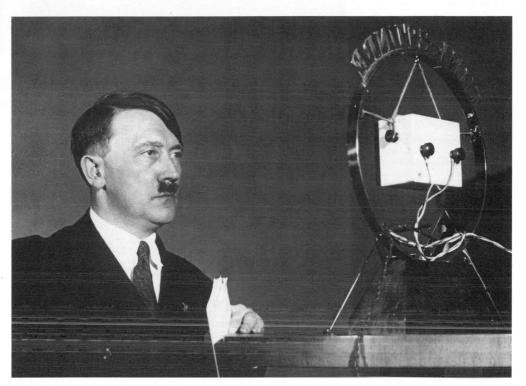

9. In this photograph Adolf Hitler looks young, dynamic and determined as he gives a radio speech on 1 February 1933 after becoming Reich Chancellor.

10. Hitler's last public appearance on 20 March 1945 is meant to show a leader who is resolute and unbroken. However, his posture is bent and his face puffy. Eye witnesses were forced to wonder whether it was just because he had aged so much or whether he was incurably ill.

**11.** Snapshots of Hitler wearing reading glasses are rare and the propaganda machinery deliberately avoided showing these typical signs of aging. Hitler often used a magnifying glass to study maps, and speeches and draft decisions were typed in large print on the 'Führer typewriter'.

**12.** This typical pose was a result of Parkinson's disease. Hitler held his left arm so as to mask the increasing tremor. Dr. Morell, Hitler's personal physician, pictured here in the background, noted the trembling a few days after he started keeping records in summer 1941. Attendant surgeon Dr Brandt (right edge of the photograph) was convinced until his death in 1948 that Hitler did not have Parkinson's disease. The photograph was taken in Austria in April 1941. Hitler is holding on to his left wrist. In earlier photos his hands were loosely crossed in front of him.

13.  Snapshots taken during a walk on the Mooslahner Kopf in January 1937 with personal physician Theo Morell, adjutant Wilhelm Brückner and architect Roderich Fick on the way to the planned Kehlsteinhaus. It is no coincidence that the doctor was allowed to accompany Hitler on this walk, although he had only been attending the Führer for a year. Hitler trusted him from the outset and believed him to be particularly gifted.

14.  In a break in negotiations during the Bad Godesberg conference in September 1938 Hitler and his entourage took a trip on the Rhine. His personal physician was always present at important diplomatic events.

15.  Dr. med. Theodor Morell, here in uniform, used his closeness to Hitler for his own business purposes. His 'unappetizing' appearance fostered the suspicion that he was a charlatan and a quack.

16.  Berlin, Kurfürstendamm at Fasanenstrasse. Dr Morell had a dermatology and venereal disease practice on the first floor of this well situated building. In treating venereal diseases he did not just rely on the recently developed sulphonamides but also espoused a holistic approach. In 1936 he cured Hitler's chronic skin complaint. Courtesy of Sammlung Peter-Alexander Bosel.

17. Hitler's birthday on 20 April 1938, with personal photographer Heinrich Hoffmann, attendant surgeon Dr Brandt and orderlies in the background, and Dr Morell on the right. The birthday reception in the Reich Chancellery did not follow the classic diplomatic protocol. Hitler accepted the congratulations not only of political figures but also of his courtiers. Courtesy of Hans-Joachim Neumann.

18. This photograph was published when Hitler awarded Morell the Knight's Cross of the Cross of Military Valour on 24 February 1944. In fact the picture was taken in 1938 when Morell became a professor. The head of state in Germany was allowed to award this honour and it did not necessarily mean that the holder had a chair in a university.

Courtesy of the Archiv der
Humboldt-Universität Berlin

Above: Attendant surgeons Karl
Brandt and Hanskarl von Hasselbach
(both Charité Berlin)

Middle: Ludwig Stumpfegger,
attendant physician from 1944

Below: Dentist Hugo Blaschke (private
practice, Berlin) and ENT specialist
Erwin Giesing (reserve military
hospital, Karlshof)

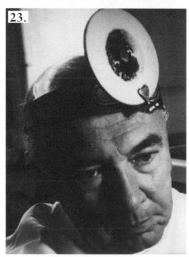

24.

25.

26.

Courtesy of Bibliothek der
Humboldt Universität

Courtesy of Bibliothek der
Humboldt Universität

Courtesy of Alfred Nissle
– Gesellschaft

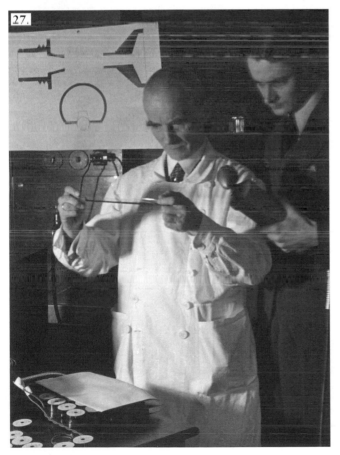

27.

Consultants: ENT specialist
Carl Otto von Eicken (Charité
Berlin), ophthalmologist Walter
Löhlein (Charité Berlin),
Alfred Nissle (University of
Freiburg) and Arthur Weber
(Bad Nauheim, University of
Giessen)

28.  Karl Brandt's wedding in Hermann Göring's Berlin apartment on 17 March 1934. The bride, Anni Rehborn, a sports teacher, and the artist Sophie Storck had both been members of Hitler's entourage since 1925. The adjutant Wilhelm Brückner had been Hitler's commanding officer during the First World War. The photograph demonstrates the close private links between leading National Socialists.

29.  One of the few photographs of Hitler in which he is shown confronting the consequences of his war. On 15 March 1942 'Heldengedenktag' or Memorial Day he took the salute at a parade of wounded soldiers in wheelchairs in Unter den Linden in Berlin. He is escorted by SS Obergruppenführer Hanns Oberlindober, head of the Nazi association for wounded veterans, attendant surgeon Karl Brandt, and field marshal Wilhelm Keitel.

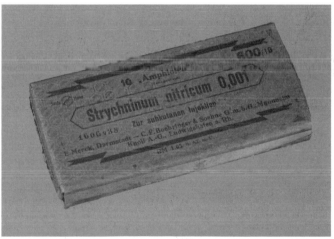

30. The Engel-Apotheke building in Mohrenstrasse, Berlin, purchased in 1928 by Allianz Versicherung, was burnt to the ground in the last hours of the war. All of the doctors in the government district of Berlin, including Hitler's personal physician, obtained their medicaments there, regardless of whether they were treating diplomats or high-ranking officials or politicians. The term 'SS-Apotheke' (SS pharmacy) that is sometimes seen is incorrect. The pharmacist Ernst Just took over the pharmacy in 1930 and was not removed until 1955, for a violation of the trading regulations between East and West Germany. Courtesy of Berlin Mitte Archiv.

31. Strychnine, a component of Dr Kösters Antigas-Pillen, provoked a dispute among the doctors in the Führer's headquarters in 1944, which resulted in the dismissal of Brandt, von Hasselbach and Giesing. Courtesy of Charité Berlin.

**32.** A selection of the many drugs prescribed by Morell. He often treated Hitler with several drugs simultaneously without considering possible interactions. Hitler was not interested in this aspect either and merely demanded that his personal physician restore his ability to act without delay. Courtesy of Charité Berlin.

a)

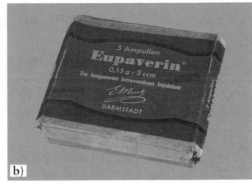

b)

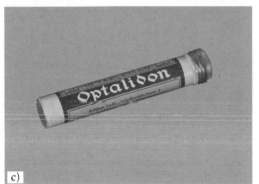

c)

d)

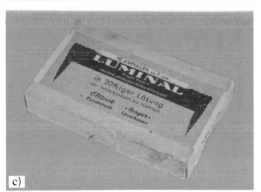

c)

33. Morell frequently injected the morphine derivative Eukodal together with the spasmolytic Eupaverin in order to treat Hitler's intestinal spasms. Optalidon was an effective drug in tablet form for treating headaches. Hitler took Sympatol to stabilize his blood circulation. It is not known whether Hitler ever took the barbiturate-containing soporific Luminal and there is no documentation to that effect. Courtesy of Charité Berlin.

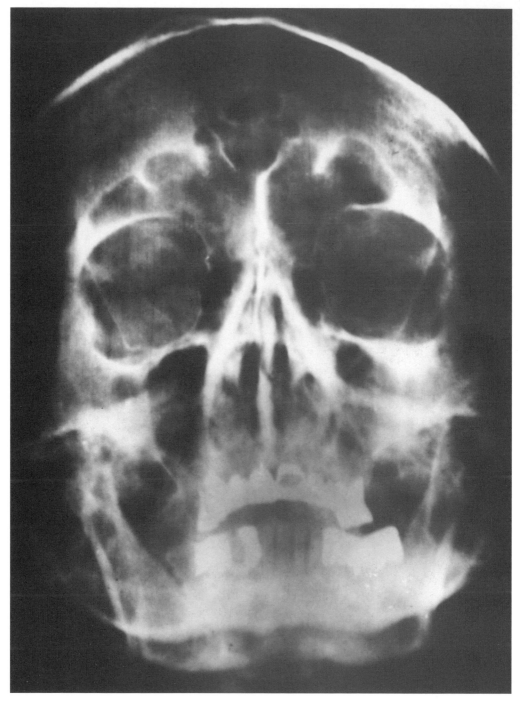

**34.** The left maxillary sinus is partially shadowed. The X-ray was taken after the assassination attempt on 20 July 1944.

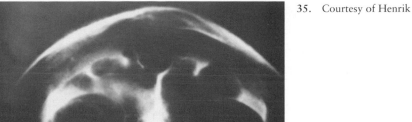

35. Courtesy of Henrik Eberle.

36. Courtesy of Henrik Eberle.

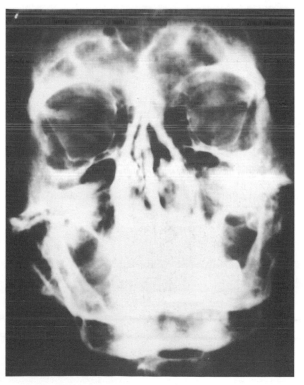

The upper X-ray from 22 September 1944 shows that both maxillary sinuses are well aerated. In the lower X-ray incipient lateral shadowing of the left sinus can be discerned.

**37.** On 7 October 1941 Hitler congratulated Reichsführer-SS Heinrich Himmler on his birthday. Himmler had returned a few days earlier from his inspection tour of the mobile killing units and reported on it to Hitler. In September and October 1941 they planned the extermination of the Jews together.

**38.** Hitler with Mussolini on the way to Feltre north of Venice. For the meeting with the wavering Axis partner Morell had 'armed' Hitler with Vitamultin tablets, which might have contained the stimulant Pervitin.

**39.** Briefing on the eastern front in March 1945. Hitler was marked by Parkinson's disease and could not stand for more than half an hour. The trembling left hand is concealed under the table. His intellectual capacities were not affected by the disease.

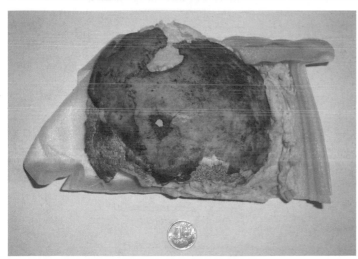

**40.** Remains of Hitler's skull found by officers of the Soviet secret service NKVD. The cranial vault shows an exit hole caused by a pistol shot (Prof. Dr. Gunther Geserick, Charité Berlin). A DNA analysis would establish for certain whether it is actually Hitler's skull, but to date the Russian State Archive has not agreed to such a test. Courtesy of Henrik Eberle.

Right after the German capitulation, the Allies attempted to establish for certain that Hitler was dead. Soviet officers exhumed the remains of his burnt corpse and confirmed its authenticity on the basis of dental records. These remains are currently kept in the archive of the former KGB in Moscow. The American investigators questioned numerous eye witnesses including Morell and Brandt, who shared a cell in the investigation camp in Oberursel near Frankfurt. The picture below shows a Christmas card drawn by internees in 1945.

41. Courtesy of Henrik Eberle.

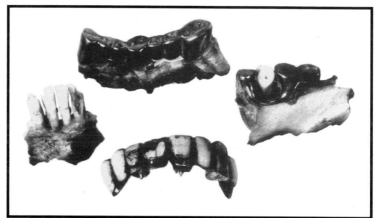

42. Courtesy of Sammlung Franz Gajdosch

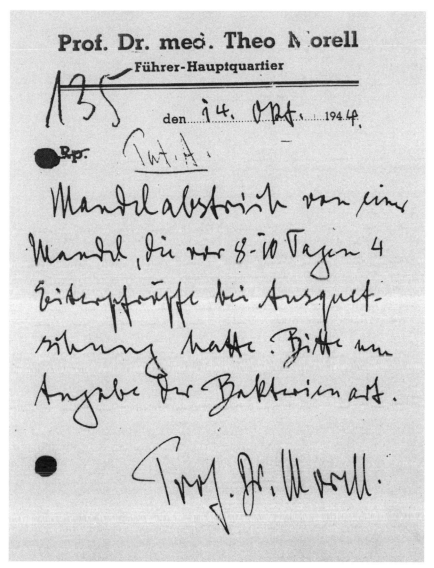

**44.** In October 1944 Morell squeezed the septic tonsil of 'Patient A.'
On 14 October he requested identification of the bacteria.

with Neo-Pyocyanase' and 'swab with Lugol's solution'. In mid-October 1944 he also submitted a smear from one of Hitler's tonsils that 'when squeezed had (probably four detritus plugs)' for pathogenic analysis.[61] As Hitler's acute recurring inflammations gradually became chronic, Morell considered a tonsillectomy and wrote in his diary: 'If the tonsil does not improve soon, removal after healing.'[62] The tonsillectomy was not performed, however. Because of the chronic tonsillitis, Hitler had had severe halitosis since March 1945, which Morell was not the only person to notice.[63] This had also been remarked on occasion as early as 1942.

## Conclusion

All in all, Hitler did not suffer extensively from acute illnesses. The occasional colds and tonsillitis, the injuries and buzzing in the ears required treatment, but did not have any lasting effects. His tremor, of course, needs to be taken into consideration, but cannot be described as an acute disease. Hitler's irritability and increasingly frequent tantrums at the slightest provocation in the last months of his life were intolerably difficult for his entourage but understandable in view of the course of the war.

Hitler was concerned about his voice and he was tormented by a fear of cancer in the light of the fate of Kaiser Frederick. The two operations to remove polyps on his vocal cords were harmless, and the microscopic analysis confirmed Professor von Eicken's clinical diagnosis. By contrast, he was resigned to the reduced mobility of his left arm as the result of the injury in 1923 in front of the Feldherrnhalle in Munich.

He was confined to bed on account of illness only twice: the dysentery in summer 1941 and the jaundice in early autumn 1944. In both cases he recovered quickly and was able to attend the daily briefings again. Even when he was indisposed, however, he did not relinquish his control of events at any time.

## Chronic Diseases

Apart from the acute illnesses, Hitler also suffered from other complaints requiring treatment. His medical history started with irritable bowel syndrome, which was already causing him trouble in 1929.[64] This condition is also known as spastic or irritable colon or colonic neurosis. Other conditions requiring treatment were coronary sclerosis diagnosed in 1941, hypertension and the shaking palsy observed by Morell for the first time in 1941, which neither he nor Hitler's attendant physicians associated with Parkinson's disease.[65]

## Irritable Bowel Syndrome

Chronic irritable bowel or colon is a functional intestinal disorder without demonstrable structural abnormality. It produces colic-like abdominal pain, mainly in the lower abdomen. It can also include symptoms affecting the biliary system (gallbladder). The main clinical symptom is abdominal pain relieved by defaecation. The patient has a distended abdomen, feels full and nauseous and needs to belch frequently. Bowel evacuation is typically irregular, alternating between constipation and diarrhoea. The patient also has the feeling that the bowels have not been completely evacuated. The gastrointestinal spasms can be triggered by a low-fibre diet with protein and vitamin deficiency and occasionally also by cold drinks. More frequently, however, chronic irritable bowel syndrome is caused by emotional tension and stress. This was probably the case with Hitler. In most patients the disorders do not go away but they do not reduce life expectancy. Therapy should be preceded by an explanatory discussion of this basically harmless but not trivial condition. A detailed diagnostic examination should also be carried out at all events to exclude other diseases like cancer of the colon or ulcerative colitis.[66] A diet high in dietary fibre to provide the bulk needed to transport the contents of the intestines is also urgently recommended. Although Hitler consulted Morell on his diet, he adamantly refused any further diagnostic examination. The only medicinal treatment he allowed was spasmolytics and analgesics (Eupaverin and Eukodal).

There are four other clinical syndromes with symptoms similar to that of irritable bowel syndrome.

### Roemheld syndrome
This set of gastrocardiac symptoms, named after the German physician who first described it, is more frequently observed in men than in women. The patient experiences a feeling of constriction and left ventricular discomfort caused by upper abdominal meteorism and an accumulation of air in the left colonic flexura. Cardiac symptoms including angina pectoris attacks, tachycardia and extrasystoles can occur along with gastric pain, nausea and hot flushes.[67]

### Porphyria
Porphyria is an inherited or acquired haemoglobin biosynthesis dysfunction. Certain forms can make urine turn red.[68] Tachycardia and hypertension are also observed.[69] The disease has different forms, the symptoms of acute intermittent porphyria being most similar to those

119

of irritable bowel syndrome. The main symptoms of porphyria are abdominal difficulties with spasms, colic and intense pain. Vomiting, constipation or diarrhoea complete the clinical picture. Manifest neurological symptoms including paralysis can occur, as can agitation, psychotic and delirious states, which are not infrequently mistaken for hysteria.

### Diabetic enteropathy

Non-diagnosed diabetes mellitus and high blood sugar levels can produce the symptoms of chronic irritable bowel syndrome. Once other causes have been excluded, the irritable colon can in fact be diabetic enteropathy, mainly with type 2 diabetes, which is often associated with gastroduodenal symptoms, particularly constipation, diarrhoea, nausea and vomiting, and stool incontinence.[70] Hitler's sweet tooth and fondness for cakes could have produced a temporary increase in his blood sugar level, but it is nevertheless rare for diabetes to trigger irritable bowel symptoms. Morell regularly monitored Hitler's blood sugar levels from 1940 until the end of the war so as to preclude the possibility of diabetes. They were consistently in the normal range between 90 and 120 mg/dl (5.0 to 6.66 mmol/l). Hitler's urine status was also normal in this regard. Diabetes will not therefore have been the cause of Hitler's gastrointestinal spasms.[71]

### Abnormal intestinal flora

The Freiburg bacteriologist Nissle believed that pathological processes could also be triggered by abnormal intestinal flora. Hitler's digestive disorders could thus have been a consequence of dysbacteria, i.e. abnormal enteric bacteria. Nissle's research showed that the abnormal bacteria could be suppressed and replaced by biologically tested coliform strains (Escherichia coli). These coliform strains were among the ingredients of Mutaflor (see Chapter 4) prescribed by Morell as a course of treatment.

All treatment was preceded by an analysis of Hitler's excrement in Nissle's Bacteriological Research Institute in Freiburg. Practically all of Hitler's stool samples revealed abnormal intestinal flora, and both Nissle and Morell believed that Mutaflor was indicated. Hitler himself claimed that the course of treatment with Mutaflor improved his condition and relieved the gastrointestinal problems. Morell continued to submit stool samples in the last months of the war, which would seem to indicate that he believed there was a connection between Hitler's spasms and the abnormal intestinal flora. It is highly likely that the ongoing administration of 'healthy' bacteria strains will have helped to recolonize Hitler's intestine, but Morell was nevertheless obliged to prescribe spasmolytics repeatedly to relieve the discomfort.[72]

*Summary*
Even if other diseases have similar symptoms, Hitler's colic was unquestionably a case of chronic irritable bowel syndrome. Roemheld syndrome and porphyria can be excluded. Diabetic enteropathy is also rare and can be discounted. The attempts by Morell and Nissle to replace Hitler's intestinal flora were effective only for a short while and had little impact on the chronic complaint.

## Digression: Hitler's Vegetarian Diet

The fact that Hitler was a vegetarian should also be considered in connection with his chronic digestive disorders. After 1930 Hitler barely ate meat and he himself blamed meat for his discomfort. In their book, *Medical Casebook of Adolf Hitler*, the American doctors Leonhard and Renate Heston consider that vegetarianism was the sole cause of Hitler's digestive disorders. The dictator apparently suffered such severe cramps after eating that he ultimately developed an 'eccentric diet' that became 'nearly vegetarian' and caused even greater digestive problems.[73] According to the Hestons his basic diet was vegetables and cereal (muesli). This assertion is not borne out, however, by eyewitness statements or Morell's frequent references to diet. It has also been testified that Hitler sometimes got 'carried away' and abandoned his vegetarian diet and that he was in any case no fan of vegetables and cereal on their own. In other words, he did not keep consistently to his diet.

A strict vegan eats only plant food. A more moderate form, lacto-vegetarianism, allows animal products like eggs, milk and dairy produce, and also fish. Eggs and dairy products were frequently served in the Reich Chancellery. Hitler was thus not an orthodox vegan but rather a liberal vegetarian. He was also not completely consistent in his refusal to eat meat products. He was fond of the liver dumplings made by Anni Winter, his housekeeper in Munich, and her half-sister Angela. Some authors also write that Hitler was not averse to Bavarian sausages and pigeon. The only genuine vegetarian in Hitler's entourage was probably Rudolf Hess.[74]

One often cited speculative reason for Hitler's apparently sudden change from an omnivore to a vegetarian was the suicide of his niece Geli Raubal in 1931, which is said to have caused so much emotional turmoil in Hitler that he never again ate meat and meals prepared with animal fat.[75] According to Geli's brother Leo, he did not attend her funeral in Vienna because he was in no mental or physical state to do so.[76]

From a medical point of view, Hitler's abrupt switch to vegetarianism is difficult to understand. It would have been explicable perhaps if a post-mortem had been performed on Geli Raubal in his presence. The Munich forensic pathologist Professor Dr Wolfgang Eisenmenger wrote in this regard on 31 May 2007: 'A post-mortem was not performed on Geli Raubal . . . The police and public prosecutors did not demand it at the time in clear cases of suicide.' There is no file and because 'Ms. Raubal was not brought to the institute', there was no need, even during the Nazi era, to remove evidence.[77]

The Berlin forensic pathologist Professor Otto Prokop also considers the connection between vegetarianism and a severe emotional shock as coincidental and difficult to explain if there was no postmortem. The connection would have been more plausible if Hitler had witnessed the slaughtering of an animal. Prokop wrote of suicide and vegetarianism in 2007: 'Neither I nor my students can say anything definite. My students and friends at the Charité also have *nothing* to say! Sic est!'[78] It is therefore highly questionable whether Geli Raubal's death was the real reason for Hitler's abrupt transition from partial to full vegetarian.[79]

A further interpretation is possible, however, if one considers the social surroundings. Here, too, Hitler adapted to what was accepted in the circles he valued. The highly traditional family of Richard Wagner, to which he was introduced by Dietrich Eckart in 1923, for example, was semi-vegetarian.[80] The composer himself presented the renunciation of meat as an alternative to a Jewish materialist way of life. Animal experiments, vivisection and the killing of 'fellow creatures' in general were rejected in conservative nationalist circles and by young representatives of the 'conservative revolution' alike. Animal protection was regarded as a 'moral obligation' of the 'Germanic peoples'.[81]

It is no longer possible to determine whether Hitler was already a vegetarian during his imprisonment in 1924. Monika Gross, head of the Landsberg am Lech prison, stated on 31 July 2007 that 'no documents to this effect exist'.[82] Eyewitnesses nevertheless regularly recall that Hitler was already a vegetarian in the 1920s.[83] Later on, high-ranking guests would often be served spaghetti in the Reich Chancellery with chopped mushrooms being used instead of meat.[84] According to Traudl Junge, Hitler's favourite dishes were millet gruel with linseed oil (regarded as poor man's fare) or curd with linseed oil, with caraway or apple peel tea to drink. It is not uncommon in the diet proposals for Hitler in Morell's notes from 1941 to 1945 to find items like gruel, crispbread, asparagus salad, mashed potatoes, stuffed pancakes, mashed carrots and the like. Thanks to Morell, Hitler's diet became even more frugal than it had been before the personal physician's appointment.

When Hitler was staying at Obersalzberg he obtained his vegetables from Dr Zabel's sanatorium for natural healing in Berchtesgaden. Zabel wrote a letter of criticism to Morell on 29 June 1943 complaining that he was not being informed about Hitler's health, appetite, weight and other matters and could not therefore determine the quantities for Hitler's meals. He also disapproved of Nissle's suggestion that lettuce be blanched, on which Morell himself had made no comment. The letter indicates that Zabel, a former ophthalmologist, was asking to be consulted on Hitler's diet, something that Morell did not desire, since he had 'little idea' about the cardiovascular system.

Morell therefore suggested a new dietary assistant, who had looked after the Romanian head of state Antonescu for several years to his great satisfaction. Hitler approved and the Viennese dietary chef Marlene von Exner joined Hitler's services on 15 July 1943 for a monthly salary of RM 800. The monotonous menu changed immediately. The meals were tastier and more varied, nutritious and full of vitamins, and still completely in line with the dictates of vegetarianism. Hitler was very taken with his young and friendly new acquisition whom he also invited to his nightly tea session on account of her self-assured Viennese manner, which delighted him no end.

The situation changed overnight: von Exner was suspended unexpectedly in February 1944 and dismissed in May of that year – not because of any lack of quality or conscientiousness, but because of her Jewish grandmother or great-grandmother. Morell, who had attempted to prevent her dismissal, wrote to her in a letter on 15 April that all officers and important staff members at the headquarters had to produce a complete genealogy going back several generations and continued regretfully: 'I can assure you in confidence that I argued strongly with one instance and it was considered changing your status at a later date to full Aryan.'

This one 'instance' was probably Martin Bormann, who had more power than Morell. According to Traudl Junge, Hitler had a last meeting with von Exner and is said to have arranged her Aryanization in March 1945.[85] Before that, however, Constanze Manziarly from

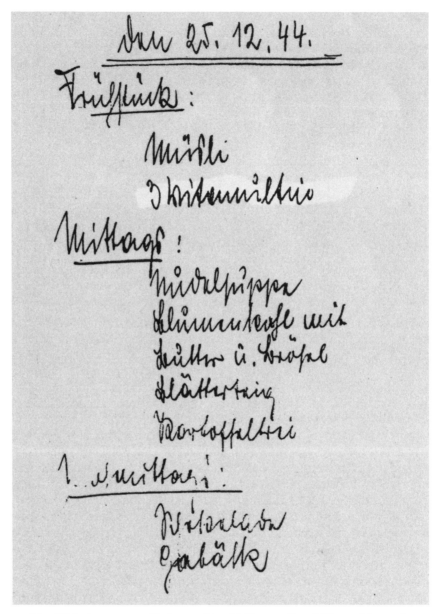

45. Hitler's menu on Christmas Day 1944: muesli and Vitamultin tea for breakfast, noodle soup, breaded cauliflower, flaky pastry and mashed potatoes for lunch, and chocolate and pastries in the afternoon. For the nightly tea session there were pastries and sandwiches and celery soup. As usual there is the comment 'The F. ate well.'

Abends:

der F. hat gut

gegessen

Dr Zabel's sanatorium was hired in August 1944 as Hitler's dietary assistant. She stayed with him until the end in the Reich Chancellery and prepared his last meal on 30 April 1945, which he ate together with his secretaries and her. Manziarly disappeared in Berlin and was probably raped and then killed by Soviet troops.[86]

It can thus be said in conclusion that Hitler was a vegetarian for the most part. The sometimes monotonous selection and occasional unprofessional preparation might have contributed to his abdominal spasms but on the whole they influenced his health far less than some authors claim. His diet was never 'eccentric'; on the contrary, in an era of 'meat scandals' like BSE, it may even be considered healthy.[87]

Traudl Junge and others doubt, however, that Hitler renounced meat for the sake of the animals, as the Nazi propaganda claimed. Hitler's former adjutant Otto Günsche is also sceptical in this regard.[88] It is true that Hitler appears to have liked dogs, but the German shepherd was in any case a popular pet. He liked to be photographed with Wolf, his first dog, and with its successors, all of which were named Blondi.

The Nazi propaganda is understandable, however. Anyone who has such a close relationship with animals must also have had one with his fellow men and women. Thus, animal protection, which was also anchored in the law, helped to increase Hitler's popularity with the citizens of the Third Reich.[89] His alleged love of animals fits in well with the stylization of the dictator as an ascetic revolutionary and role model who did not smoke or drink, ate no meat and had no women.

### Coronary Sclerosis

The site Hitler chose for his Wolf's Lair headquarters proved to be less than ideal.[90] He suffered during the intolerably hot and humid summer days in the marshy Masurian forests and complained of difficulty in breathing and nervous heart trouble. He confided in Eva Braun, Albert Speer and Joseph Goebbels that his heart was causing him increasing problems. His condition took a sudden turn for the worse during a heated discussion with his foreign minister on the progress of the war with the Soviet Union at the end of July 1941. Ribbentrop apparently even questioned Hitler's decision to attack Russia at all. When the foreign minister then said: 'God doesn't let people take a look at the cards he's holding!', Hitler thought he was going to have a heart attack. He was thunderstruck by Ribbentrop's gaffe. Only when the colour gradually returned to his face did Hitler, still sitting and looking directly at Ribbentrop, reply softly and placidly: 'I thought I was having a heart attack. Promise me that you will never again question my decisions.' Ribbentrop gave him his word.[91] His entourage had never seen anything of the like before. During the French campaign in 1940, Hitler had been in the best of health and he had also been robust in spring 1941 in the course of the fighting in Yugoslavia and Greece. Now, in summer 1941, Morell noted oedema on Hitler's legs and detected signs of a weak heart.[92]

As there is no record of this heated discussion apart from eyewitness reports and not even the date can be reliably determined, the events must be questioned. Hitler's apparent heart attack could have been an angina pectoris incident or a purely functional disorder. After the heart attack on 14 July, an ECG was finally recorded on 14 August. Other examinations were also carried out, although pulse and blood pressure were normal.[93] Morell submitted Hitler's ECG anonymously to the renowned cardiologist Professor Arthur Weber, director of the Balneological University Institute in Bad Nauheim, for analysis. Weber sent his findings to Morell on 20 August, saying that the most likely diagnosis was *coronary sclerosis*, unless digitalis[94] had been administered or there had been an infection. The letter ended with a personal comment: 'Trusting that you remain well, I offer you my best regards, Heil Hitler, A. Weber'.[95]

Weber thus suspected coronary sclerosis, hardening of the coronary arteries, provided that nothing else was causing a constriction. As Hitler never again had symptoms such as those during the argument with Ribbentrop, the findings are not dramatic; after all, Hitler was fifty-two years old. Morell was nevertheless aware of the danger of an angina pectoris attack or cardiac infarct.

Coronary sclerosis results in insufficient blood circulation because of constriction or obstruction of the coronary arteries. In its acute form it can lead to a reduction or interruption of the blood flow (myocardial ischaemia) or an angina pectoris attack characterized by feeling of tightness or heaviness behind the sternum. The attack occurs suddenly and is accompanied by pain in the chest, which can last for seconds or minutes, and a belt-like feeling of constriction. Respiratory distress, a choking sensation and feeling of impending doom are also typical symptoms.[96]

As Weber did not suggest any treatment, Morell was not unduly concerned by the ECG findings. Despite the recommendation for a control ECG at regular intervals, none was carried out, because Hitler

127

**Balneol. - Universitäts - Institut**
Direktor: Prof. Dr. A. Weber
Fernruf 2964

Bad-Nauheim, den .............20...8........... 194..1

Sehr geehrter Herr Kollege Morell!

Es freut mich,dass es Ihnen trotz der sicher sehr
grossen Beanspruchung gut geht.Hoffentlich sind wir bald so weit,
dass wir uns alle eines guten Frieden freuen können.

Das übersandte Ekg zeigt:Sinusrhythmus.Linkstyp.
Übergang zu Linksverspätung.Beginnende Senkung von S-T$_I$ und S-T$_{II}$.
Erhebliche Abflachung von S-T$_I$ und S-T$_{II}$.Falls nicht Digitalis
oder eine Infektion eingewirkt haben,muss man in I.Linie an Coro-
narsklerose denken.Weitere Ekg-Aufnahmen in Abständen von je 14
Tagen sind zu empfehlen.

In der Hoffung,dass es Ihnen weiter gut geht
bin ich mit den besten Grüssen

Ihr

46. In August 1941 the cardiologist Artur Weber from Bad Nauheim assessed
the ECG sent to him of a 'gentleman from the Foreign Office'. Weber diagnosed
coronary sclerosis and suggested regular check-ups.

almost always refused diagnostic measures. Morell was relatively
unconcerned, however, and assured Hitler that his heart and other
organs were healthy and that the changes in the coronary arteries
were normal for his age. He acted on Weber's findings, however, to
the extent that he consulted with other heart specialists and carried
out his own research in the relevant literature.

Weber's findings – there were two further analyses in 1943 and
1944 – led some Hitler biographers to claim that Hitler was suffering from 'rapidly progressive coronary sclerosis' (Werner Maser) or
a 'practically incurable coronary disease' (John Toland). There is
no indication of this in Weber's findings, despite the fact that in his
accompanying letter of 17 May 1943 he noted that there had been
an evident deterioration.[97] This was the first time that Weber offered
treatment recommendations. He advised 'patient A.', whose identity
he apparently did not know, to rest for three or four weeks. If he was
a smoker he should also stop smoking and ensure that his diet contained little fluid and salt. He also recommended 'regular afternoon

rest for at least an hour and as much sleep at night as possible'. At the end of the letter he admitted: 'I realize that a person in a responsible position will find it difficult or even impossible today to follow these absolutely indicated measures.' As Weber mentioned smoking, it can be assumed that he was unaware of the person whose ECG he was studying, since it was common knowledge that Hitler was a non-smoker.

In his last report on 4 December 1944, Weber mentioned 'signs of slowly progressive left coronary insufficiency' and urged that it be treated. Once again, he was reluctant to hazard a prognosis. He had already written to Morell in 1943 that 'in such cases it is impossible to give a definite prognosis'.[98] The conclusions of a reassessment of the ECG in February 2008 were somewhat different to Professor Weber's in the 1940s. According to the cardiologist Dr Swertlana Möller,[99] Hitler did not have 'coronary heart disease' but a hypertensive heart disorder due to a microvascular dysfunction of the myocardium associated with hypertension.[100] In July 1941, therefore, Hitler probably suffered from an acute functional heart disorder without organic aetiology occurring typically between the ages of forty and fifty.[101]

*ECG assessment: findings 1941, 1943, 1944 and 2008*

*Weber 1941*: 'The submitted ECG shows sinus rhythm, slight left axis deviation, transition to left cardiac conduction delay, incipient depression in $S\text{-}T_I$ and $S\text{-}T_{II}$. Unless caused by digitalis ("no" handwritten by Morell) or infection, probably indication of *coronary sclerosis*. Further ECGs recommended at fourteen-day intervals.'

*Commentary by Möller 2008*: 'Estimated interval (l. PQ 0.115–0.123, QRS 0.09s, QT 0.36s) normal. The shallower T peaks could be a normal variant. Relatively deep S [diagram] III, which could indicate left ventricular hypertrophy (e.g. hypertension).'

*Weber 1943*: 'Sinus rhythm, slight left axis deviation, perhaps incipient left cardiac conduction delay, slight depression in $ST_I$ and $ST_{II}$ drifting negative, $T_{II}$ at baseline. Manifest deterioration compared with 1941 in that the ST drop has become clearer and $T_I$ was positive and now negative. $T_{II}$ also clearly positive then, now almost at baseline. The ECG on 11 May this year confirms my earlier diagnosis. Coronary sclerosis, evidently progressive. I would urgently recommend three to four weeks' rest. It is never possible to give a definite prognosis in such cases but the course will probably not be very

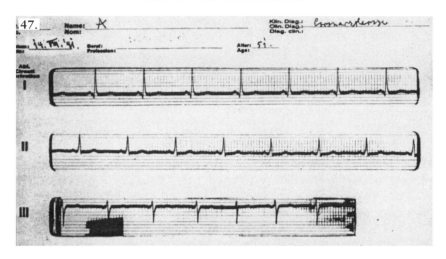

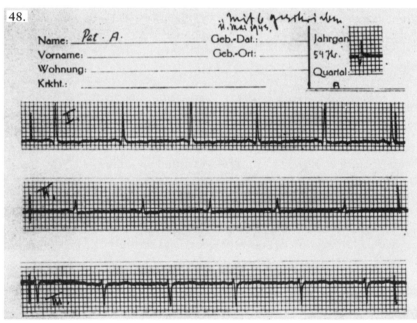

favourable. Impossible to give a more precise time forecast, however. I recommend control ECG every three months and intermittent courses of treatment, either with Theominal or Deriphyllin or Jod-Calcium-Diuretin. Three weeks with one of these drugs then three weeks off and so on. Absolute smoking ban, low fluid and salt diet if at all

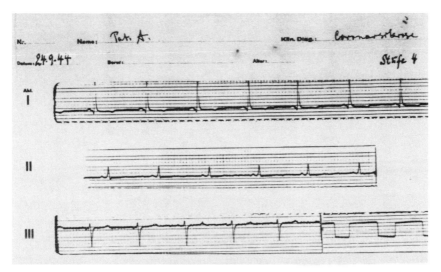

49. Morell recorded Hitler's ECG in 1941, 1943 and 1944 and sent them to Professor Weber under the name 'Patient A.' for evaluation. His clinical diagnosis was 'coronary sclerosis'.

reconcilable with work, one fruit juice day (1 litre) per week with no food and drink in these twenty four hours and work restricted to the absolute minimum. Regular afternoon rest of at least one hour and as much sleep as possible at night. I realize that a person in a responsible position will find it difficult or even impossible today to follow these absolutely indicated measures, but they should be observed as far as possible in order to conserve energy for work.'

*Commentary by Möller 2008*: 'Slight left axis deviation, sinus rhythm, heart rate 87/min (here I think the paper speed of 25 mm/s is correct), PQ 0.11–0.12s, QRS 0.09s, QT 0.36s, slight T inversion in I, shallow T in II and III.'

... *Weber 1944*: 'Now to patient A ... findings 24 September 1944. Left axis deviation more manifest. Depression of S-T in I, now showing the start of an upward convex course. T in I clearly negative. ST in II also more depressed. QRS difficult to determine with certainty, but appears longer than in 1943. Indication of slowly progressive left coronary insufficiency and also left cardiac conduction delay.'

*Commentary by Möller 2008*: 'Slight left axis deviation, sinus rhythm, heart rate 107/min (assuming paper speed of 25 mm/s), sinus

131

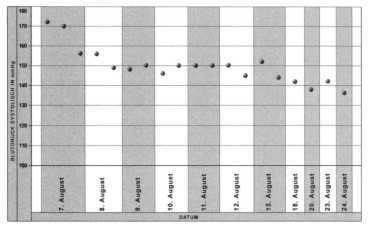

50.  August 1941: At the beginning of the war against the Soviet Union Hitler's blood pressure was already high. Morell noted only the systolic values, which was not unusual at the time as the diastolic values were considered to be of lesser significance. According to the WHO and German medical associations a systolic blood pressure of 150 mmHg is classified as mild hypertonia (stage 1) and 120 to 129 mmHg as normal.

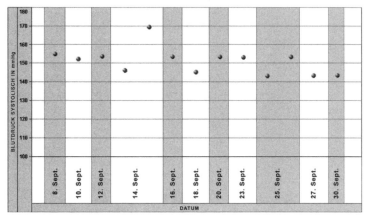

51.  Hitler's blood pressure readings in September 1944 show mild hypertonia. Throughout the war his blood pressure was around 150 mmHg.

OKTOBER 1944

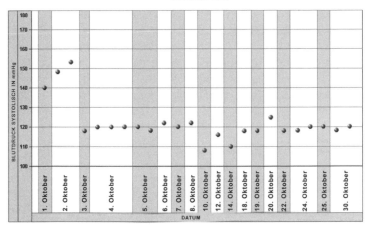

52.   The systolic values measured by Morell in October were between 108 and 120 mmHg. Hitler's blood pressure thus tended to be too low. The hypertonia that Hitler had from August 1941 to September 1944 gave way in October and November to hypotonia. It is difficult to explain why, not least because it would have been thought that during the preparations for the Ardennes offensive Hitler would have been sympathicotonic with elevated blood pressure.

NOVEMBER/DEZEMBER 1944

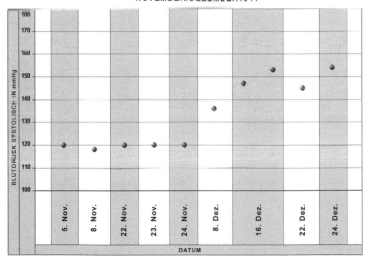

53.   In December 1944 Morell's diary has entries with 'no treatment' on thirteen occasions. The blood pressure, which Morell measured only fourteen times, had returned within a short time to its accustomed hypertonic levels of around 150 mmHg after the hypotonia in October and November.

133

tachycardia, PQ 0.11–0.12s, QRS 0.10s, QT 0.40s. Slight T inversion in I (unchanged from 1943). Slight ST depression in II.

The changes could be indicative of myocardial ischaemia in connection with a coronary heart disease or left ventricular hypertrophy as a function of hypertension or possibly in connection with ischaemia. In theory, any form of hypertrophy (e.g. aortic stenosis or hypertrophic cardiomyopathy) or digitalis therapy could cause similar changes.'

## Hypertension

Apart from the coronary sclerosis diagnosed at the time, the possibility of a hypertensive disease must also be considered, particularly in view of the reassessment of the ECG. A chronic increase in blood pressure to 140 to 150 mmHg systolic and 90 to 99 mmHg diastolic[102] is symptomatic of arterial hypertension. Hitler had high blood pressure practically throughout the war and was normal or hypotonic only in October and November 1944.

The World Health Organization – which did not exist at the time – defines mild hypertension as a diastolic value of 90 to 99 mmHg. From Morell's notes, as far as they exist, Hitler's diastolic and systolic values were both above the norm. In the 1930s the systolic values were considered more important and the diastolic values were frequently disregarded. In Hitler's case they were usually around 100 mmHg or higher. Today, systolic values have a special significance and isolated systolic hypertension is a clinical syndrome in its own right.[103]

Morell measured Hitler's systolic blood pressure nineteen times in 1941 and the average value was 150 mmHg, above the normal range. He noted the diastolic values only sporadically. The higher of the two readings was 111 mmHg, above the WHO 'mild hypertension' threshold. In 1942 the average systolic values were 146 mmHg, slightly lower than the previous year's average, but still elevated. The highest of the five diastolic readings noted by Morell was 110 mmHg. The average of the twenty-six systolic readings taken the following year was 149 mmHg. The average for the six diastolic readings was 101 mmHg, the highest being 110 mmHg. Except for October and November both the systolic and the diastolic blood pressure readings in the penultimate year of the war were elevated.[104] There are no records of diastolic pressure in 1945 and the average of the four systolic readings was 150 mmHg.

According to the definitions of the WHO and relevant associations (Deutsche Hochdruckliga, European Society of Hypertension) the diastolic readings for the years 1941 to the end of September 1944 put Hitler's hypertension not in the mild but in the moderate stage (stage 2) of 100–109 mmHg.

It is difficult to explain why Hitler's blood pressure was in the normal to hypotonic range towards the end of 1944, because in the run-up to the Ardennes offensive the commander-in-chief would be expected to have been sympatheticotonic. The sedatives he was taking do not provide an adequate explanation either, because he had been using them since the start of the war against the Soviet Union.

It is not possible to tell from Morell's records whether Hitler was taking higher doses of the prescribed drugs, or had also been pre-scribed a diuretic for the oedemas caused by his constant deskwork. New anti-hypertensive agents can also be excluded. Why would Morell have used them only in October and November 1944 when Hitler had had high blood pressure for years? In view of the tension that Hitler was under, his blood pressure should have been consist-ently high. For all their unlikelihood, it would appear that fluctua-tions took place.

The forced confinement to bed following the jaundice attack could have produced a drop in blood pressure, as Hitler was obliged in October and November 1944 to delegate authority for the conduct of the war. During this time Morell forbade visits by many politicians and generals so that while Hitler was not completely cut off from information he was no longer able or permitted to make day-to-day decisions.

When the Ardennes offensive got underway, Hitler's blood pres-sure once again rose to the customary elevated level. In planning this military operation, Hitler became hopeful again for a favour-able outcome. This hope was not completely unfounded, as can be concluded from an assessment by British Field Marshall Bernard Montgomery at a press conference on 7 January 1945 at which he stated that the Allied armies had been on the verge of disaster.[105] Hitler's blood pressure rose steadily in December 1944, reaching the levels of August 1941, similar to all readings until September 1944. The blood letting by Morell in August 1944 (200 cc) and 12 February 1945 (230 cc) did not actually appear to him to be necessary, but as Hitler requested it he obeyed. In February 1945 Hitler's blood pres-sure did in fact drop from 156 mmHg to 143 mmHg. The dictator's subjective wellbeing improved but a correlation with the state of the war cannot be established.

## Parkinson's Disease

Morell had observed a tremor in Hitler's left arm as early as August 1941. It was also to be seen soon afterwards in the left leg. It started on one side, which is typical of Parkinson's disease. Hitler himself described the tremor as a 'severe nervous complaint'; Morell described it as a 'kind of shaking palsy', which he thought might be a sign of hysteria. He wrote the word 'hysteria' in his diary entry on 18 August 1941 without drawing any further conclusions.[106] Hitler's tremor does not appear to have been a consequence of the First World War, which left many soldiers shell-shocked. There is no mention in the discharge report from the Landsberg prison doctor Dr Brinsteiner of a tremor.[107]

The tremor nevertheless existed. It is generally assumed today that Hitler suffered from Parkinson's disease.[108] The origins of this disease are unclear and it likely that a number of factors play a role. Symptoms can be triggered by encephalitis, pesticides or insecticides, carbon monoxide or methyl alcohol, or possibly by drugs such as neuroleptics or antiemetics as well.

Three main symptoms characterize Parkinson's disease. The first that normally appears is akinesia (difficulty in initiating movements) together with bradykinesia (slow movement). There is also festination (short, shuffling step) and decreased range of motion – the patient blinks less frequently, and writing becomes increasingly illegible and small. Speech is monotonous, softer and can ultimately cease altogether.

Rigidity, the second main symptom, is characterized by stiffness and inflexibility of the muscles, while the third main symptom is tremor, a beating or oscillating movement of individual parts of the body. The tremor is classified as coarse, moderate or fine and it starts on one side of the body. Resting tremor can extend to the legs and other parts of the body and can typically be in the form of what is known as a pill-rolling phenomenon. Other possible symptoms include melancholy, dementia and sensitivity disorders. A tremor can have other causes, however. People who have celebrated through the night often have the shakes the following morning. Tension and emotional stress can also produce a tremor.

Hitler did not have all of the symptoms of Parkinson's disease. His stride was shorter than it had been in his younger years and he tended to shuffle somewhat, although Traudl Junge denied this.[109] From mid-1941, however, his resting tremor and anomalous posture could not be overlooked. Ellen Gibbels analysed these after studying eighty-three episodes of the *Deutsche Wochenschau*.[110] According to Karl Brandt, Morell attempted to treat Hitler's tremor with spasmolytics without, however, considering the possibility of Parkinson's.[111] Even after 1945 he doubted that Hitler was suffering from Parkinson's disease.

In her monograph published in 1990, Ellen Gibbels concluded that Hitler had a typical Parkinson syndrome, even if some of the symptoms were discrepant. The fact that his doctors failed to consider it may perhaps be explained by an inadequate neurological background or by the fact that slow or monotonous speech were not evident. Nor did observers notice a shuffling gait.[112] Until his suicide, Hitler revealed none of the standard psychological symptoms of Parkinson's disease: his thought processes were not retarded nor were there any signs of dementia. He did, however, tend increasingly towards depression, the most frequent psychological disorder in idiopathic Parkinson's syndrome. It is possible that this was due to his high drug consumption. Brom-Nervacit, which contained barbituric acid, for example, was used as a daytime sedative, although it was generally indicated as a soporific to help sleep. Optalidon, Hitler's analgesic, also contained barbiturate, and Hitler's enormous stress should also be taken into account.

All of this does not correlate with the 'manifest organic psycho-syndrome' claimed by Heston, who based his claim on the errone ous assumption of 'chronic amphetamine intoxication',[113] which he alleged had a marked influence on Hitler's military decisions from summer 1942. Ellen Gibbels, by contrast, explains these changes 'at best' by a 'possible organic psychosyndrome in the form of an "aggravation" of certain primary personal characteristics'. She concludes: 'Altogether according to our research the supposed psychopathological changes in Hitler are so small that they are likely to have had a negligible influence on his military and political decisions during the last years of the war.'[114]

### Chronic Hypermetropia and Acute Eye Diseases

Finally, it should be mentioned that from 1941 onwards Hitler had problems with his eyes – in itself a normal physiological process, since after the age of forty a person with emmetropic (normal) sight will tend to develop presbyopia (middle-aged vision), often requiring the use of reading spectacles. The strength of these spectacles is also like to increase with age.

As the photographs approved by Hitler for publication reveal, he was well aware of the importance of his gaze. Many men in Hitler's entourage emphasized that they were not susceptible to his 'hypnotiz-ing gaze',[115] but more naive respondents answered differently. Christa Schroeder, Hitler's secretary from 1933 to 1945, wrote in September 1949: 'When I entered his study I was struck by the intensive gaze of his blue eyes.'[116] She found Hitler's eyes 'expressive' and confirmed that they could 'look warm-hearted or express outrage'.[117] Traudl Junge shared this impression when she recalled his 'warm friendly gaze' in 1997.[118] Dr von Hasselbach, Hitler's second attendant surgeon, wrote in 1946: 'It is senseless to claim that Hitler's gaze was fixed or dead . . . In reality Hitler's eyes were extremely lively and fascinating and the most important aspect alongside his words of his exceptional power of suggestion.'[119]

However, we are not interested in Hitler's 'expressive' eyes, which could appear radiantly blue or grey, depending on the way the light fell on them, but on his eyes as sensory organs. Dr Giesing's claim in November 1945 that a 'vitreous opacity . . . had been diagnosed by an ophthalmologist' in 1935 and 1944 cannot be confirmed, even if Giesing referred to an alleged statement by Hitler himself. It is indeed quite possible that Hitler had had his eyes examined ten years earlier and that the vitreous opacity mentioned by Giesing had been diag-nosed. Whatever the case, Hitler was prescribed reading spectacles in 1935. Professor Dr Walter Löhlein, director of the Eye Clinic at Charité, first diagnosed a vitreous opacity in Hitler in March 1944 and it was not until a year later, in April 1945, that he examined and treated him again.

For reasons of vanity, Hitler rarely wore the spectacles prescribed in 1935. He also prohibited the publication of pictures showing him wearing them. Although their existence was kept secret, there are a number of photographs showing him wearing them. On one he is reading a document, on another he is sitting at a desk writing a military report, and a third one shows him with his birthday guests. There is also a photograph taken after the Allied landing on 6 June 1944.[120] David Irving's claim that Hitler was 'practically blind . . . in the right eye' is not correct. According to the available findings, Hitler was hypermotropic in the right eye (approx. 4.5 dioptres) and had 50 per cent vision.[121] He helped himself out, however, with a typewriter designed specially for him with 12 mm letters.[122]

Hitler complained of eye problems after 1941. A year later, in July 1942, he suffered from a pain in the eyes in the Werewolf headquar-ters, which Morell attributed to encephalitis, which Hitler was not in fact suffering from. Morell noted in his diary:[123] 'States that vision in his right eye is somewhat impaired' and wrote in the evening: 'Pain behind his right forehead has subsided and the impairment of vision has also gone.' The entry for the next day reads: 'No eye pain any more. Wants an eye check-up soon, particularly for focus, as in his opinion one eye sees worse than the other; he presumes it's the right one.' According to Morell, Löhlein was not consulted in 1942, but only on 2 March 1944, when he examined Hitler's eyes and diagnosed the vitreous opacity – normally a harmless condition found in many people after a certain age (floaters). These changes are irksome for the individual but are not normally of pathological significance.[124]

Löhlein advised Hitler, who was sensitive to light, to wear sunglasses. He can be seen wearing them in a photograph taken during a stroll with Himmler and his entourage on the snow-covered Obersalzberg in March 1944. Morell noted: 'Eye examination of patient A., new spectacles on account of slight turbidity of the right vitreous humour.' Löhlein attributed this turbidity to 'minute haemorrhage' and commented that the spectacles prescribed in 1935 were no longer adequate. A detailed letter from Löhlein to Morell of 2 March 1944 and the results of the examination have been preserved. In both he noted that Hitler's reading glasses were no longer strong enough and 'glasses for near vision . . . need to be stronger'.[125] Hitler, who did not have new spectacles made but preferred to use a magnifying glass, appears to have had eye problems once again in December 1944, so that Morell wrote on Saturday, 9 December: 'Prof. Löhlein planned for Sunday.' Löhlein could not be reached, however. Hitler did not press the matter further, as he was completely absorbed in the Ardennes offensive, and Löhlein only appeared shortly before the end of the war on 7 April 1945. At midnight on 22 March Morell noted: 'Conjunctivitis probably caused by wind and dust as there is a lot of building debris in the courtyard. The Führer said that he had only very limited vision in the right eye. I put some drops of cocaine adrenaline solution in his eye.'

On 4 April Morell reminded Hitler about Professor Löhlein and noted in his pocket diary: 'can consult with him. F. has not fixed date or time for examination.' On Saturday, 7 April, he wrote: 'Eye examination by Prof. Löhlein in the evening . . . Slight vitreous opacity in right eye as earlier . . . Prof. L. talked later with us (Dr Stumpfegger and I) about the tremor . . . Asked if the F. had had a speech disorder, which had never been the case.' Löhlein concluded his own report with the words: 'Follow-up examination in a week, possibly removal then of chalazion from left upper eyelid.'[126] It is surprising that Hitler should ask for an eye examination just as in peacetime.

On 10 April 1945 Morell made a last entry on an instruction from

Löhlein: 'At lunchtime I rewrote the prescription from Dr Löhlein as he had put at the bottom "for the Führer" and instructed that it be filled at any pharmacy except for Engelapotheke. It was finally filled at the sixth pharmacy (at the Zoo) and can be collected tomorrow (it appears impossible to obtain adrenaline anywhere).'

## Teeth

Hitler's teeth were in constant need of treatment. Whether for hereditary reasons or because of deficient or incorrect diet, he already had teeth missing in 1933. Some teeth had caries and others were loose. Hitler subsequently received several jacket crowns (porcelain or plastic) and bridges, as the Soviet forensic pathologists from the NKGB were told by the technician Käthe Heusermann.[127] Two teeth were extracted in autumn 1944 and the gold bridge in the upper jaw replaced. The dentist, Hugo Blaschke, probably used dental gold from Jewish concentration camp victims, of which he had a personal supply of approximately 50 kg.[128]

When Blaschke was summoned for the first time in 1933 he found Hitler's dentition to be in terrible shape. The surviving teeth had fillings and crowns and the gaps had been 'bridged'. Blaschke had to remove and replace all the fillings in the upper jaw. He attempted to stabilize the teeth with a bridge. Hitler insisted on fixed replacements and refused removable dentures. According to the description of the KGB historian Lev Bezymenski, which tallies almost entirely with Blaschke's description to the American interrogation officers, nine new teeth were fitted in the upper jaw.[129] These were said to have been connected by a 'bridge', but this cannot be right. The reports also speak of molars when in fact premolars are meant. Eyewitnesses agree, however, that Hitler had both gold and porcelain teeth. Apart from a bridge, he might therefore have had single crowns – either metal banded or jacket crowns.

Blaschke said of his first visit that Hitler's lower jaw had one painful and four loose teeth. This description also tallies with Bezymenski, who mentioned fifteen teeth, of which ten were false. According to the Soviet post-mortem report, the bottom front teeth were intact. Blaschke fitted a bridge in the left lower jaw extending from the canine tooth and two premolars to the wisdom tooth. The right canine and second premolar were fitted with crowns, which Blaschke had connected by means of an arched plate to close the gap next to the first premolar.[130] Blaschke's statement was once again confirmed for the most part in June 1945 by Dr Giesing, who had a surprisingly good recollection of Hitler's teeth. Professor von Eicken, Hitler's ear, nose and throat specialist, recalled only that Hitler had had 'mostly false teeth in the upper and lower jaw but no removable dentures'.

It can be said with certainty that the few natural teeth were connected until Hitler's death by bridge constructions. It is also likely that Hitler would sooner or later have needed dentures. The question remains only where and how his dentist, however skilful he might have been, could have fitted fixed replacements in his mouth.

# — 6 —

# HITLER'S HEALTH AND THE WAR

As Führer and Reich Chancellor with dictatorial powers, Hitler made countless decisions between 1933 and 1945. The main focus in the first years of his chancellorship was on domestic policy as a means of consolidating the Nazi dictatorship and his personal power. His repressive measures were accompanied by incisive changes in social and economic policy. At this stage the dictatorship was extremely popular and was seen by the German people not as the precursor to war but as the fulfilment of a social vision. They apparently accepted the fact that some people were excluded from this national community, that political opponents and 'asocials' were put in concentration camps and that thousands of people were killed. The decision to wage war against Poland, by contrast, was unpopular on account of the anticipated retaliation by the Western powers. According to British historian Ian Kershaw, it was not until the victory of France that Hitler's popularity began to rise again in 1940.[1] He was unable to achieve a political solution in the form, for example, of peace with Britain, however. On the international scene he was rightly thought of as a gambler, liar, fraud and violator of diplomatic agreements. His domestic policy was regarded as criminal and discredited the German Reich to such an extent that peace with democracies like the United States of America and the United Kingdom was impossible and made the continuation of war inevitable.[2]

It was not as though Hitler were acting from a defensive position. The German Reich dominated the European continent, neutral countries were well disposed, and a useful treaty of friendship had been concluded with the Soviet Union. The international stalemate is evident from the decisions made at this point by Hitler. He stepped up the persecution of the Jews and was preparing a decisive war with the Soviet Union. The instructions for the coming war were unambiguous. Before terminating the war with Britain the army must be prepared to 'crush Soviet Russia in a rapid campaign'. The aim of the war was to create a 'shield against Asian Russia' by advancing as far as the 'Volga-Archangel line'. The campaign would end with the taking of Leningrad and Moscow, with the only remaining Soviet armaments region in the Urals to be 'neutralized by the air force'.[3]

The war with the Soviet Union turned out differently than had been expected, however. After initial victories, the German advance halted before Moscow. Leningrad was not taken, and the Volga was not reached until Stalingrad in 1942. The catastrophic defeat at Stalingrad was followed by a terrible series of hard-fought victories and defeats that ended with the overthrow of the Nazi regime by the Soviet Union, USA and Britain. The war cost the lives of at least thirty-nine million people.[4]

At the time Hitler embarked on war in 1939, he did not require any special medical treatment. His personal physician Theodor Morell still had his practice on the Kurfürstendamm and not one single eyewitness reports regular visits to the Reich Chancellery. Morell's notes also give no indication that Hitler was treated regularly at the time. Morell's notes do not start until 1941 during the war with the Soviet Union. Regardless of whether Morell, who was vain enough to do so, intended to write a history of the health of the Führer (whom he usually referred to in his notes as 'F.') or simply wanted to cover himself, it can be assumed that it was only after this time that Hitler required a doctor on a regular basis. It is only in retrospect that those involved deduced that Hitler was in need of treatment. Hitler's deputy attendant surgeon Dr Hanskarl von Hasselbach recalled after 1945: 'Until 1940 Hitler looked much younger than he really was. Thereafter, however, he aged quite quickly. Until 1943 he looked his age, but later his rapid physical deterioration became apparent.'[5]

Von Hasselbach deliberately refrained from using the word 'illness', preferring the vaguer term 'deterioration', because he did not want to or could not commit himself, perhaps because he was too frequently in Hitler's presence. By studying the decisions individually and comparing the notes by his personal physician with the military and political events at the time it is possible to correlate them with Hitler's medical history.

## Hitler's Health and the Decisions In 1941

The desire to annihilate the 'Jewish race' was at the core of the Nazi ideology. This plan needed to be carried out in several stages, however, and was characterized by tactical considerations and political constraints. There can be no doubt that Hitler envisaged the murder of the Jews as early as 1924. In his book *Mein Kampf* under the heading 'The neglected accounting with Marxism', he stated his desire that 'twelve or fifteen thousand of those Hebrew corrupters of the nation' be subjected to 'poison gas'. Twelve thousand 'scoundrels', he claimed, 'opportunely eliminated' would have saved the lives of millions of Germans.[6] In 1941, in contrast to his position during the First World War, Hitler had the power to make his vision come true. Was his decision to annihilate millions of people made by a healthy or an ill person?

The history of Hitler's health in 1941 was comparatively commonplace and starts in August 1941. SS-Sturmbannführer Walther Hewel, Hitler's permanent representative at the Reich Foreign Ministry, noted on Hitler's visit to Ukraine on 6 August: '4 a.m.: flight to Berdichev. Three hours over Russia . . . Met General Antonescu . . . Walk through Berdichev. Destroyed abbey. Open coffins . . . ghastly town. Many Jews, ancient hovels.' When Hitler returned to the Wolf's Lair that evening it was intolerably hot. The next day he was ill and did not appear for lunch or for the daily military briefings. This was a sensational occurrence: Hitler had never been so ill before that he could not take part in the day's events.[7] Now, however, he was confined to bed with dysentery.

On 7 August Hitler was very unwell, as described. At 1.30 p.m. he suddenly felt dizzy while sitting in the map room. Morell noted that he had recently been looking poorly and pale. His suggestion that he examine Hitler was refused by the Führer, who said he felt fine. Then Hitler's orderly Hans Junge phoned telling Morell to come *immediately*. Hitler had gone to the bunker and said to his personal physician: 'I feel very unwell, more than ever before. I suddenly felt dizzy over there [in the map room]. I don't know what it is. Up here [indicating his left temple] I feel so strange. During the flight it kept bothering me.'

During this examination Morell noticed the tremor in Hitler's left hand for the first time but did not associate it with Parkinson's disease. (According to other accounts the tremor did not appear until 1942–3 and Morell's notes are therefore of particular significance.) Morell came to the following diagnosis: 'Facial spasms with rush

144

of blood to the temples due to various causes.' He prescribed 'cold compresses to the temple and left side of the head, hot leg poultices'. He also injected Vitamultin-Calcium, Glyconorm and Septoiod – substances belonging to his basic programme – and three Yatren laxative pills, because Hitler now complained of constipation. He further prescribed twenty drops of Dolantin for the pain and two Phanodorm sleeping pills for the night.[8]

Morell's 'diagnosis' is more a general description of the symptoms. He was probably unable to make a proper diagnosis on the spot or even afterwards. Nicolaus von Below, Luftwaffe adjutant in Hitler's headquarters, infers from remarks made by Morell that Hitler had had a mild stroke.[9] There is no indication to this effect in Morell's notes.[10]

On 8 August Hitler got up at 11 a.m. Without waiting for instructions from Hitler's valet, SS-Sturmbannführer Heinz Linge, as was customary, Morell had already visited his patient, who was feeling terrible, saying that he had never had a day in bed since being gassed in the World War.[11] In spite of the two Phanodorm tablets, Hitler had not had a good night's sleep. He said he couldn't stand being in a confined space and had to get up and about. He told Morell straightaway that he didn't want any more injections. The injection site hurt so much that it put everything else into the shade. Morell had unfortunately bent the needle the day before while administering the injection, although he was usually very skilful.[12] Hitler dismissed his personal physician after a short while and went to the map room. He ignored the recommendation to eat crispbread and unsweetened tea for lunch and ordered spaghetti and strawberries instead. Morell was so disturbed by Hitler's mood that morning that he added in his notes: 'I've never seen the Führer so hostile towards me.'[13]

On 9 August Morell gave Hitler three Vitamultin tablets, possibly containing Pervitin. Morell often mentioned Vitamultin, but in most cases it was Vitamultin-Calcium and not the tablets or Vitamultin forte, which was used later.[14] He was summoned to Hitler at 1 a.m. on 10 August. Blood pressure and pulse were normal again but the abdomen remained distended and there was still a buzzing in the ears. On Sunday, 10 August, Morell visited Hitler from 12 noon to 1 p.m. He had slept a little that night and the buzzing in the ears had stopped. His digestion was unchanged and his mood was not good but better than the previous Friday. After taking Calomel powder he had had five successful bowel movements, which had provided relief.

Morell was summoned again at 1 a.m. on 11 August. The gastrointestinal region was still tender but soft. Morell suggested the application of leeches to reduce the blood pressure further and an electric heating pad. He injected Vitamultin-Calcium and Tonophosphan to help with the digestion before leaving for the night. He returned that morning and noticed the tremor, as he had done on four days previously. Hitler informed him that he had had two bowel movements in the night. The meal that day was gruel, porridge and strawberries. On 11 August Morell also started the Mutaflor treatment recommended in Nissle's letter of 8 August.[15] Between 4 and 8 p.m. he also set two leeches on the mastoid process behind the left ear and in front of the left ear. After removal of the rear leech, the site continued to bleed for about two hours until Morell was able to staunch the flow with a pad of cotton soaked in iron chloride and a plaster dressing. The buzzing in the ears had stopped following Morell's treatment and Hitler, who did not appear for dinner because of the dressings, was able to take part in the evening briefing without problem.[16]

After the treatment with leeches, Hitler no longer complained of buzzing in the ears at the nightly tea discussions. Morell checked his pulse and blood pressure at 2 a.m., noting that they were practically normal, and departed for the day, leaving Hitler at work as usual. He returned at 12 noon to remove the iron chloride pad on the front leeching site, and the renewed bleeding was staunched by dabbing with Suprarenin solution. Hitler continued to feel well, however: his abdomen was soft, the dysentery had passed and the buzzing in the ears had stopped. When Morell returned at 7 p.m. blood pressure and pulse were almost normal. Hitler complained of throbbing on the left side of his head, no doubt on account of the tiring discussions with the Army High Command generals that afternoon. In contrast to his customary habits, he retired early.

Hitler slept well that night and felt fresh, apart from some ringing in the ears. As usual Morell administered Tonophosphan and Vitamultin-Calcium to promote digestion. At 1 a.m. on 14 August – Morell refers to this as 'evening' on account of Hitler's working habits – Hitler once again summoned his personal physician but would not permit an examination, saying that he was fine except for some ringing in the ears. That day he finally allowed the ECG that Morell had been urging since the heart trouble in July. Hitler also agreed to further examinations in the night.[17]

On the evening of 14 August, Morell left for Berlin, arriving at his home on Schwanenwerder island on the Havel river at noon the following day. He phoned the headquarters to ask about Hitler's health and was told that he was well. He looked at the analysis of the blood

146

samples from 14 August and found the red blood cells to be normal and the white cells slightly below. At around 1 p.m. on Sunday 17 August he returned to the headquarters and observed that Hitler was in good health. He informed him of the blood analysis and continued the treatment with Mutaflor and Vitamultin-Calcium. He also gave Hitler the multivitamin preparation Intelan and recommended Brom-Nervacit, a barbiturate-containing sedative, for the night. In the evening Morell, whose own cardiac problems were causing him increasing difficulties, was so 'tired and drawn' that he took his leave as 'early' as 1.30 a.m.

On 18 August Hitler no longer had any problems. Pulse and blood pressure were normal and the heart tones quiet. Morell now discussed the ECG findings from 14 August, which he had determined independently of Weber, whose letter was dated 20 August. After administering Tonophosphan, Glyconorm and Vitamultin-Calcium, he tried to persuade Hitler that he lacked fresh air and sunshine and was suffering from a chronic oxygen deficiency. Morell believed that the bunker was too humid and unhealthy and represented an ideal breeding ground for fungi. He said that his boots had developed a mould after standing for two days and that the clothes in the bedroom were damp. The climate was ideal for rheumatism and also for sciatica and aching joints, from which Morell himself suffered.[18] He had informed Hitler of the unsatisfactory situation after four days in the bunker and noted: 'Everybody disagreed with me, now they all agree with my judgement.' According to Morell the humid atmosphere in the bunker inevitably led to 'chest constrictions, anaemia and bunker psychosis'. Hitler himself was undisturbed by the bunker atmosphere. Perhaps the accommodation in the Masurian Forest reminded him of his war years in Flanders, where the dugouts had also not been comfortable. The spartan lifestyle was also an expression of his solidarity with the front soldiers. Morell attempted to persuade Hitler to take a holiday for a week or two on the Obersalzberg and also suggested excursions to the nearby woods. Hitler persistently refused, however, and put off making a decision.

While Hitler felt fine on 19 August, he reported to Morell the following day that his head felt a bit dizzy after all the work on the previous day and that everything irritated him. The tremor in his hands was also more pronounced. He had nevertheless slept well without any medication. Morell continued his treatment as usual and was generally happy with Hitler's condition.[19]

On 22 August Hitler slept soundly from 4 to 11 a.m. and his health gave no cause for concern. On that day Morell gave him a booster injection with 20 per cent glucose solution, Tonophosphan and Vitamultin-Calcium. Although Hitler's pulse and blood pressure were normal on 23 August, Morell set three leeches requested by Hitler: 'My head must be clear.' The desired effect was achieved this time as well and his head did apparently become clearer and 'lighter'. On 24 August Morell once again administered a booster injection and recommended a sedative for the night since Mussolini was arriving at the Wolf's Lair the following day for a visit of several days and Hitler needed to look fresh.[20] Mussolini arrived at the Wolf's Lair at 11 a.m. on 25 August and took part in the lunchtime briefing in the map room of the army staff headquarters. The following day he flew with Hitler from Rastenburg (Kętrzyn) to Terespol near Brest-Litovsk to inspect the troops and visit the destroyed fortress in Brest.

From 7 a.m. to 5 p.m. on 28 August Hitler and Mussolini inspected the Italian expeditionary corps front line in Ukraine after driving around for some time to find it. This, together with the poor military performance of the Italian allies, put Hitler in a bad mood. Mussolini urged Hitler to fly in his four-engine Focke-Wulf Condor D 2600 to distract him from the embarrassing impression that his fellow countrymen had left with the Germans. Hitler was also overcome with panic and annoyed with himself for having given in to Mussolini and flying in his Condor.

Morell had a further explanation for Hitler's bad mood. The intense summer sun had also left its mark on the Führer. Morell noted: 'His face was burnt beetroot red, his forehead with painful sunburnt patches, so he was very grumpy.' Although Hitler had remained in the vehicle and the sky was mostly overcast, the sensitive skin on his face was not only red but also swollen. He set off by train for the return journey to the Wolf's Lair at 8 p.m., pausing the following afternoon in Deutsch-Eylau (Iława), where Hitler was given another booster injection. The train arrived at the Wolf's Lair in the late evening and Hitler's entourage was invited for tea as usual. Morell left at 1.30 a.m. while the rest remained.[21] Except for a note mentioning a normal urine analysis on 6 September, Morell's records for 1941 end here.

The records for 1941 show that Hitler's health was compromised during the summer. To judge from Morell's notes, the three-week bout of diarrhoea appears to have been caused by bacterial dysentery. Heart problems are mentioned for the first time, and Hitler's blood pressure was also too high. Apart from this, Hitler does not seem to have suffered from any particular health problems.

Hitler's staff were concerned in early August at the state of the

**Prof. Dr. med. Theo Morell**

Sprechstunden: Werktags 11—1 und 5—7 Uhr
außer Sonnabend-Nachmittag

Berlin W 15, den  6. Sept. 1941.
Kurfürstendamm 216 (Ecke Fasanenstr.)
J 1 Bismarck 7382 U.-Bahnhof Uhlandstr.

Rp. *Führer - Hauptquartier.*

Pat. A. Morgen - Urin.

spez. Gew. 1020

Reaktion : alkalisch

Albumen : —

Saccharo. : —

Gallenfarbstoff :

Blut : —

Sediment : ganz wenig weißt
Leukos. u. Epith. B. i. ?

54. Morell's records end in 1941 on 6 September with a note that the
morning urine was normal.

149

'boss' [Chief] as they called him among themselves. During his illness he only had a few decisions to make, however. One regarded the introduction of the yellow star for Jews demanded by propaganda minister Joseph Goebbels, who had flown to Rastenburg (Kętrzyn) on 18 August 1941 to persuade Hitler of the need for all Jews in the Reich to be visibly identifiable. Hitler had been reluctant to take this step hitherto because of the possible reaction by other countries. In view of the military successes in the east and the west and the start of the mass extermination of the Jews he now realized that he no longer needed to worry about foreign opinion. As a result of this decision, the Jews now experienced a new public humiliation. The police regulation on the identification of Jews in the Reich territory entered into force a month later on 19 September 1941, making it compulsory for Jews to wear a yellow star with the word 'Jude' (Jew) on it.[22] All subsequent steps regarding the deportation and killing of the Jews in gas chambers were agreed by SS head Himmler with Hitler in September and October 1941. Morell was not in Hitler's headquarters at this time and Hitler did not suffer from any illnesses.[23]

Did Hitler make any misjudged decisions with an impact on the war while he was suffering from dysentery at the beginning of August? As has been mentioned, the disease did not weaken his powers of leadership in any way. He has been repeatedly criticized, however, for one military operation, which became known as the Battle of Kiev and later the fateful departure from the primary military objective.[24] On 21 August 1941 Hitler gave an order that the four Soviet armies at Kiev should be encircled and destroyed. Tank Group 2 of Army Group Centre swung south to complete the encirclement of Kiev, which surrendered on 26 September with the capture of 660,000 soldiers. It is questionable, however, whether the Battle of Kiev slowed down the German advance to such an extent that the Russian campaign could not be completed before becoming bogged down in the mud. In reality, it had already become clear in August that it would not be possible to achieve the primary military objective in spite of the massive territorial gains and the millions of Soviet prisoners of war.[25]

This is where the basic 'mistake' in the strategy was made. The Soviet Union did not collapse as had been hoped. On the contrary, the Soviet high command, the Stavka led by Stalin,[26] proved extremely flexible and quickly realized that space, time and weather could become decisive military factors. As a result of the skilful Soviet holding tactic – and the unscrupulous readiness to sacrifice millions of soldiers in order to gain time – the German offensive was held up before Moscow in December 1941.[27] The long planned

Soviet counter-offensive was carried out against exhausted and overstretched German fighting units that were ill-equipped for the wintery conditions. They were incapable of doing more than holding the retreating front. Hitler himself reacted frenetically and ordered small-scale tactical retreats and a number of changes in personnel. It is questionable whether Hitler's insistence prevented the immediate collapse of the German front; nor can it be demonstrated, however, that his actions had a negative impact on the course of the war for the German army.[28] It was not Hitler who determined events on the eastern front but his counterpart Stalin.[29]

A further decision by Hitler that was to have a fateful impact on the course of the war also had nothing to do with an acute illness or his megalomania, as is often claimed,[30] namely the declaration of war on the United States of America on 11 December 1941. It is regarded as a turning point in the war if for no other reason because of the fact that the military balance tilted clearly in favour of the Allies as a result. In fact, it was only a de facto recognition of a state of war that had existed between the two countries since summer 1941 following a series of incidents in the Atlantic. Germany merely anticipated the expected entry into the war by the USA on the side of Britain.[31] For the Americans, the war against Britain in any case threatened the vital interests of the USA, prompting President Roosevelt to advocate active involvement. Consequently, he did nothing to de-escalate the situation in the Atlantic. As Kershaw describes it, the USA was already waging an undeclared war in summer and autumn 1941. According to the 'Victory Program' by the Roosevelt administration announced to the public in September 1941, it would be necessary to send millions of soldiers to Europe in order to destroy the Nazi regime. Hitler's declaration of war merely determined the official beginning.[32]

## Late 1942 / Early 1943 and the Battle of Stalingrad

Except for occasional headaches and difficulty in sleeping, Hitler appears to have been healthy in subsequent months. Plans for a new offensive on all fronts were developed together with the military leadership. The main thrust was the war against the Soviet Union. This focus has been characterized as a mistake. The Austrian military historian Heinz Magenheimer, for example, argues that greater success could have been achieved with little effort in other theatres of war.[33] The Soviet leadership shared Hitler's belief, however, that

151

the eastern front would be the decisive arena in 1942. Stalin expected victory that year. The Stavka therefore regrouped all available forces in January 1942 and prepared for an offensive with a view to driving the Germans westwards 'without pausing for breath' in the early part of the year. This offensive broke down in February, however, and for a short while the front did not move.[34] On 5 April 1942 Hitler issued order no. 41 outlining the objectives for the German summer offensive on the eastern front. They reflected the existing German fighting forces and were relatively limited. The advance was to proceed from the south while a holding campaign was to be conducted in the north, albeit with plans for taking Leningrad and linking with the Finnish allies.[35]

During this time Hitler's health deteriorated, not least because the interminable briefings were draining his strength. The Army Group commanders shared Hitler's strategic aim of attempting to conquer territories that would give access to raw materials. Major infrastructure centres, such as Stalingrad, which was a vital communications hub, were also targeted. The desired destruction of enemy forces in further encirclement operations was not achieved, however. After the conquest of the Kerch peninsula and the capture of 170,000 Soviet soldiers in May 1942 and the disastrous defeat by the Red Army at Kharkov with 170,000 dead, the Stavka changed its tactics. Instead of confrontation it now opted for flexible defence, which included large-scale evasive movements but spared men and material.[36]

The practically unceasing advance by the Germans made it necessary in July 1942 to set up a new Führer headquarters near Winnyzja (codename: Werewolf). Hitler fell ill there shortly after the move, probably with influenza. Morell was flown in and in his daily records, which he resumed on 22 July 1942, he once again noted his patient's fluctuating blood pressure. Hitler complained above all of severe headaches, which might have been triggered by the pungent tar odour of the carbolineum used to protect the wood.[37] Morell once again prescribed leeching, used frequently to alleviate the headaches. He noted anew that Hitler's 'translucent, fine, hypersensitive skin' was extremely prone to sunburn.

Overall Winnyzja appears to have been even more unbearable for Hitler than the Wolf's Lair. On 22 July, Morell wrote that the climate in East Prussia and the mountain air were more suitable. For all Hitler's abhorrence of winter, he found the 50-degree temperatures in summer in his new headquarters intolerable. Keitel also attributes Hitler's lack of self-control and insufferable irritability to the hot continental climate in Winnyzja, which 'literally went to his head'.

This, at least, is the way that Morell described it to Keitel, adding that drugs were ineffective.[38]

It is worth mentioning the deterioration in Hitler's sight and the 'blurred vision in the right eye', which prompted him of his own accord to request an eye examination. Apart from this, the entries for July give no indication of serious illnesses. On the contrary, Hitler was sleeping relatively well and Morell even noted on 23 July: 'In excellent form'. There are brief entries for 22 to 24 July and again for 26 to 28 July but nothing concerning Hitler's health. August and September also seem to have passed without any health problems, as Morell's records do not begin again until October 1942.

The decision to continue the war in the south of the Soviet Union was made on 22 July 1942, before what appears to have been an attack of influenza. Although the order to attack Stalingrad is dated 23 July, it had been planned hitherto, occasioning fierce discussion in the general staff.[39] Chief of Staff Franz Halder did not realize that the Soviet tactics had changed despite it having been pointed out to him by Field Marshal Fedor von Bock, commander of Army Group South. Bock noted this divergence of opinion in his diary, stating that Halder was ordering 'the encirclement of an enemy who is no longer there'.[40] Von Bock had already been relieved of his command on 15 July and replaced by General Maximilian von Weichs, a commander who seldom contradicted Hitler.[41]

Von Weichs, high-ranking general staff officers and General Friedrich Paulus, commander of the Sixth Army, nevertheless conducted intensive discussions as to how the advance on Stalingrad was to take place, and it was only after thorough preparation that Paulus ordered the offensive.[42] A German infantry spearhead reached the banks of the Volga in mid-September 1942, and the city centre was later taken with massive bombardments in which over 40,000 civilians were killed. Only a few narrow bridgeheads in the ruins of industrial sites in the north of the city were still held by Soviet troops. The German attack had stalled, however, and the Soviets under the new commander of the 62nd Army, Lieutenant General Vasily Ivanovich Chuikov, fought from house to house to defend the city. In early November the city was still not completely taken.

The Red Army used the overstretched flank on the wide bend in the Don for a counterattack, Operation Uranus. The careful planning by the Soviet general staff provided for a wide encirclement of Stalingrad. More than one million soldiers were mustered in the north and south-east and equipped with some 13,500 guns and 900 tanks.[43]

In spite of careful efforts to conceal the deployment, Hitler already knew of the concentration of Soviet troops on 9 November and the following day ordered the 48th Tank Corps to reinforce the Third Romanian Army. The tank corps in question had very little combat strength, however, something that Hitler was unaware of. Moreover, the extent of the deployment was underestimated, a misjudgement that General Jodl described after the war as the greatest error by the German military intelligence.

The attack in the north began on 19 November and in the south the next day. The two thrusts met on 22 November on the Don around one hundred kilometres to the west of Stalingrad. The 6th Army, i.e. 250,000 German soldiers, was encircled. Considerable discussion has taken place on the subsequent mistakes, notably the arrogance of Hermann Göring who boldly guaranteed that the Luftwaffe would be able to supply the encircled army. Hitler's order that Stalingrad should be held at all costs is also cited as a cause of the loss of the 6th Army. It is questionable in any case, however, whether it would have been able to break out in view of the fact that it only had a hundred tanks available. The most promising solution did indeed appear to be to relieve the besieged troops, but this proved to be impossible in view of the superior Soviet power and the stuttering advance of Manstein's reinforcement.[44]

The mood in the Führer headquarters in autumn 1942 was correspondingly tense, not least as the German strategy was also coming to grief on other fronts. On 23 October the British under Field Marshal Montgomery launched an attack at El Alamein and inflicted a heavy defeat on the Afrika Korps. On 8 November the British and Americans landed in north-west Africa and progressed eastwards.

In spite of this crisis, Hitler's health remained stable. His blood pressure fluctuated in October and he could have suffered from intestinal dysbacteria, but his health was otherwise undisturbed, as can be seen from Morell's sporadic notes, which resumed on 1 October. Apart from the lack of sleep because of the heavy workload – or as Morell wrote on 23 November because of the 'huge responsibilities and overwork' – there were no health problems in November either. In December, however, Hitler suffered from chronic and attritional insomnia, almost certainly on account of the deteriorating situation in Stalingrad and Tunis. Morell saw it this way, providing sedatives and writing on 15 December: 'slept poorly (because of the military situation)'. On 9 December he had already noted: 'The intestinal problems were almost certainly attributable to the aggravation over the dire overall situation.'[45]

On 17 December Morell reported an interesting conversation with

Hitler, whose health at this time was not good and his mental state extremely tense. In this uncertain and dramatic situation he asked Morell to tell him directly if there were serious problems, as he still had vital decisions to make on Germany's account. Morell reported extracts of the conversation: 'He [Hitler] is not afraid of death, as it would be a release for him . . . He lives only for his Fatherland, for Germany. He knows that there is no cure for death, but if his health is ever endangered I [Morell] should tell him.'

Morell reassured him and reminded Hitler of a critical day when he had felt very bad with a systolic blood pressure of 200 mmHg and alarming dizziness. After Hitler had again assured Morell of his confidence in him, Morell took the opportunity of broaching the subject of coronary sclerosis. As the narrowing of the coronary arteries can produce angina pectoris attacks, Morell gave Hitler nitroglycerine tablets and Esdesan cum Nitro in case of emergency.[46] Hitler finally demanded of Morell not only selfless medical assistance but also immediate relief for all health impairments.

At the end of the year Morell provided the following summary diagnosis: 'Variable blood pressure through arterial spasms and coronary sclerosis – vascular spasms (head).' He also noted that the tremor in the left-side extremities had become worse in 1942 and could now be seen for the first time at rest. Morell still did not suspect Parkinson's disease, however.

Hitler's frequent tantrums at this time gave rise to considerable speculation among journalists that Hitler had become 'insane' in view of the defeats.[47] Indeed, Hitler could not understand why the 6th Army wanted to break out rather than succumb. He expected General Paulus to die a soldier's death, not least as he had promoted him by radio to field marshal on 30 January 1943. He also hoped that Paulus would 'save the last bullet for himself' rather than surrender, as he anticipated that the entire German officer corps would be totally demoralized if he were taken prisoner by the Soviets.

Eyewitnesses note that Hitler looked pale and hunched over. His gaze was stony and his eyes without lustre. He had a tremor in his left arm and leg, which he dragged. Joseph Goebbels wrote on 2 March in his diary: 'He [Goering] also thinks that the Führer has aged fifteen years in the three and a half years of the war.'[48]

In spite of the outward deterioration, the visible aging and the toll taken on his mental strength, Hitler did not have any diseases in the first months of the new year. Apart from an occasional headache, the continuing insomnia and sporadic abdominal pains, Morell found nothing extraordinary to report in his January records. Coronary sclerosis, vascular spasms in the head and abdomen, and dysbacteria remained the primary health issues – a continuation of Hitler's multi-factorial and diffuse complaints. This situation remained unchanged during the first months of 1943.

## The War in 1943: The Battle of Kursk

The tragedy of Stalingrad does not seem to have put a brake on Hitler's activity. On the contrary, in a four-hour meeting on 6 February 1943 he dissuaded Field Marshal von Manstein from continuing to insist on changes in the command structure. Von Manstein had demanded no less than a surrender of the supreme command to a marshal designated by Hitler so as to guarantee coherent leadership, an indispensable prerequisite, in his opinion, for achieving victory over the Soviet Union after all. He noted later that the meeting did not produce an outcome. Hitler skilfully directed the conversation away from this main concern and discussed the situation in the south instead. They conducted an intensive debate on the situation at the front and developed plans for avoiding large-scale incursions by the enemy in Ukraine. They also considered various ways of going on the offensive again. Von Manstein found Hitler to be a 'tough' opposite number capable of forming diverse arguments to back his case and of conducting the conversation in a 'psychologically skilful' manner.[49] In the next few weeks Hitler turned to combating the dejected mood in the population and army. He gave a speech to the Gauleiter and coordinated the propaganda with Goebbels for the impending 'total war', which Goebbels announced in a speech at the Sportpalast in Berlin on 18 February 1943.

Hitler himself took care of motivating the military leadership. He visited the headquarters of Army Group South in Zaporozhye from 17 to 19 February and met there with Field Marshal von Manstein and many other officers. He also reintegrated Kurt Zeitzler, Chief of Staff of the Army General Staff, and Alfred Jodl, Chief of the Operations Staff of the Armed Forces High Command, re-establishing close contact again and even effecting a 'reconciliation' with the latter. Here, too, Hitler demonstrated his psychological skill by once again befriending and allying himself with the brilliant staff officer. Jodl was in fact the perfect ally. After the victory over France he was highly respected in the army and was unconditionally loyal, sharing Hitler's penchant for risky operations, which in view of the impending war on two fronts appeared unavoidable.

Hitler then went on to the Werewolf headquarters in Ukraine, where he rehabilitated General Heinz Guderian on 21 February by appointing him Inspector General of Armoured Troops. Guderian was another commander willing to take the greatest risk if success could be achieved in that way.[50]

Morell's entries for February give no indication that Hitler was affected by the wearying travel, and he does not appear to have suffered any ill health. He was also increasingly more balanced mentally after the stabilization of the situation with Army Group South. Goebbels noted on 9 March: 'He is in excellent health, thank God. He looks a bit tired but otherwise very active.'[51]

On 24 March 1943, two days after his arrival at the Obersalzberg, Hitler once again suffered from 'very strong headache', probably caused by the foehn [warm mountain wind]. Morell also found the temporal artery badly swollen. As usual, he resorted to an injection, administering Septoiod, Brom-Nervacit and Optalidon to provide relief. Hitler returned immediately to his unhealthy daily rhythm, reflected in the following entry by Morell: 'Sat up after eating in animated conversation until 2.30 a.m. at the fireside (but no fire!) and made sure he got fresh air. F. kept telling me he felt much better again.' The eight days proposed by Morell and the attendant physicians for Hitler to spend resting in the mountains turned into three months.

On 26 March Morell, who spared no effort to improve Hitler's wellbeing, once again suggested a masseur, which Hitler once again declined. He said of his health that he got better in any case when the worries stopped. This statement epitomizes the state of his health. Hitler believed that his complaints were psychosomatic and he demanded of his personal physician that he remove the symptoms. He expected of himself and of others the smooth running of a machine that he had helped to create and was now making excessive demands. We can say cynically that Hitler's worries did not let up in early 1943 but his complaints remained within bounds.

As the entries for March indicate, Morell continued the daily glucose and vitamin injections and blood pressure measurements. He also advised Hitler to go to bed early and repeatedly suggested massage, without success. As far as others could tell, Hitler was nevertheless in good shape.[52]

Intensive discussion took place in early 1943 within the military and political leadership. The lack of success in the Atlantic and North Africa called for decisions, as did the discernible shortage of labour in the armaments industry and the dramatic situation in the Luftwaffe, which demanded effective weapons to combat the Allied bombers.

There was also the question of whether a political solution could be achieved with the Soviet Union, a separate peace agreement like the Treaty of Brest-Litovsk in March 1918. The diplomatic initiatives by Japan and Italy were no more enthusiastic than German efforts, however. Hitler's opinion prevailed that peace negotiations with the Soviet leadership were futile.[53] Recent research by British and Russian historians confirms this view. Stalin did not even consider the possibility of a separate peace agreement but was rather considering the restructuring of Europe that, in agreement with the Western Allies, called for the complete neutralization of the German Reich as a power factor.[54]

Hitler, von Manstein and Zeitzler were therefore all in favour of an offensive. They selected the Red Army front that had penetrated as far as Kursk, 120 km deep and 200 km wide, in which eight Soviet armies were concentrated, preparing for an advance. The possible starting date for Operation Citadel, as it was called, was dictated by the weather and the end of the mud period, and could not take place before April at the earliest. Difficulties in equipping the reinforced troops, particularly with assault guns and tanks, meant that the date was repeatedly postponed.[55]

The endless debates at Berghof caused insomnia and constipation, as Hitler's personal physician reports. On 11 May Morell carried out a thorough examination and various analyses. He did a blood count, blood sugar and urine analysis and took pituitary and adrenal gland readings. He also finally persuaded Hitler to have another ECG, which he initially evaluated himself before sending it two days later to Professor Weber in Bad Nauheim. The 1941 diagnosis of coronary sclerosis was confirmed and was described by Weber as 'evidently progressive'.

On several occasions, as on 28 May, for example, Morell found Hitler to be 'easily aroused' and 'very irritable'. His patient's abdomen was hard, and Morell therefore prescribed a strict diet and laxatives. Hitler refused massage, short wave treatment and even enemas, however. Because of the gastrointestinal cramps, Morell administered an intravenous Eupaverin injection on 28 May, which brought about immediate relief. Hitler reported a 'large bowel movement' in the evening. He claimed to have lost four kilograms in the preceding few days. He was cheerful and 'very lively' at the evening meal, however, and the tea session went on until 2.30 a.m.[56]

Nissle reported to Morell by telephone on 2 June that he had again found 'large amounts' of aerogenic bacilli in patient A.'s stool. Morell therefore commenced a further Mutaflor treatment on 17 June, which

Hitler had always been amenable to. On 20 June Morell described him as 'looking very good'.[57]

A few days later Hitler left Berghof and returned after a good three months to the Wolf's Lair, his headquarters in East Prussia. On 1 July he gave a speech to all commanders and generals involved in Operation Citadel, the assault on the Kursk/Orel region. In the early morning of 5 July, Army Group South (von Manstein) and Centre (von Kluge) launched the planned operation, which was to become the largest land battle in military history. The fighting involved over four million soldiers, 69,000 guns and mortars, 13,000 tanks and self-propelled artillery vehicles, and almost 12,000 aeroplanes. Even the Battle of Stalingrad appeared 'small beer' in comparison, as military historian Karl-Heinz Frieser comments.[58] Hitler believed that the battle would be decisive. When Josef Kammhuber, commander of the 12th Air Corps and coordinator of the night fighters, asked in early summer 1943 for a reinforcement of the Jagdwaffe [fighting arm of the Luftwaffe] to combat the Allied bomber formations, Hitler therefore replied: 'When I have defeated Russia you can have everything for the defence of the Reich. However, then you will no longer need it.'[59]

In retrospect, as the Bundeswehr Military History Research Institute concluded in 2007, the attempt to force a decision at Kursk was 'forlorn'.[60] The Soviet positions were too strong and the amount of men and material that the Stavka was willing to employ was too great, exceeding the German potential by several orders of magnitude. Sepp Dietrich, commander of the SS-Leibstandarte Adolf Hitler, realized: 'We are not going to break through.'[61] On 13 July the offensive was indeed called off and on 17 July the Soviet general offensive got underway, bringing the Red Army to the north of Ukraine by the end of the year. Kiev, the prestige target in 1941, fell on 6 November 1943.

Hitler accepted the failure of the 'decisive battle' with fatigue, as eyewitnesses report, but also ultimately impassively, because by this time the situation in Italy was giving cause for concern. Field Marshal Albert Kesselring, Commander-in-Chief South, had already informed Hitler in June that the Allies were about to invade Sicily and that Mussolini's regime would collapse. Right after Kursk, Hitler therefore travelled to Berghof to arrange a meeting with Mussolini. Morell once again noted at 10.30 a.m. on 18 July: 'very painful spastic constipation' and also observed that Hitler 'looked very bad and rather faint'. As far as Morell was concerned his patient was completely overworked and overstrained. The spasms were relieved with intravenous Eupaverin and intramuscular Eukodal injections.

On 19 July Hitler flew to Italy to meet Mussolini at the villa belonging to Senator Gaggia in Feltre near Treviso, north of Venice. He managed to persuade Mussolini not to abandon the alliance with Germany. During the two-hour meeting Hitler appeared euphoric and barely allowed Mussolini a word in edgeways.[62] Hitler survived the visit well and had no health problems, for which he thanked Morell, who had phoned to recommend Vitamultin tablets, that evening at Obersalzberg. This is one of the few occasions in which it can be assumed that Hitler was supplied with the Pervitin-containing Vitamultin tablets.[63]

Six days later, on 25 July 1943, Hitler's Italian ally Mussolini was deposed. The Grand Council of Fascism asked King Victor Emmanuel III to take command of the Italian troops. Mussolini submitted his resignation and was arrested as he left the Quirinal Palace. This news caused great concern at the Führer headquarters and the idea of retribution against the traitorous Italy was immediately considered, despite the fact that Mussolini's successor Marshal Pietro Badoglio announced that he would honour Italy's commitment to the Axis. When General Eisenhower announced an armistice with Italy on 8 September, however, Hitler had Rome occupied. On 12 September Mussolini was 'liberated' by a parachute unit under SS-Hauptsturmführer Otto Skorzeny from the ski resort hotel Campo Imperatore in Abruzzo. He arrived the same day at Hotel Imperial in Vienna, called Hitler and set off for Munich. On 14 September he flew to Rastenburg (Kętrzyn), where the two Axis partners rethought Italy's political landscape at their leisure. Mussolini initially had the idea of forming a republican-fascist party and of establishing a new government for north and central Italy under German supervision on Lake Garda. The Repubblica Sociale Italiana, also known as the Salò Republic, was to survive as a German puppet state in northern Italy until April 1945.[64]

As far as Hitler's health was concerned, this development merely meant an increase in his gastrointestinal cramps and miserable mood. For the German Reich, however, it was the beginning of the end. Once again Hitler attempted to influence military developments and spread optimism through his personal presence in the various headquarters and command posts. At 7 a.m. on 27 August he flew to Winnyzja to meet with von Manstein and other army commanders, returning that evening to Rastenburg. On 8 September he flew to Army Group South in Zaporozhye, where he once again met with von Manstein and the other army commanders. Hitler was in top form physically, prompting Goebbels to note on 10 September that the

Führer 'surpassed himself physically, emotionally and intellectually in crises', while Morell noted on 15 September that he looked very well. Hitler's entourage appear to have known nothing of his health problems, as an entry in Goebbels' diary on 23 September indicates: 'The Führer seems to be in excellent health.' Morell, by contrast, observed extreme flatulence and spasms caused by the immense agitation. Following administration of Eupaverin and Eukodal, however, Morell noted that after a few hours 'everything wa in order'.[65]

During these months Hitler's health problems were limited to the chronic sleeping disorders and painful abdominal spasms, which Morell once again attributed to mental factors because Hitler had to put up with 'increasing agitation'. From this time onwards, this comment is found frequently in Morell's notes, sometimes on a daily basis.

The last entry by Morell in 1943 was on 12 December, the fifth year of war, when he wrote that Hitler looked 'very well, excellent appetite'. It can therefore be assumed that apart from the chronic gastrointestinal complaints Hitler was in good health in December 1943 and that he required Morell's services less often in the last months of the year. Apart from the colic-like abdominal pains, which had increased continuously over the years since 1941, Hitler's health in 1943 left nothing to be desired. There were no new or serious illnesses. In spite of a series of defeats, Hitler remained in control and demonstrated unbroken energy and performance capability.

There are no indications whatsoever by Morell of a new illness, even if the increase in gastrointestinal cramps sometimes affected Hitler's health to the point of rendering him incapable of working. Even though he supported Nissle's dysbacteria theory, Morell did not fail to mention his suspicion that the spasms might also have been psychosomatic. He also noted some changes in Hitler: he was more irritable and nervous and became derailed quite quickly. He had become so manic compared with previous years that conversations frequently turned into monologues.

Although such judgements must be made with caution, it would appear that Hitler was transformed after the defeat at Stalingrad and became more thin-skinned and unpredictable. The defeat affected him deeply but did not reduce his determination. Morell became increasingly indispensable but not, it should be emphasized, because Hitler was becoming addicted. Morell's records indicate that he was summoned more frequently in 1943 than hitherto, but there were no particular health problems, and Morell's thoughts centred repeatedly on the gastrointestinal spasms that both he and Hitler believed to be psychosomatic. He was concerned about Hitler's general health but did not undertake any radical change of treatment.

## Strategic Decisions: 1944

Morell noted in his diary on 27 January: 'Spa House, speech by boss'. 'In a two-hour speech to his generals, Hitler painted a grim picture of the future and informed the generals that if the worst came to the worst he expected them to close ranks around him with swords drawn.'[66] On 11 February Morell diagnosed 'catarrh in upper respiratory tracts, particularly left tonsil, and bronchitis, influenza' and once again noticed the marked tremor in Hitler's left leg. On 22 February, however, he wrote: 'Tremor in left leg and shaking of hands gone.'[67] The entire entourage moved to the Berghof near Berchtesgaden, where a 'second Reich Chancellery' was set up with offices of all the main government bodies and a military infrastructure that included not only a large-scale bunker network but also smoke-generating installations to protect it from air raids.[68]

It was here that the decisions were made that cemented Germany's 'downfall', as writer Joachim Fest put it. It was also here for the first time that the Wehrmacht generals began to criticize Hitler, while still remaining subordinate to him. Their protests were not about the killing of the Jews or the war of extermination in the east. In keeping with their 'professionalism', which saw killing as something political (for which they were not 'responsible'), the only aim pursued by the general staff officers and troop commanders was to achieve a favourable outcome for Germany. Thus general staff chiefs Zeitzler and Guderian and even Alfred Jodl, Chief of the Operations Staff of the Armed Forces High Command and Hitler's most important adviser, opposed individual decisions that they believed were wrong.

Hitler himself had other priorities. He was concerned that the genocide of European Jews could continue. He also hoped to be able to regain the initiative, hence the development of new weapons such as the V-2 rocket [standing for 'Vergeltung' or retaliation], the Messerschmitt Me 262 fighter aircraft and the XXI and XXIII submarines.[69] It is now clear that these developments came much too late and should, according to British historian Richard Overy, have been accompanied much earlier by a marked increase in the mass production of standard weapons. Efforts were indeed made to do this, but they were thwarted to a large extent by the Anglo-American air raids from 1943 onwards. The bombardment practically put a stop to the production of vehicles, and aircraft and tank production was reduced in 1944 by 31 and 35 per cent respectively. The resources for the German armaments industry – concentration camp inmates, forced labourers in occupied territories, factories in remote areas – nevertheless remained considerable.[70]

There can nevertheless be no doubt that the German Reich had already lost the war in 1944. The Normandy invasion and the collapse of Army Group Centre on the eastern front in summer 1944 signalled victory for the Allies. Thereafter it was just a question of how the German defeat would take shape.

As had been the case previously with the Allies, the course of the war in 1944 was determined by a series of bad decisions by the Germans. Hitler's strategy in summer 1944 was simple: fight in the west, hold on in the east. Military historian Karl-Heinz Frieser likened the war in Europe as a whole to a room with two doors, one of which – in the east – was to be barricaded to keep out the attackers on one side (at least temporarily), while on the other side the intruders were to be repelled with all possible force. The problem, he pointed out, was that the eastern front could not be simply 'barricaded' because the enemy was stronger and had superior armoured forces.[71] Hitler himself made the mistake of choosing an unfavourable line for this defence. The most radical proposal in this regard was made by General Jodl in early 1944: withdrawal to the shortest line between the Baltic and the Black Sea and taking up position between Riga and Odessa. By straightening the line in this way, twenty divisions or 300,000 soldiers would have been made available immediately, who could have formed a reserve to counter the anticipated invasion and also used as mobile fighting units behind the shortened eastern front.

Hitler was adamant, however, that none of the conquered territories should be relinquished. On 8 March 1944 he gave a decisive order for the formation of a system of fixed defensive positions as a basis for successful counter-operations.[72] The southern section of the eastern front was forced to retreat under the onslaught of the Soviet spring offensive. By April the fighting had already shifted to the Odessa region, and on 12 April Hitler forbade retreat from the Crimean peninsula, which was subsequently encircled by Soviet troops. The Red Army also used the exposed fronts in the centre and north to encircle German armies. Three divisions of the 3rd Panzer Army were destroyed in Vitebsk. Attempts at breaking out of the encirclement, such as the one at Kamenets-Podolsk, proved to be extremely costly in terms of men. For this and other reasons, Zeitzler tried to dissuade Hitler from pursuing this static strategy, which led to heated arguments.[73]

In early May Hitler's gastrointestinal cramps recurred. As usual, Morell resorted to spasmolytics. Apart from medication, he urged Hitler to go to bed earlier, but was told by his patient that he would not be able to sleep peacefully until there were no more fighter planes in the airspace over Germany. On 9 May, Morell noted: 'Headache on left side, legs trembling (invasion imminent, but where?)'. This would appear to imply that Morell saw the imminent invasion by the western Allies as an explanation for the recurrence of the shaking palsy, thus admitting the possibility of a psychosomatic influence.[74]

On 23 May 1944, Morell suggested some new treatment strategies with Vitamultin tablets, Glyconorm, Luizym and Euflat and anti-gas pills. Apart from the regular intake of Vitamultin tablets, which he had recommended sporadically in the past, there was in fact nothing new about the treatment. Hitler once again categorically refused massage, more fresh air and earlier retirement to bed. Morell also recommended daily oxygen treatment, intravenous glucose injections, and intramuscular Strophanthin and Testoviron injections. Finally, he advised ten to fifteen drops of Cardiazol in the event of an acute deterioration in his patient's general wellbeing.[75]

News of the invasion of Normandy on 6 June 1944[76] was received with relief in the Führer headquarters, and Hitler himself appeared to observers to be relaxed and in a good mood. He told Göring optimistically that the Anglo-Americans would be thrown out.[77] Hitler's good mood quickly dissipated, however, as a conversation between Hitler and Goebbels on 21 June 1944 demonstrates. Goebbels noted in his diary that Hitler 'made no bones' about the military situation and realized that Germany had reached 'the eleventh hour'. While he was still hoping for victory, he now admitted that the eastern front was in danger of collapsing. Even in the west, where the Allied landing in Normandy had begun on 6 June 1944, a retreat might now have to be contemplated.[78]

It was not immediately clear, however, that the invasion of British and American forces would put an end to the Nazi regime and seal the fate of the German Reich. The Allies were very concerned at the outcome of the Normandy landings. Supreme Commander General Dwight D. Eisenhower even prepared a press statement explaining the reasons for failure. He did not need to publish the statement, however, because the Allied supremacy in the air and the uncompromising efforts by the British and American infantry made it possible to establish a bridgehead in Normandy. It was not until 24 July, however, that the Allies managed at great expense to stabilize the new front.[79]

Hitherto, on 22 June, the long-awaited major Soviet offensive (Operation Bagration) commenced, bringing about the destruction of twenty-eight German divisions. The collapse of Army Group Centre opened the way to the Baltic and East Prussia. The holding strategy ordered by Hitler in White Russia made the situation worse. The ratio of 1:23 tanks, 1:10.5 ground-attack aircraft and 1:3.7 men made the outcome of Bagration a foregone conclusion.[80] The front was stabilized again in September 1944 after fierce and costly defensive actions. The Germans managed to bring up reserves, and the Soviet offensive swung northwards. Its aim was not to liberate an insurgent Warsaw but to reach the Baltic and cut off the connection between Army Group Centre and North.[81]

Zeitzler pointed out the seriousness of the situation on 30 June, when he told Hitler that a military victory in the war was no longer possible. According to Zeitzler's account, Hitler reacted with an 'immoderate' tantrum, accusing the general staff of defeatism.[82] The ongoing conflict between Hitler and his generals once again centred on the question of rigid or mobile defence.

Hitler interfered increasingly in the conduct of the war, not in general, however, but only in the case of commanders whose unconditional loyalty was in question. He frequently replaced commanders or transferred them elsewhere, and the command of particularly sensitive sections of the front was entrusted only to certain generals whom he trusted to encounter the enemy by employing zone defence tactics [Grosskampfverfahren].[83] For the rest Hitler's order was to hold on at all costs.

## Medical and Political Consequences of the Assassination Attempt

In spite of the building work in the Wolf's Lair, Hitler and Morell flew back from Salzburg to Rastenburg on 14 July 1944. Hitler arrived well rested in his East Prussian headquarters and the late-night tea session took place as usual on 19 July, with the result that Morell had only two hours' sleep. After he had given Hitler his usual booster injection at 11.15 a.m. on 20 July, he went to bed exhausted and did not even hear the explosion of Stauffenberg's bomb at 12.42 p.m. during the midday briefing in the conference room. The explosion was described by eyewitnesses as a powerful blast accompanied by a jet of flame. The room was considerably damaged and a hole with a diameter of 50 cm opened up in the floor. The massive oak table collapsed. The blast was diverted by the table, and some of the pressure escaped through the hole in the floor. The open windows also contributed to the failure of the attempt.

After just a few seconds officers with minor injuries helped the others out of the room. Field Marshal Keitel shouted: 'Where is the Führer?' He found Hitler just afterwards and helped him out into the open air. Personal adjutant Julius Schaub and valet Heinz Linge accompanied him to his bunker. Linge quickly obtained a new uniform and called Hanskarl von Hasselbach, who performed first aid.[84] He reached Morell at around 1 p.m. and summoned him saying: 'Quickly, quickly, professor, you must come to the Führer straightaway!'

Despite his considerable injuries, Hitler was in top form. A possible psychological explanation for this is that he had survived a long-announced threat and could now move against an enemy that had finally revealed itself. Luftwaffe adjutant Nicolaus von Below recalls that warnings of an assassination attempt by a general staff officer had already been received from Sweden in February 1944.[85]

Hitler reacted quickly. Half an hour after the attempt Himmler arrived at the Wolf's Lair and after consultation with Hitler set the police operation in motion.[86] In the meantime the Reich Security Service, Hitler's personal bodyguard, had started investigations. Even before Graf von Stauffenberg arrived at Berlin-Bendlerblock at 4.30 p.m., the basic features of the assassination plan were known, and while the investigations were taking place Hitler received Mussolini and showed him the destroyed conference room. He received a telephone call at around 6.35 p.m. from Ernst-Otto Remer, commander of the Grossdeutschland guard battalion, who wanted to check whether he should really arrest Goebbels. Hitler asked Remer if he recognized his voice. Remer said yes. At 6.45 p.m. the first radio announcement was made stating that a 'bomb attack' had been carried out on the Führer. The resistance quickly collapsed thereafter. At around 1 a.m. Hitler spoke to the German people on the radio, cleverly reducing the resistance to a 'very small clique of ambitious, unscrupulous and stupid, criminal officers'.[87]

Hitler took the opportunity presented by the assassination attempt to rid the army of unpopular and 'unreliable' officers. The reserve army in the Reich now had a new supreme commander, Reichsführer-SS Heinrich Himmler. The SS also took command of other Wehrmacht institutions. The Abwehr (military intelligence), whose leaders had been aware of the plot, came under the control of the Reich Security Head Office.[88] Arrests in connection with the plot continued throughout the autumn. Around 7,000 people were arrested and at least two hundred were convicted and executed in show trials lasting until April 1945. Hitler had escaped death, as he had in earlier assassination attempts, however, and in his speeches he invoked 'providence' and thanked his 'creator' for giving him the opportunity to 'continue his work'.[89]

The actual injuries that Hitler suffered, which he sought to play down both physically and mentally in the next few weeks, can be seen in Morell's notes on the examination he made at 8 p.m. on 20 July. Hitler's pulse was strong and regular but fast (100 beats per minute), the systolic blood pressure was also elevated at 165 to 170 mmHg. Morell recorded the following injuries as a result of the explosion: right forearm badly swollen, which the doctor treated with an aluminium acetate poultice; bruise on the right lower leg; large burn blisters on the back of the third and fourth fingers of the left hand, which were dressed by Morell; hair singed partially on the back of the head and completely in the ears; palm-sized second-degree burn on the thigh; the left forearm was badly swollen from an internal bruise and thus difficult to move; there were also a number of open flesh wounds and many splinters to be removed.

Hitler received first aid from von Hasselbach until Morell arrived and took over the treatment. Morell found Hitler to be in good general shape and he therefore prescribed only two Optalidon tablets for the pain and recommended two tablespoonfuls of Brom-Nervacit before retiring. Of the twenty-four people present at the explosion Hitler had the fewest injuries. He was therefore in relatively good condition when he went to meet Mussolini at 3.30 p.m. at Görlitz station near the Führer headquarters.

Paradoxically, Hitler's tremor disappeared after the bomb. He noted this side effect with gratitude and said to Jodl eleven days later: 'The miracle is that the shock got rid of my nerve complaint almost entirely.' The trembling of the left leg had 'vanished almost completely as a result of the attack – not that I would recommend this kind of remedy.'[90]

On 21 July, the day after the assassination attempt, Morell discovered that the results of the injury were more severe than he had first suspected. Hitler was deaf in the right ear and he had difficulty hearing with the left. He also complained of a taste of blood in the mouth. That night his right ear started bleeding and he had severe pain in the ear. As Professor von Eicken was not available, Professor Brandt, who had come from Berlin right after the assassination attempt, asked Dr Erwin Giesing, senior staff physician and head of the ear, nose and throat department of Karlshof hospital, to come to the headquarters. He treated Hitler for around two months. Von Eicken also arrived at the Wolf's Lair on 23 July. He basically confirmed Morell's findings and noted: 'Consultation in Führer headquarters with Prof. Morell, 20 July: bomb attack . . . both eardrums ruptured, lots of blood in right ear . . . some blood in the nasopharynx.' Dr Giesing was left to carry out treatment.

Giesing's ear examination showed a slight rupture with bleeding of the left eardrum. After removal of the blood, the right ear proved to have a major injury to the eardrum that was bleeding quite severely. A balance test revealed that the inner ear had also been involved. Hitler wanted to know how long the treatment would last. Giesing reckoned it would take six weeks and suggested cauterization of the rim of the eardrum.

The cauterization took place the following day. Hitler had refused a local anaesthetic and wanted to put up with the torture without assistance. But the bleeding was not stopped although Morell prescribed Nateina in addition. Giesing had to cauterize the eardrum a second time. Because of the danger of a middle ear infection Hitler demanded a booster dose of sulphonamide with Ultraseptyl as a precautionary measure. Giesing refused to use a chemotherapeutic drug for prophylaxis. Although the ENT specialist ultimately acquiesced, Hitler nevertheless developed otitis. The consequences were difficult to put up with for Hitler's entourage because the chronic insomnia and the throbbing headaches made him even more irritable than usual. As always, he refused his doctors' suggestion that he take a walk in the evenings, saying that it was too damp and misty.

It is interesting to note from Morell's records during this time that Hitler continued his night-time tea sessions even after the assassination attempt. He wrote: 'Invited to tea, slept only two hours'. When Giesing gave Hitler a more thorough examination on 30 July after treating his ear, the local condition had improved but Hitler's general health was still considerably diminished. His face was extremely pale and he had diffuse swellings. He was unable to sleep in spite of taking Phanodorm. The middle ear infection was noticeably slow in healing, making it difficult for Hitler to take part in the daily briefings. The general staff officers observed at these briefings that Hitler's tremor was now more pronounced. He said ironically to his secretary: 'Before the attack I had this tremor in my left leg. Now it's moved to the right hand. I am very glad that I don't have it in my head. It would be bad if my head was shaking all the time.'[91]

Ultraseptyl, Morell's panacea, had no effect and instead of a slow improvement Hitler showed clinical manifestations of an inflammation in the head. At all events he complained of a feeling of pressure and pain in the head, particularly the forehead. Giesing reckoned the most likely cause to be frontal sinusitis or pansinusitis (see section on acute diseases). Hitler's skull was therefore X-rayed at Rastenburg hospital in the evening of 19 September.[92] Two frontal views and one lateral view were taken. These three X-ray pictures have survived. The left maxillary sinus and ethmoidal cells were shadowed but all other paranasal sinuses were free of inflammatory processes.

Morell urgently recommended oxygen to improve Hitler's general health and suggested that he spend eight to ten days on the Obersalzberg. He said that a similar effect could be achieved with a drive in an open vehicle with stops for a thirty-minute walk in the Masurian woods. Morell believed that additional massage would stimulate the blood circulation and help bring down the swelling on the left lower leg and ankle. He further recommended that the left leg be raised. As always, Hitler rejected suggestions of this kind.

## The Ardennes Offensive and Morell's Notes

In summer 1944, when the military situation in Normandy was becoming increasingly difficult and the loss of France looking imminent, Hitler had already decided on a counter-offensive that winter. On 19 August he informed the participants of the briefing that an offensive would be launched in November – when the enemy could not fly. From the orders issued by Hitler at the time, it can be seen that he had already given intensive thought to the matter.[93] He explained the operational details to a small group of trusted confidants on 16 September, prompting forceful protests by Guderian because of the precarious situation in the east and by the Luftwaffe representative in the Führer headquarters because of the possibility of failure.[94] Hitler was insistent, however, and at a meeting on 25 September appointed Field Marshal Gerd von Rundstedt as commander and selected the terrain on which the operation would be carried out. The idea was to advance through the Ardennes towards Antwerp and encircle and destroy the British forces. Hitler even spoke of a 'second Dunkirk'.[95] Hitler deliberately chose the difficult terrain in the Ardennes because he reckoned that this would give the German troops an advantage. He was also playing on the possibility of confusion in the command structures and communications between British and American units. Altogether he was counting on Germany regaining the initiative on one section of the front at least. In view of the masses of troops available to the Soviets, it was unlikely that a decisive advantage could be achieved in the east. If it were possible to destroy twenty to thirty of the sixty-two divisions belonging to the Western Allies, the overall situation could change 'abruptly' – at least that is what Hitler hoped.[96]

The date for the offensive was set on 25 September for the last ten days of November.

It was not until a few days after this decision had been made that Hitler fell ill with jaundice and was confined to bed. Thus General Jodl's claim that Hitler formulated the idea for the Ardennes offensive when he was already lying sick in bed is incorrect. Morell was not summoned until 6.30 a.m. on 28 September and it was on this occasion that he noticed Hitler's striking yellow colour.

Hitler reported to Morell that he had experienced severe colic and nausea after lunch. The examination showed that the abdomen was very taut and the pit of the stomach very tender to the touch. Hitler also told his personal physician that his urine had been 'as brown as beer'. Morell injected Eukodal and Eupaverin and recommended an electric heating pad and hot, unsweetened tea. He was summoned again in the night and stayed from 12.15 to 1.30 a.m. on 29 September with Hitler, who was still complaining of nausea and gastrointestinal cramps and was bathed in perspiration. The urine was still dark. Did Hitler really have jaundice? Morell and the attendant physicians all tended to this conclusion. As has been discussed earlier, Morell discounted the possibility of strychnine poisoning, and the most probable explanation in his view was an obstruction of the gallbladder.[97]

When Morell visited Hitler at 11.50 a.m. on 29 September, his patient informed him that he had slept only three hours that night. He reported agonizing flatulence and complained about the general staff and the complete failure of the Luftwaffe.[98] Hitler was so unwell that on 29 September Morell was summoned four times. In the afternoon he ordered Hitler to bed.

The situation remained unchanged during the night. There was no question of Morell going to bed, although he was in urgent need of sleep on account of his own ill health. He was obliged to keep Hitler company from 1.30 to 5 a.m. and then started his day by administering an enema, which finally brought the long-awaited relief. Morell was called back at noon when Hitler reported that he was not getting better but was worse than before. In objective terms, however, an improvement had taken place because the abdomen was much softer and even the pit of the stomach and gallbladder region were less tender, although there was still discomfort from gas in the intestine, as Morell noted.

Hitler flatly refused an oil or camomile enema in bed but agreed to an irrigator camomile enema, which he administered himself in the WC. When Morell was summoned at 6.30 p.m., Hitler announced that he had had four bowel movements between 4 and 6 p.m. He had only called Morell to announce the good news. Hitler's diet was limited to gruel soup, but Morell did not prescribe any drugs, merely camomile tea administered from time to time with a rectal syringe, which the patient wished to carry out himself.

Morell once again suggested a change of air and walks and proposed a two-day visit to Berlin. He also recommended a fourteen-day stay on the Obersalzberg. As always, Hitler prevaricated.[99]

At 1 p.m. on 1 October Morell reported that Hitler was looking well and the natural colour was gradually coming back. He ordered his patient to remain in bed as he was still obviously weak. For lunch there was gruel soup and steamed fruit. Morell administered his booster injection of 20 per cent glucose solution and vitamins. At 6.30 p.m. he once again brought up the idea of a change of air, suggesting two to three days in Berlin then twelve to fourteen days in the mountains, or just Berlin for eight to ten days. Hitler finally rejected Obersalzberg out of hand and said that Berlin was unsuitable because he would have to keep going down to the bunker but he was too weak to walk much. Morell took the occasion to point out that the new bunker, which Hitler had had built in the Wolf's Lair in spite of the dangerous proximity to the front, was completely unsuitable. Morell's day ended with a final visit at 10 p.m. and his next visit was at 1 p.m. on 2 October. Hitler's health still left something to be desired: he felt weak and complained of much belching. Pulse and blood pressure were slightly elevated and the temperature of 37.3 degrees was subfebrile. There was the usual discussion on the frequency of bowel movements and sleeping problems, which were still much in evidence.

On 2 October Morell noted: 'Yellow skin coloration now gone.' At 9 p.m. Hitler ate some gruel and stewed fruit, and Morell once again administered his collection of drugs to fortify his patient, who had been gradually debilitated by the diet.[100]

Morell himself had a minor stroke in the night on 6 October. As he noted, he had a cerebral oedema and slight bleeding behind the left eye, impaired vision and reduced field of vision, and also dizziness when walking. It was not until 8 October that Hitler informed him of the dismissal of attendant surgeons Dr von Hasselbach and Dr Brandt following the doctors' dispute about the strychnine-containing anti-gas pills.

While Morell remained handicapped by the consequences of his stroke, Hitler appeared much better, despite having lost thirteen pounds in weight in two weeks. Since 14 October, however, he had had an inflammation of the left tonsil and his voice was husky and abrasive. Professor von Eicken was summoned to the Wolf's Lair on 21 October and after examination ordered an X-ray of the nasal sinuses, which was performed at 6 p.m. at the hospital in Karlshof. The result was once again slight shadowing of the maxillary sinus, the other sinuses being non-inflamed.

Hitler's own subjective symptoms improved in the next few days but his voice remained husky for five weeks. He complained repeatedly as it made it impossible for him to speak to the German people. Unlike Hitler, however, Morell was of the opinion that he had just a slightly throaty voice, which he attributed to the cold air from the extractor fans in the bunker.[101] Perhaps it was not his voice that held Hitler back from speaking to the German people. What should he tell them? The course of the war was disastrous and he wanted to keep the forthcoming offensive secret.

Morell was summoned at 6 a.m. on 30 October to Hitler, who had worked through the night on a 'very important decision'. He was now permanently occupied with the Ardennes offensive and was continuously confronted by operational details. Because he had reserved important decisions for himself, he now had to deal with the matter of fuel supplies, arms and 'refreshing' the fighting units. As a result of his efforts he was suffering from severe gastrointestinal cramps. Morell administered an intravenous injection of Eupaverin and Eukodal. The spasms eased as the injection was being administered, upon which Hitler pressed Morell's hand and said: 'How lucky we are to have Eupaverin.' When Morell was summoned again at 2 p.m., Hitler was contemplating the general staff, whose failure to perform was a constant thorn in his side. He commented that the old Prussian slogan 'Be more than you appear to be' had been born of false modesty, since 'if you are capable of something you should be proud to show it'. Morell took up this comment and expressed the opinion that the bad habits of the general staff had evolved after the

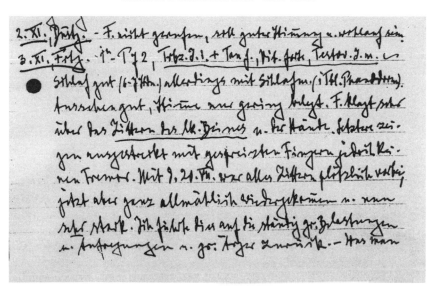

55. On 2 November 1944 Morell noted that Hitler was 'well and in a good mood'. On 3 November he noted 'Slept well but with sedative (Phanodorm tablet). Appearance good, voice only slightly hoarse. F. complains a lot about the tremor in his left leg and in his hands. However, the latter, when extended with fingers spread, shows no tremor.' He continues that after 20 July 'all tremor suddenly disappeared but was now gradually returning very strongly.' Morell attributed it to the 'constant burdens, worries and arguments'.

First World War. Hitler disagreed, pointing out that this clique had already set itself apart during the war.[102]

It is surprising to note how much Hitler confided in his personal physician, but it is unlikely that he was speaking sincerely. As with others, he employed a characteristic and successful tactic of blaming those who were not there and motivating those who were. While Hitler's voice was only slightly throaty, the tremor in his left leg and hand had noticeably increased, which Morell attributed to the constant burdens, worries and arguments.[103]

On 8 November Morell's records take up five whole pages. The day began at 12.30 a.m. Hitler complained of colic-like pain in the upper abdomen that he believed had arisen because he was facing the 'biggest decisions of his life'. As usual, Morell provided immediate relief with Eukodal and Eupaverin. He suggested insistently that Hitler should take a short break of eight or ten days, which he urgently required because of the chronic lack of daylight and fresh air in the bunker atmosphere. The doctor was used to receiving evasive responses. Hitler's reaction on this occasion was typical: 'I'll see what I can do in the next few weeks.' Morell also once again urged Hitler to have an X-ray taken of his gastrointestinal tract, saying that he would even arrange for an X-ray machine to be set up in the bunker so as to avoid any undue concern. Because of the frequent cramps, Morell's colleagues would make an issue of it if he didn't have the X-ray taken. Surprisingly, Hitler agreed, but the examination was ultimately not carried out.

Morell's notes for 8 November indicate that it was on this day that Hitler decided to move to the large bunker. A short while later he transferred to the bunker in the garden of the Reich Chancellery, originally intended merely as an air-raid shelter. The ceiling was reinforced to a thickness of over 3.5 metres. The bunker system was independent and had its own water and power supply, and Hitler also had a large living room and sleeping area for himself. He refused to move anywhere else, such as the enlarged Luftwaffe site near Potsdam. The Wolf's Lair was evacuated on 20 November.[104] In spite of intense discussion by commander-in-chief von Rundstedt with Hitler's close aide Jodl about the aims of the planned offensive, Hitler signed the detailed order to attack on 10 November.

Much to Morell's delight, Hitler went for an hour-long walk every day in the garden of the Reich Chancellery. Morell was also happy with the midday meals and noted that Hitler often ate with a good appetite. On 28 November, for example, he wrote: 'Führer went for a brisk one-hour walk. Voice good and determined.' In view of the many strenuous and intensive discussions, Hitler explicitly requested a continuation of the booster injections with 20 per cent glucose solution every two days. As he had also mentioned in November that Homoseran helped his tremor, Morell administered several injections in December, albeit without success.

On 3 December, the first Sunday in Advent, Hitler visited the Goebbels family for the first time in four years. Goebbels' secretary Naumann was also present at the tea session and he made an enthusiastic note of Hitler's physical, mental and emotional state. This impression coincides with Morell's own.[105] On 8 December, however, Morell noted 'bile colic!', which he was once again able to treat successfully with Eupaverin and Eukodal. Hitler did not allow himself to be influenced by his health problems. On 10 December a final examination was carried out by ENT specialist Carl von Eicken. Morell noted that these were 'the most dramatic days in his life', adding 'we *must* achieve a great victory'.[106]

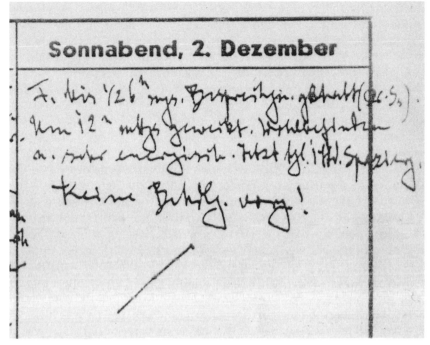

**Sonnabend, 2. Dezember**

56   Entry in Morell's diary for 2 December 1944. The Führer had had meetings at 6 a.m. He woke at noon and looked fit and very energetic. One-hour walk, no treatment.

At 5 p.m. on 10 December Hitler left Grunewald station, arriving at 2.42 a.m. at an unspecified station on the Werra, from where he drove to his new Eagle's Nest headquarters, built in 1939, in the Taunus, arriving at 6.30 a.m. on 11 December. Hitler's western headquarters were at the end of an isolated valley, two kilometres north-west of Ziegenberg near Bad Nauheim.[107] In the afternoon of this first day in the new headquarters he had a three-hour meeting with around fifty generals, the last one before the great offensive, which began at 5.30 a.m. on 16 December. According to the personal physician's notes, the Battle of the Bulge, code-named Watch on the Rhine, clearly made Hitler nervous in the extreme and the tremor in his left hand had visibly increased.

Hitler continued the walks at his new headquarters, making daily trips to the forest and meadowed valleys of the Taunus. His health was good. He still received his daily booster injection but had

175

no gastrointestinal cramps or other complaints, slept satisfactorily without medication and had a good appetite. The promising start to the Ardennes offensive clearly played a role, particularly the grey and rainy weather, which obstructed the enemy air force. The offensive was initially kept secret and it was not until 18 December that the Wehrmacht high command announced that an offensive had started on the Siegfried Line on 16 December.[108]

Hitler, who was in fine form, called Goebbels at 1 a.m. on 19 December. The success of the Ardennes campaign had put him in a good mood and his health also left nothing to be desired. He informed Goebbels euphorically that the German Luftwaffe had confronted the enemy with tremendous courage. But, even as Hitler was speaking with Goebbels, the Ardennes offensive was coming unstuck and on 24 December it came to a complete standstill. It was therefore already clear in December that the offensive would fail, but it wasn't abandoned until the massive American counterattacks in January 1945.

In the sixth year of the war there had thus been no significant change in Hitler's health. The assassination attempt had failed, even if it had left its mark. The injuries were insignificant and the diseases in 1944 were merely a continuation of earlier years. The gastrointestinal cramps had increased markedly due to Hitler's emotional state, which was clearly linked to the military successes – or lack thereof in 1944. Hitler ultimately set his faith in the Ardennes offensive. He had no problems with his health as long as the offensive was running well, as it did in the beginning.

On 2 January 1945 Hitler asked his personal physician to take a closer look at the tremor in his hand. Morell considered sedatives as a possible solution, but was reluctant to use them as he feared they would interfere with Hitler's mental processes. In January 1945 he therefore did nothing and did not even consider it necessary to act. Hitler appeared strong and energetic and was even continuing his nightly tea and biscuit sessions, which gave him an opportunity for his endless monologues. The session on 12 January 1945 did not finish until 5 a.m. Asked by Morell how he felt, Hitler knocked on wood three times and said 'very good!'[109]

## In the Bunker: How Irrational were Hitler's Decisions in 1945?

On 16 January 1945 the Führer headquarters moved one last time, back to the Reich Chancellery. Keitel and Jodl occupied their quarters in the 'alternative Army High Command post' in Berlin-Dahlem. As the Reich Chancellery had been badly damaged by air raids, Hitler moved into the bunker underneath it, the Führer bunker, as it was called, which had been enlarged and deepened in 1943 and had connections to the Ministry of Foreign Affairs and the Ministry of Propaganda and to Hitler's apartment. Hitler must have known that defeat was inevitable. From now on he busied himself with constructing the nature of the 'downfall'. It was not a question of a collective yearning for death by the German people, somehow embodied in Hitler's person, however, but rather the honour of the Prussian military, a concept that is difficult to understand today.

Hitler, who had studied the writings of Carl von Clausewitz, quoted frequently from his 1812 *Bekenntnisschrift* against Napoleon's foreign rule. Clausewitz said in this text that a nation should 'defend the dignity and freedom to exist with the last drop of blood' since the 'shame of cowardly submission' can never be 'erased'. 'Downfall' after a 'bloody and honourable fight', by contrast, ensured the 'rebirth of a nation'.[110] Like Clausewitz, Hitler saw his task as ensuring that this bloody and costly struggle would be 'honourable'.[111] In his view this meant having no regard for the soldiers, who were being sent to the slaughter in increasingly hopeless rearguard actions, nor for the civilian population or the opponent, who was an 'enemy' to be destroyed.

For the German officers this concept of honour was clear. There could be no question of accepting such another affront to German honour, as had taken place after the capitulation in 1918, as Hitler remarked on 31 August 1944 to future chief of staff Hans Krebs.[112] Krebs's suicide in the bunker on 1 May 1945 is sufficient indication of the fact that he also subscribed to this view. In his biography of Hitler, Ian Kershaw described these statements as 'obsessive'.[113] But 'honourable defeat' and suicide as an alternative to living with the 'shame' is considered acceptable in many civilizations. The suicides in the wake of the global economic crises of 1929 and 2008, the Japanese kamikaze attacks during the Second World War and suicide bombings by the Islamic Jihad all testify to this.

At all events, Hitler's 'yearning for death' was shared at least by some of the Prussian and Nazi officer corps, and in 1944–5 Hitler therefore saw his task as one of managing this 'honourable' defeat. The stability of his health helped in this regard: in the days leading up to the final disaster his appetite was good, he had no gastrointestinal cramps and his blood pressure was relatively normal. On 16 January 1945 he appointed Ferdinand Schörner, the most uncompromising and devoted of his field marshals, as commander-in-chief of Army Group Centre. He once again rejected the suggested evacuation of the Courland Pocket and also ordered the deployment of the 6th SS Panzer Army to Hungary.[114] On 19 January Hitler issued what in retrospect was a fateful order that committed the commanders in chief of the armies and army groups and the commanding generals and division commanders even more strongly to him and to his decisions. Every major operation had now to be notified 'as early as possible' to enable him to 'intervene if necessary' and ensure that 'contrary orders would reach the front in good time'. Hitler also pre-empted the personal right to make every decision on redeployment and retreat and on the abandonment of a position or fortification.[115]

The evening briefing now became ever more protracted. In the night of 24 January it did not finish until 3 a.m., and the ensuing tea session went on for another two hours. Whereas Morell's notes indicate that Hitler was relatively healthy in January and February, the hopeless military situation in his opinion led to an increase in Hitler's shaking palsy. He still refused to see it as a symptom of Parkinson's disease but sought psychosomatic causes instead. Hitler's astonishing energy and tangible presence in the bunker must have confirmed this point of view.

Hitler repeatedly opposed the suggestions of his military advisers. Guderian, for example, informed foreign minister von Ribbentrop on 24 January 1945 of the hopelessness of the situation on the eastern front and asked him to persuade Hitler to seek a ceasefire. Hitler regarded the suggestion as treasonous and during the briefing of 28 March he had a dispute with Guderian, with those present looking on in silence as Hitler dismissed his chief of staff with the words: 'General Guderian, you need sick leave. I don't think your heart can stand the strain. Come back in six weeks.'[116]

Hitler's radio address on 30 January 1945 to mark the twelfth anniversary of his coming to power also gave no indication of physical or mental weakness. In this last speech to the people, he appealed once again to the 'immutable will' to continue the fight. He called on every German 'to fulfil his duty to the utmost and to make every sacrifice demanded of him' so that 'Europe' and not 'central Asia' would be the winners of this fight.[117]

The relentless bombing of German cities appears not to have gone unnoticed by Hitler, however. Petrol, coal and arms production was almost at a standstill. The rapid advance of the Soviet troops on the eastern front did the rest. In early February they had established themselves in East Prussia, Upper Silesia and Pomerania despite a

German counter-offensive on 4 February, which halted the advance at Frankfurt an der Oder, under 100 km east of Berlin. Hitler was extremely depressed at this time. He was noticeably calm and detached. To observers he appeared withdrawn, as on 9 February, for example, when the architect Hermann Giesler presented a model of Linz, his favourite city where he was to have retired. Eyewitnesses recall him as being a disillusioned dreamer and compare him with a fallen Icarus.[118]

Hitler was abrupt with his personal physician. Morell suggests in his notes that Hitler's depressive mood was caused by the military situation in the east and the attacks on Dresden. On 17 February he described the Führer as pensive and tired. He therefore decided on a course of Strophthantin to strengthen Hitler's heart. The treatment continued until well into April. Although Hitler's blood pressure was stable according to Morell's notes, he had asked for blood letting, which Morell carried out on 10 February. It was unsuccessful. Two days later 230 cc of blood were taken, reducing the blood pressure from 156 to 143 mmHg. Hitler was nevertheless steadily declining. Although he carried out carefully orchestrated visits to the front on 3 and 11 March 1945 as evidence of his optimism, his left arm and hand now shook uncontrollably and he could barely sign documents with his right hand. His spine was bent, his face mask-like. Naval captain Heinz Assmann, who saw Hitler during his last days, said: 'His handclasp was weak and soft, all his movements were those of an old man; only his eyes retained their flickering gleam and penetrating look.'[119]

The description by the former naval adjutant was not far off the mark. The dictator's physical decline was evident. Everyone was able to see his behaviour and actions, which in retrospect can only be interpreted as irrational and regressive. Hitler's depressive mood and emotional outbursts have been the subject of countless books and several successful films. The actors portray Hitler in line with public expectations as a raging and disappointed dreamer. Writers and film makers trained in classical tragedy, not least the journalist Joachim Fest, recognized the potential and created dense, powerful and tense scenarios. The comparison with Richard Wagner's musical dramas was inevitable – and they naturally played their evocative film operas as a 'twilight of the gods'.[120]

The many absurd – although historically authenticated – scenes would seem to confirm this interpretation. It is incredible to think that in this hopeless military situation, Hitler and his cohorts would turn to the great king of Prussia. Goebbels read Hitler passages from

Thomas Carlyle's biography of Frederick the Great in the hope that the Führer would imitate the king's stoical bearing and composure. In the Seven Years War, the death of Czarina Elizabeth of Russia brought about an outcome favourable to the Prussians. Hitler's 'czarina', President Franklin D. Roosevelt, died on 12 April 1945. Did this strengthen his belief in destiny? Why shouldn't the miracle experienced by Frederick the Great be repeated?[121]

There is no doubt that Hitler suffered bouts of depression after the Ardennes offensive. At the same time, he still managed to persuade many independent and rational people to yearn, like him, for this 'decline' and to hope for a Wagnerian twilight of the gods. It is unlikely that his memory was impaired in the last weeks and months, as has been claimed. Statements by members of Hitler's entourage, such as Otto Günsche or Traudl Junge, to whom he dictated his political testament two nights before his death, indicate the contrary. The descriptions of general staff officers, who were by Hitler until the end, also cast doubt on these impressions. For them, Hitler's occasional lapses were the result of the genuine strain he was under and a justified anger at those who had no 'backbone' or who simply wanted to give up.

To counter this defeatist attitude, Hitler issued an order on 19 March 1945, known as the Nero order, calling for the destruction of all military transport, communications, industry and supply facilities and assets within the Reich territory that could enable the enemy to continue the fighting.[122] This order, which would result in the destruction of the entire infrastructure, had the opposite effect to the one intended. Even Hitler's most loyal supporters like armaments minister Albert Speer regarded the instruction as a crime against the German people. Speer managed a few days later to persuade Hitler of the impracticality of the order and the implementing regulation, which was also signed by Hitler, took some of the sting out of the original by stating that industrial facilities were now only to be 'disabled' and, like supply utilities, were only to be destroyed if they were *directly* threatened by the enemy.[123]

Morell was summoned to Hitler at midnight on 22 March because he was suffering from conjunctivitis, which he (Morell) believed to be due to the dust from the surrounding debris in the Reich Chancellery courtyard. Otherwise Hitler's health on 31 March still left nothing to be desired. During a conversation with Hitler, Morell said that he wanted to write down his medical history. Hitler's reply was short and crisp: 'I've never been ill. There is nothing to write about.' In principle he was right, and Morell also seems to have seen it that way.

But he stood by his intention and reminded Hitler of the injury to his left shoulder in 1923, which had immobilized his left arm for a long time. As Hitler had exercised strenuously to regain full mobility, he maintained that there was still 'nothing to write about'.

The fronts were approaching inexorably and were threatening the government district. On 2 April, Easter Monday, Morell noted: 'Military situation very grim.' Morell's notes in the last days of the Third Reich sound unworldly. He appears to have been unmoved by the impending downfall that was taking place before his very eyes. It must be assumed that he just did not want to face up to the reality of the collapse. He remained doggedly by his usual subjects, paying attention to the last to Hitler's blood pressure, bowel movements and stomach cramps as if there was nothing wrong with the world. He reminded Hitler repeatedly about the X-ray of the gastrointestinal tract, the long-overdue ECG and the need for Professor Löhlein to look at his eyes. Löhlein appeared on 7 April, found Hitler to have slight conjunctivitis and otherwise confirmed his earlier findings. He advised Hitler to wear goggles when walking in the garden.[124]

Goebbels, who was in despair about the situation on the front, wrote on 9 April: 'One might ask . . . where this is all leading.' For security reasons, the major military briefing now took place directly in the Führer bunker. On 9 April the night briefing did not end until 6 a.m. and this rhythm became customary. Hitler invited those present to drink tea with him afterwards, which Morell noted in his diary with an exclamation mark. He added quite casually: 'Let's hope there is no early air raid warning so there is enough time for sleep.'

Morell continued to be in poor health, at all events worse than his patient. On 10 April he wrote: 'I myself have been very short of breath and gasping for air, particularly when climbing stairs.' It was not until 15 April, however, that Morell mentioned Hitler's tremor, which he described for the first time as a variety of shaking palsy and which he was now treating with daily subcutaneous injections of Harmin and Homburg 680. Morell's entries in the last few days are increasingly scant. On 18 April he noted that a major Russian assault had begun three days previously near Küstrin (Kostrzyn) and Frankfurt an der Oder. He does not comment on it but merely notes the state of Hitler's health. Hitler had been taking Tempidorm to help him sleep and appeared tired during the day. On his birthday, the injections of Strophanthin and Harmin were administered by Dr Stumpfegger 'because I was too shaky'. Morell made no mention of the birthday celebration on 20 April, to which all of the leading Nazis were invited for the last time, and on 21 April he was dismissed.[125]

The day after Morell's dismissal, Hitler was told during a briefing in the Führer bunker that in this disastrous situation no external help could be expected and it was illusory to expect Berlin to be relieved. Hitler reacted with a tantrum. He also talked of suicide, screaming: 'The war is lost! But if you gentlemen think that I am going to leave Berlin you are making a very big mistake! I'd rather blow my brains out!'[126] It took the intervention of Martin Bormann and Wilhelm Burgdorf, the adjutant in chief of the Army High Command, and Hans Krebs, the last chief of staff, to gradually calm him down. He now ordered his confidential files to be burned. At Hitler's behest, Magda Goebbels and her six children left the air raid shelter at her apartment on Herman-Göring-Strasse (now Friedrich-Ebert-Strasse) and moved into the Führer bunker, while Goebbels himself attempted to build Hitler up again. On 23 April Hitler summoned General Helmuth Weidling and appointed him commander of Berlin. He was the third commander in four weeks and realized, of course, that his position was hopeless. After the war he told the Russians during an interrogation that he had seen Hitler a year previously and was horrified at his physical decline. He sat in his chair completely absorbed in himself. His hands shook and his speech was faltering. In short, Weidling felt that the man sitting opposite him was at the end.[127]

Hitler went up one last time to the Reich Chancellery on 23 April and looked down from the terrace at the ruins of his office. He then returned to the bunker and was not to leave it again alive. The Russians disconnected the last underground telephone cable in the night of 26 April, cutting off the bunker from the outside world.

## Testament and Death

The following events have been described frequently in memoirs published by the survivors and the extensive reports written by the two competing Soviet secret services, SMERSH and the NKVD, for their military superiors and for the Soviet dictator Josef Stalin.[128] The journalist Joachim Fest used these eyewitness accounts to create a fascinating report, which formed the basis for the Oscar-nominated film *Downfall*.[129]

In medical terms there are only two questions of interest: the nature of Hitler's suicide on 30 April 1945 and his mental state at the time of his death. The numerous rumours surrounding Hitler's suicide (or even his successful escape to South America) were dispelled in 1949 by officers of the NKVD, whose report supplies a reliable account of

Hitler's death. In their three-year inquiry, the investigators looked carefully at the scenarios of escape, suicide by shooting or with cyanide, and carried out a meticulous reconstruction of his last days.

It describes the state in which Heinz Linge, Hitler's personal valet, found the body of the dictator and his wife in Hitler's private quarters in the bunker. '. . .on the left-hand side of the sofa sat Hitler. He was dead. Next to him was a dead Eva Braun. In Hitler's right temple gaped a bullet wound the size of a Pfennig and two streams of blood ran down his cheek. On the carpet next to the sofa a puddle of blood the size of a plate had formed. The wall and the sofa was besplattered with blood.' Next to Hitler's right foot was a Walther 7.65 mm pistol. By his left foot was the pistol Hitler had once given to Eva Braun, a 6.35 mm calibre Walther. Eva Braun had not shot herself, however. Her lips were pressed tightly closed: she had taken cyanide.[130]

The analyses by the Soviet army 291st Medical Epidemic Front Laboratory in June 1945 failed to confirm that either Hitler or Eva Braun had poisoned themselves (tissue sample no. 12 and 13). SMERSH refused to allow a new post-mortem of the two bodies. The officers of the rival NKVD therefore revisited the sites where Hitler had died and been burned. Pyotr S. Semenovski, a competent forensic pathologist, examined the splattered blood and reconstructed the path of the bullet. His finding was confirmed by two skull fragments. He found part of the right and left parietal bone at the site where SMERSH operatives had found Hitler's corpse a year earlier. The left parietal bone had a defect identified by Semenovski as typical of an exit wound. He also determined that the bullet had travelled upwards and backwards from right to left.[131] It can therefore be confirmed that Hitler shot himself.

It is not clear whether he took cyanide as well. As the NKGB insisted to Stalin on this version, however, and continuously presented further evidence in support, this version of the suicide cannot be excluded.[132] The cyanide capsules issued from 1944 to a large number of officers, officials and technical staff like radio operators and secretaries, were approximately three centimetres long and one centimetre in diameter. They were made of glass and coated in paraffin. They came in a brass casing. Each batch contained between 0.7 and one gram of potassium cyanide. The lethal dose is 2.857 mg per kilogram body weight. The smaller dose would therefore have been sufficient to kill a person weighing 245 kg.[133]

Hitler's greatest opponent in the NSDAP, the pharmacist and later Reich Organization Leader Georg Strasser, predicted back in 1933 that Hitler would commit suicide. His brother Otto claims to have added: 'Only if there's a sufficient audience to applaud him.'[134] The American psychiatrist Walter C. Langer also opined in his psychological analysis for the US intelligence service OSS in 1943 that Hitler would commit suicide if Germany were defeated.[135]

It is difficult to determine what exactly prompted Hitler to commit suicide. It is known that he was depressive, and even when he was imprisoned in Landsberg in 1924 one of his co-inmates believed that he would take his own life. After his failure to form a cabinet in December 1932, his entourage also feared the worst – from their point of view.[136] He described to the officers and staff in the bunker how he imagined Stalin displaying him in a cage on Red Square during the victory parade. It was certainly not beyond the bounds of possibility.[137]

Information on Hitler's mood in the hours before he committed suicide is provided by his will. He dictated his last political testament impromptu, firmly and in full possession of his senses 'as always'.[138] He dictated to his secretary Traudl Junge, who took notes in shorthand and then typed them up, that he had been actuated solely by 'love and loyalty' to his people. He entered the room several times and urged his secretary to hurry up so that he could sign the testament. He had had to make the most difficult decisions, he said, and had spent his 'time, working strength and health'. It was 'untrue' that he had wanted the war in 1939. It was desired and instigated exclusively by those international statesmen who were either of Jewish descent or worked for Jewish interests. He continued by stressing once again that he had wanted peace, pointing out that he had called to account and punished the Jews, who were the 'real criminals'.

The war itself, the 'six-year struggle', had been 'the most glorious and valiant demonstration of a nation's life purpose'. He admitted that he had failed, stating that forces were 'too small' and at the same time describing those who were weakening the resistance of the German people as 'deluded' and 'lacking in initiative'. He had chosen death 'of his own free will' and would die 'with a happy heart'. He appealed to the people 'on no account to give up the struggle' but rather to 'continue it against the enemies of the Fatherland, no matter where'. Then 'the seed of a radiant renaissance of the National Socialist movement and thus of the realization of a true community of nations' would spring up. Finally, he described his flight from responsibility as a duty. As the 'founder and creator' of the Nazi movement he 'preferred death to cowardly abdication or even capitulation'. The

German leaders should thus 'march ahead as shining examples', ful-filling their duties 'unto death'.

In the second part of the testament he expelled Göring and Himmler from the party and appointed Admiral Dönitz as Reich President and Supreme Commander of the Armed Forces. He also appointed the members of the cabinet. Goebbels was to be Reich Chancellor, the loyal field marshal Ferdinand Schörner commander-in-chief of the army, and Martin Bormann Party Minister.[139] At the end of the testament was a sentence that once again formulated the core of his ideology: 'Above all I charge the leaders of the nation and those under them to scrupulous observance of the laws of race and to merciless opposition to the universal poisoner of all peoples, international Jewry.'

# — 7 —

# CONCLUDING DIAGNOSIS

The term 'disease' was defined by the German Federal Social Court in 1972 for the purpose of insurance claims as an 'irregular physical or mental condition requiring medical treatment'.[1] When it was constituted in 1948, the World Health Organization defined health as 'a state of complete physical, mental and social wellbeing and not merely the absence of disease or infirmity'.[2]

Hitler's health until his suicide on 30 April 1945 has four main medical focuses:

1  Hitler suffered from gastrointestinal cramps, an irritable bowel syndrome that seemed to depend on his mental constitution.
2. The tremor in his left arm and leg was not what Morell described as a 'variety of shaking palsy' but a symptom of Parkinson's disease that first manifested itself in 1941.
3. Without doubt he also suffered from high blood pressure and a deteriorating coronary sclerosis.
4. There is no scientific medical proof that Hitler suffered from any mental illness.

Under the Federal Social Court definition, Hitler was without a doubt 'ill' since he certainly required frequent medical treatment, particularly in the last three years of his life. He was also not 'healthy' according to the WHO definition because it is doubtful whether he was in 'a state of complete physical, mental and social wellbeing' over long periods.

Historians, philosophers, journalists and doctors have considered the question of Hitler's health not because they are interested in his wellbeing but rather, like Hitler's contemporaries, the victims and the perpetrators, because they seek explanations as to how 'it' could have happened. The millions of deaths, the outbreak of the Second World War and the boundless suffering demanded a justification that was to be sought not in vague diseases but also in Hitler's personality.

This is one reason why Hitler's former employees invented the myth that the dictator had originally 'meant well' but had become 'megalomaniac' or 'mentally ill'. In doing so they were completely in line with the spirit of the times. In 1955, no less than 48 per cent of the German population believed that had it not been for the war Hitler would have been one of Germany's greatest statesmen.[3] Moreover, the idea that their leader was mentally and emotionally impaired relieved them of responsibility. Whether destroyed by drugs or illness, Hitler would not then have been answerable for his actions, something that the German people could not have known at the time.

In reality, this was not the case. Hitler was well aware of what he was doing. He was not handicapped by illness or drugs. On the contrary, he was obsessed until the last by his fanatical belief in his mission. His gradual physical and mental decline was the result of an age-related arteriosclerosis and his Parkinson's disease. There is no evidence that these two conditions affected his decisions.

Hitler's ill health from the beginning of the Russian campaign until the assassination attempt on 20 July 1944 was characterized increasingly by gastrointestinal spasms and colic together with alternating diarrhoea and constipation. He also suffered from circulation problems and from summer 1941 at the latest from a tremor in his left arm and leg. These symptoms were not observed at all times, however, but occurred following long periods without problems. Hitler's chronic insomnia was also in part of his own making because for years he had worked through the night.

Hitler's personal physician Theodor Morell treated practically all of the health conditions himself, calling on specialists only for stool and ECG examinations. If Hitler had had serious diseases, Morell would almost certainly have consulted other specialists. He did so in any case, calling on Professor Walter Löhlein from the Charité hospital for eye examinations, and his colleague Carl von Eicken for treatment of ear, nose and throat diseases and the removal of Hitler's vocal nodes. He did not feel the need to consult a neurologist for Hitler's tremor, however, because he did not consider Parkinson's disease, although he gave his patient spasmolytics for 'shaking palsy'.

In spite of the basic therapy, Morell regarded his patient as being chronically exhausted. He believed that Hitler's permanent physical and mental strain had disrupted the functioning of his organs with

187

manifest vegetative stigmata. This explained Hitler's irritability, headaches, sleep disorders, dizziness and constipation alternating with diarrhoea.

On 1 December 1944, Morell noted in his diary that severe spasms always occurred after 'extreme agitation' in Hitler's life. Both he and Hitler believed that the gastrointestinal cramps were psychosomatic. He had suffered from them during the high treason trial in 1924 and again in 1929 when the NSDAP publishing company, which also printed the *Völkischer Beobachter*, was in financial difficulty, and in 1935–6 when he was in conflict with the military leadership. Morell was also of the opinion that Hitler had symptoms of dysbacteria. This extreme discomfort recurred in 1943 before the meeting with Mussolini because Hitler had a premonition of betrayal by the Italian army. The final example of the psychosomatic origins of Hitler's cramps mentioned by Hitler in conversation with Morell was the assassination attempt of 20 July 1944. On 6 December he told Morell that his disease was the result of 'eleven years of aggravation with the 20 July generals'. Two days later Hitler, whose cramps had been relieved by Morell through Eukodal and Eupaverin injections, opined that he was facing the greatest burdens in his life since the forthcoming events (the Ardennes offensive) 'and the constant terror attacks on German cities' were causing the greatest nervous tension. Hitler believed that his colon was healthy as he had never had blood in his stool or vomited blood.

It would therefore appear that Hitler's gastrointestinal complaints were mainly psychosomatic. And yet he did not suffer any marked ill health after the defeat in Stalingrad as might have been expected under these circumstances, and paradoxically Hitler's health seemed to improve during the crisis situation in 1944 and January 1945.

Although his gradual physical decline was evident, his tremor actually disappeared, albeit temporarily, after the assassination attempt of 20 July 1944. It is known that a tremor can stop at times of extreme concentration. Hitler survived the last months of the fall of the Third Reich without any appreciable health problems.

It is unclear and questionable whether Hitler's somatic diseases affected his mind and behaviour. It is more likely that the bouts of ill health were triggered by the many objective or subjective factors affecting his mental state, and his diseases are thus likely to have been of psychosomatic rather than somatopsychic origin. Moreover, Hitler's momentous decisions were taken at a time when there was no question of him being sick. The decision to wage war and rectify the consequences of 1918 was taken in 1937 at the latest. He wanted war and in doing so channelled the feelings of the generation that had experienced the First World War. This course of action was not that of an irrational man. Hitler's desire for war – at this time and in this form – and the course of the war can both be explained by his personality. The reasons for the German defeat can also be sought there. But none of the decisions taken by him was influenced by illness. The stimulants that are often blamed for Hitler's actions were not part of his treatment, if at all, until 1943.

Millions of Germans had a similar family situation: a dominating, possibly violent father, and an overly attentive and very loving mother were quite normal in families at the turn of the century. All other claimed external emotional disorders belong to the realms of mythology and deliberate lies. There is no evidence for many of the assumptions, such as Hitler's supposed repressed homosexuality. Nor is there any indication that a particular Jew or the frequently conjured up idea of an abstract 'Jew' ever caused Hitler fateful difficulties. And finally, there is no question of unconscious 'control' of his hatred or identification with any kind of 'super-ego'.

Hitler seethed with hatred, but he was always capable of synchronizing his desire to exterminate the Jews with public opinion. The various tactical manoeuvres, such as the Hitler–Stalin pact with the 'Jewish Bolshevist' Soviet Union, testify to his great flexibility. He also had a reliable intuition as to the 'right moment' for various decisions. However cynical it might sound, all of the crimes that he ordered and made possible, the genocide of the Jews, the killing of Sinti and Roma, the mass murder of mental patients, took place within a social framework that to some extent condoned them.

Hitler never suffered from any kind of obsessive mania. The real causes for these crimes are to be found in German society, its intellectual history and the social context. There is no doubt that Hitler exerted a considerable influence on this society and may be regarded as the driving force behind the German people in the 1930s and 1940s. He was well aware of what he was doing at all times during his political career and was not influenced by drugs or by some kind of hypnotic trance, the explanation sought by some after 1945. The intelligence service provided him with information about the public mood and he knew what 'the nation' thought at any given time and what objectives would motivate his supporters. He also knew what measures should be kept secret.

The historian Saul Friedländer is therefore right in his assessment that Hitler's decisions were governed by a combination of 'ideological fanaticism and pragmatic calculation'. Friedländer states: 'The ideological obsession was unwavering, but tactical considerations were no less compelling. Sometimes, however, the third element, uncontrolled fury, would burst into the open – triggered by some obstacle, some threat, some defeat – sweeping away all practical considerations. Then, fed by the torrent of ideological fanaticism, the murderous fury would explode in an unlimited urge for destruction and death.'[4]

There is no doubt that Hitler can be designated as 'sick' for having planned and carried out a genocide and unleashed a world war. But if that is the case, the society that produced and allowed itself to be led by him was just as 'sick'. Many Germans were untroubled by Hitler's anti-Semitism and they harboured a deeply felt wish for retribution for the defeat in the First World War. Those who were not excluded by the Nazi regime profited from the dictatorship, the appropriation of Jewish property and the subjugation of other nations. Hitler's personal values were accepted by society; his visions excited people because they were receptive to them. And many Germans shared his conviction that it was meaningful and honourable to sacrifice one's life for the nation. But, the willingness to die by millions of soldiers did not give a higher meaning to the German defeat but rather permitted crimes of hitherto unseen proportions to be committed.

The reconstruction of Hitler's medical biography leaves no room for any other conclusion: war was not waged and Jews exterminated because Hitler was ill, but because most Germans shared his convictions, made him their Führer and followed him.

A forensic expert would not base his assessment of Hitler's personality on the German legal definition (need for medical treatment) or the utopian vision of the World Health Organization, but on the provisions of German and international criminal law. Hitler's actions were not influenced by a mental disease or psychotropic substances like alcohol and drugs, but stemmed from his 'primary personality'. His actions until the last days of the war are not consistent with any kind of psychological disorder. It cannot be denied that Hitler often appeared fatigued in 1945, but through self-discipline and a strong will he managed to motivate himself and others.

The answer to the question 'was Hitler ill' is therefore as follows: the leader of the NSDAP, chancellor of the German Reich and commander-in-chief of the German Wehrmacht was healthy and accountable.

# NOTES

## 1 MADNESS, DESIGN AND REALITY: WHY A MEDICAL BIOGRAPHY OF HITLER?

1  In 1946, the camp in which many high-ranking Nazis were interrogated was renamed Camp King, after a colonel who had been killed in 1944. Information from Manfred Kopp, head of the project 'Erinnerungsorte der Zeitgeschichte – Das Gelände Camp King 1933–1993', memo by Brandt in Oberursel after contact with Morell, 19 September 1945 (BA kl. Erw.), 411–13.

2  See Ernst Klee, 'Euthanasie' im NS-Staat: Die 'Vernichtung lebensunwerten Lebens' (Frankfurt a. M., 1983) for general discussion; Dietmar Schulze, 'Euthanasie' in Bernburg (Essen, 1999) for local aspects.

3  Hitler had awarded both of them the title of professor: Morell as an honorary title, Brandt following his promotion to extraordinary professor at the University of Berlin.

4  This was the view of Traudl Junge in a personal statement as late as 2001. See also Karl Dönitz, Memoirs: Ten Years and Twenty Days (New York, 1997). On the basis of trend indicators, Ian Kershaw plotted a graph of Hitler's popularity, which has been confirmed by other sources. See Ian Kershaw, The 'Hitler Myth': Image and Reality in the Third Reich (Oxford, 1987).

5  Norbert Frei, Der Führerstaat: Nationalsozialistische Herrschaft (Munich, 2007), p. 211.

6  See Kershaw, The 'Hitler Myth'. A discussion of the ethical motivation for resistance is provided by Gerd R. Ueberschär, Für ein anderes Deutschland: Der deutsche Widerstand gegen den NS-Staat (Frankfurt a. M., 2006).

7  See Joachim Fest, Hitler (London, 1974) p. 9. Also Claus Jacobi, editor-in-chief, BILD (3 January 2009 – national edition), 2. For the possibilities and limitations of impartial fictional historiography see Alexander Demandt, Ungeschehene Geschichte: Ein Traktat über die Frage 'Was wäre gewesen, wenn . . .' (Göttingen, 2001). See also Hans Vaihinger, The Philosophy of 'As If' (New York, 1968).

8  Hannes Heer also discusses Fest's theses in Hitler war's: Die Befreiung der Deutschen von ihrer Vergangenheit (Berlin, 2008).

9 There is also the view claiming that practically all of the leading politicians in the Nazi regime were addicts. See Werner Pieper (ed.), *Nazis on Speed: Drogen im Dritten Reich* (Löhrbach, 2002).
10 Peter Hoffmann, *The History of German Resistance 1933–1945* (London, 1977).
11 Walter C. Langer, *The Mind of Adolf Hitler: The Secret Wartime Report* (London, 1973), pp. 211–12.
12 Ian Kershaw, *Hitler* (Harlow, 1991), 2 vols.
13 Ian Kershaw, 'Warum Hitler möglich war', in *Berner Zeitung* (22 April 2005).
14 Ian Kershaw, *Fateful Choices: Ten Decisions That Changed The World 1940–1941* (London, 2007), p. 457.
15 Refutations (i.e. the necessary demonstration of falsifiability as defined by Karl Popper) have often taken the form of personal attacks rather than scientific discussion, which has sometimes made clarification more difficult rather than easier.
16 Alan Bullock, *Hitler: A Study in Tyranny* (London, 1952).
17 Sebastian Haffner, *The Meaning of Hitler* (Harvard, 1983).
18 Brigitte Hamann, *Hitler's Vienna: A Dictator's Apprenticeship* (Oxford, 2000). Hamann refutes countless myths and falsehoods about Hitler's youth and time in Vienna and also reconstructs the political climate in the city.
19 Gerhard L. Weinberg (ed.), *Hitler's Second Book* (Ann Arbor, 2003).
20 Anna Maria Sigmund, *Die Frauen der Nazis I–III* (Munich, 2005) and *Diktator, Dämon, Demagoge: Fragen und Antworten zu Adolf Hitler* (Munich, 2006).
21 An interesting pioneering study has been made by Bernd Wegner, 'Deutschland am Abgrund', in Karl-Heinz Frieser (ed.), *Das Deutsche Reich und der Zweite Weltkrieg*, vol. 8, *Die Ostfront 1943–44: Der Krieg im Osten und an den Nebenfronten* (Munich, 2007), pp. 1165–1209.
22 For the historical discussion within Germany, which ultimately comes back again and again to the crimes committed by the Nazis, see Martin Sabrow, Ralph Jessen, Klaus Grosse Kracht, *Zeitgeschichte als Streitgeschichte: Grosse Kontroversen nach 1945* (Munich, 2003). The pros and cons of research about Hitler are discussed clearly by John Lukacs, *The Hitler of History: Hitler's Biographers on Trial* (London, 2000).
23 Apart from the access to Eastern European archives, which was only possible after 1991, the scandalous failure of German historians should also be mentioned. Raul Hilberg's standard work on the destruction of European Jewry was also unprinted for years and did not appear in German until 1990. Götz Lays sums up this polemic in 'Logik des Grauens', *Die Zeit* (1 June 2006).
24 Saul Friedländer, *Nazi Germany and the Jews: The Years of Extermination 1939–1945* (New York, 2007); Christopher Browning, *The Origins of the Final Solution: The Evolution of Nazi Jewish Policy, September 1939 – March 1942* (Jerusalem, 2004); Peter Longerich, *Holocaust: The Nazi Persecution and Murder of the Jews* (Oxford, 2010); Peter Longerich, *Heinrich Himmler* (Oxford, 2012).
25 Ernst Günther Schenck, *Patient Hitler: eine medizinische Biographie* (Augsburg, 2000). It seems certain that Schenck carried out nutrition

experiments on inmates in Dachau concentration camp, but it is not clear whether anybody died as a result. See Heer, *Hitler war's*, p. 16.

26 Fritz Redlich, *Hitler: Diagnosis of a Destructive Patient* (Oxford, 1999).

27 *Süddeutsche Zeitung*, 24 November 1998; Kershaw on the back cover of Redlich, *Diagnosis*.

28 This applies in particular to the utterances of Hans Frank, Hitler's lawyer, and Hermann Rauschning, a local politician from Danzig [Gdansk], and the notorious liar Henriette von Schirach. Frank's comments were made when he was facing the gallows and, having converted to Catholicism, wanted to make a confession. Rauschning wrote as a renegade with a view to warning foreign readers, particularly politicians, about Hitler. For the myths surrounding the ear, nose and throat doctor Erwin Giesing, see Chapter 2.

29 Redlich, *Diagnosis*, p. 336.

30 Julius Schaub, Hitler's oldest servant, burnt the contents of three safes in the Reich Chancellery and Hitler's personal papers in two filing cabinets in the Berghof. These documents have disappeared for ever. See Olaf Rose (ed.), *Julius Schaub* in *Hitlers Schatten: Erinnerungen und Aufzeichnungen des Chefadjutanten 1925–1945* (Stegen/Ammersee, 2005), p. 334.

31 Werner Jochmann (ed.), *Adolf Hitler: Monologe im Führerhauptquartier 1941–1944, aufgezeichnet von Heinrich Heim* (Munich, 2000); Henry Picker, *Tischgespräche im Führerhauptquartier* (Frankfurt a. M., 1993).

32 The reference here is to volume 1 of the two-volume work, the original title of which was 'Four and a Half Years of Struggle Against Lies, Stupidity and Cowardice'. See Othmar Plöckinger, *Geschichte eines Buches: Adolf Hitler 'Mein Kampf' 1922–1945* (Munich, 2006).

33 Morell's diary entry for 31 March 1945.

34 Fest, *Hitler*, p. 807 (note 63).

35 An example is the documentary, shown several times on n-tv, about Walter C. Langer's psychiatric assessment.

36 See Claudia Schmölders, *Hitler's Face: The Biography of an Image* (Philadelphia, 2006), which diverges markedly from conventional propaganda analysis.


2 THE DISEASED HITLER – A HISTORIOGRAPHICAL PROJECT

1 Ian Kershaw, 'Warum Hitler möglich war', in *Berner Zeitung* (23 April 2003).

2 Henrik Eberle, *Letters to Hitler* (Cambridge, 2012), p.52.

3 See the section on the three classes of the national body in Adolf Hitler, *Mein Kampf* (London, 1969). On the metaphor see Albrecht Koschorke et al., *Der fiktive Staat: Konstruktionen des jüdischen Körpers in der Geschichte Europas* (Frankfurt a. M., 2007).

4 Summary by psychiatrist Walter C. Langer of statements by former NSDAP functionaries living in the USA (Langer, *The Mind of Adolf Hitler*, pp. 171–2).

5 Otto Strasser, *Hitler and I* (Boston, 1940).

6 Alice Miller, *For Your Own Good: Hidden Cruelty in Child-Rearing and the Roots of Violence* (New York, 1983).

7 *Der Spiegel*, 10 (1964), 48–60.

8 Paul Matussek, Peter Matussek, Jan Marbach, *Hitler: Karriere eines Wahns* (Munich, 2000).

9 Ibid. pp. 205–8.

10 Langer on Hitler's masochism: 'From all this we see the constant struggle against complete degradation whenever any affectionate components enter into the picture. It now becomes clear that the only way in which Hitler can control these copraphagic tendencies or their milder manifestations is to isolate himself from any intimate relationships in which warm feelings of affection or love might assert themselves. As soon as such feelings are aroused, he feels compelled to degrade himself in the eyes of the loved object and eat their dirt figuratively, if not literally. These tendencies disgust him just as much as they disgust us.' (Langer, *The Mind of Adolf Hitler*, pp. 171–2). Masochistic and sadistic tendencies are interpreted today exclusively as a disorder of sexual preference without any other inferences about personality. See World Health Organization International Classification of Diseases (ICD-10), 2006, F65.5.

11 See Claudia Schmölders, 'Schamabwehr und Judenhass: eine psychohistorische Studie auf schmaler Ausgangsbasis', at www.literaturkritik.de, 9 (September 2000).

12 Manfred Koch-Hillebrecht, *Homo Hitler: Psychogramm des deutschen Diktators* (Munich, 1999).

13 Ibid. pp. 79f.

14 See pp. 350, 405 and 417. It is interesting that the author suggests that Winnetou and Old Shatterhand also had a homosexual relationship. 'Winnetou enchanted [Hitler's] homophile heart' (p. 371). Author J. K. Rowling was evidently cleverer than Karl May, responding to inferences that Harry Potter and Ron Weasley might have had a similar relationship by having them marry their girlfriends. The relationship alluded to by Karl May between Old Shatterhand and Winnetou's sister Nscho Tschi was sufficient in 1900 to allay such suspicions, but apparently no longer today. The film *Der Schuh des Manitu* by Michael 'Bully' Herbig in which the characters, who recall Winnetou and Old Shatterhand, are clearly homosexual was made in 2001, after Koch-Hillebrecht's book was published.

15 Matussek, *Karriere*, p. 60.

16 Langer, *The Mind of Adolf Hitler*, section 3.

17 See Josef Kopperschmidt (ed.), *Hitler der Redner* (Munich, 2003), a collection of essays on Hitler's rhetorical capabilities.

18 This talent was recognized before 1933 particularly by his opponents or those who had originally supported and then turned away from him. See the analyses by Kurt Lüdecke, Hellmuth von Mücke, Otto Strasser and Ernst Hanfstaengl.

19 Brigitte Hamann, *Hitlers Edeljude: Das Leben des Armenarztes Eduard Bloch* (Munich, 2008), pp. 45f.

20 George L. Mosse, *The Crisis of Ideology: Intellectual Origins of the Third Reich* (New York, 1988).

21 Saul Friedländer, *Nazi Germany and the Jews: The Years of Persecution, 1933–1939* (New York, 1997). Without limiting the phenomenon to Germany, the author persuasively attributes the central position of the Jews in this delusional universe to the Christian tradition rooted in the German mind. The suggestion by Ernst Nolte that Hitler's anti-Semitism was a

rational reaction to the Munich Soviet Republic is too one-sided. See Ralf Georg Reuth, *Hitlers Judenhass: Klischee und Wirklichkeit* (Munich, 2009).

22 Quoted by Ullrich Volker, 'Fünfzehntes Bild: Drückerberger', in Julius H. Schoeps and Joachim Schlör (eds), *Bilder der Judenfeindschaft* (Augsburg, 1999), pp. 212f.

23 Even nationalist-minded historians like Hans Herzfeld, who was later to be discriminated against as a 'half-Jew', subscribed to this 'stab-in-the-back' myth. See Hans Herzfeld, *Die deutsche Sozialdemokratie und die Auflösung der nationalen Einheitsfront im Weltkriege* (Leipzig, 1928).

24 His autobiographical evaluation of the German defeat in *Mein Kampf* is retrospective and influenced by the effect it had. Whether Hitler himself had such strong feelings about the defeat is another matter. He spoke quite deliberately in *Mein Kampf* of the 'most terrible certainty' in his life and suggested to the reader that as a front-line soldier he had cried for the first time since his mother's burial. Elsewhere, his analysis is quite impersonal, saying that the collapse was retribution for 'internal decay, cowardice, want of character'. This seems to confirm the 'evolution of the autobiographical memory' towards an 'increasing synchronization of the developing individual with his social surroundings' identified by social psychologist Harald Welzer in *Das kommunikative Gedächtnis: Eine Theorie der Erinnerung* (Munich, 2008), p. 119.

25 Daniel Jonah Goldhagen's analysis in *Hitler's Willing Executioners: Ordinary Germans and the Holocaust* (London, 1996) is refuted in detail among others by Richard J. Evans, *The Coming of the Third Reich* (New York, 2003). Mosse attributes the intellectual mood to its anti-Semitic content, see Mosse, *Crisis of Ideology*. This uncomfortable book for Germans was originally published in the USA in 1964. A German translation did not appear until 1979. For the failure of conservatism, see Heinz Hagenlücke, *Deutsche Vaterlandspartei: Die nationale Rechte am Ende des Kaiserreichs* (Dusseldorf, 1997).

26 For a detailed and rectifying discussion of the early history of the NSDAP, see Anton Joachimsthaler, *Hitlers Weg begann in München, 1913–1923* (Munich, 2000). For the mood in society and vivid but precise descriptions of individual personalities, see Hans-Günther Ricardi, *Hitler und seine Hintermänner: Neue Fakten zur Frühgeschichte der NSDAP* (Munich, 1991). For discussion of the Thule Society and its popular roots in general, see Nicholas Goodrick-Clarke, *The Occult Roots of Nazism: Secret Aryan Cults and Their Influence on Nazi Ideology* (New York, 1992). For a classification, see Stephan Breuer, *Ordnungen der Ungleichheit: Die deutsche Rechte im Widerstreit ihrer Ideen* (Darmstadt, 2001).

27 Claus-Ekkehard Bärsch, *Die politische Religion des Nationalsozialismus: Die religiösen Dimensionen der NS-Ideologie in den Schriften von Dietrich Eckart, Josef Goebbels, Alfred Rosenberg und Adolf Hitler* (Munich, 2002).

28 Houston Stewart Chamberlain, *The Foundations of the Nineteenth Century* (Munich, 1911), particularly on the impact of the Jews on Western history and Jewish materialism. For details of the Wagner-Chamberlain family, see Brigitte Hamann, *Winifred Wagner: A Life at the Heart of Hitler's Bayreuth* (Orlando, FL, 2005). On Hitler's Wagnerian self-dramatization and

Eckart's status in Bayreuth, see Joachim Köhler, *Wagner's Hitler: The Prophet and His Disciple* (Cambridge, UK, 1999). According to another version, it was the wife of the piano manufacturer Carl Bechstein who introduced Hitler to Bayreuth.

29  Dinter, who was convinced that Jesus was of Aryan descent, claimed in his novel *Die Sünde wider das Blut* that women having sexual intercourse with Jews just once were 'ruined' and could thereafter give birth only to 'Jewish bastards'. Over 200,000 copies of the book were printed. For discussion of Streicher, see Randall L. Bytwerk, *Julius Streicher: Nazi Editor of the Notorious Anti-Semitic Newspaper 'Der Stürmer'* (New York, 2001).

30  Eberle, *Letters to Hitler*, pp. 13–49.

31  Hamann, *Winifred Wagner*; Christian Hartmann (ed.), *Hitler, Reden, Schriften, Anordnungen* (Munich, 1997), vol. 4/III, pp. 74–110. Photographer Heinrich Hoffmann claims that there was a picture by the Jewish artist Wilhelm Löwith in Hitler's apartment. Hoffmann was a gifted narrator who often entertained Hitler with tall tales, and his testimony is therefore of questionable reliability. See Joe J. Heydecker (ed.), *Das Hitler-Bild: Die Erinnerungen des Fotografen Heinrich Hoffmann* (St Pölten, Salzburg, 2008).

32  Hans Mommsen, *Beamtentum im Dritten Reich* (Stuttgart, 1966).

33  This is something that commentaries on the laws, particularly after 1945, point out. See Norbert Jacobs, 'Der Streit um Dr Hans Globke in der öffentlichen Meinung der Bundesrepublik Deutschland', dissertation (Bonn, 1992).

34  John M. Steiner and Jobst Freiherr von Cornberg, 'Willkür in der Willkür: Befreiungen von den antisemitischen Nürnberger Gesetzen', in *Vierteljahrshefte für Zeitgeschichte* 46 (1998), 143–87.

35  See Goldhagen for discussion of 'eliminatory anti-Semitism'; for economic aspects, see Götz Aly, *Hitler's Beneficiaries: Plunder, Racial War, and the Nazi Welfare State* (New York, 2006).

36  Eugeni Xammer, *Das Schlangenei: Berichte aus dem Deutschland der Inflationsjahre 1922–1924* (Berlin, 2007), pp. 146ff.

37  Werner Maser, *Hitler's Letters and Notes* (London, 1974).

38  The most powerful version of this myth was created by the dramatist George Tabari. His play, *Mein Kampf*, was a gigantic success. It was translated into several languages and filmed in 2008 with Götz George in the role of Hitler's paternal friend Schlomo Herzl.

39  Hamann, *Hitler's Vienna*, p. 164.

40  See Hitler, *Mein Kampf*, vol. I, ch. 2.

41  Richard Wagner, *Judaism in Music* (London, 1984).

42  Longerich, *Holocaust*, pp. 254–5.

43  Friedländer, *Years of Persecution*, p. 307.

44  Aly, *Hitler's Beneficiaries*.

45  Ben Barkow, Raphael Gross, Michael Lenaz (eds), *Novemberpogrom 1938: Die Augenzeugenberichte der Wiener Library* (Frankfurt a. M., 2008).

46  Browning, *Origins*, p. 31.

47  Ibid. p. 89.

48  Minute by Theodor Dannecker on 21 January 1941, see Browning, *Origins*, p. 103.

49  Walther Hubatsch (ed.), *Hitler's War Directives (1939–1945): Dokumente*

*der Oberkommandos der Wehrmacht* (Utting, undated – reprint, 1983), p. 89.
50 Ibid. p. 84.
51 Browning, *Origins*, pp. 426–8.
52 Longerich, *Himmler*, p. 538.
53 Diary entries for August to December 1941 in Peter Witte (ed.), *Der Dienstkalender Heinrich Himmlers 1941/42* (Hamburg, 1999).
54 Browning, *Origins*, p. 454.
55 Henrik Eberle, Matthias Uhl, *The Hitler Book: The Secret Dossier Prepared for Stalin from the Interrogations of Hitler's Personal Aides* (London, 2005), pp. 104–5.
56 For discussion of the local group dynamics and the ever-changing frame of reference in which the perpetrators acted, see Harald Welzer, *Täter: Wie aus ganz normalen Menschen Massenmörder werden* (Frankfurt a. M., 2005).
57 Jochmann, *Monologe*, p. 99.
58 Hitler, *Mein Kampf*, pp. 272–9
59 Critics generally described the film as banal or a failure. See Marianne Kestler, '*Mein Führer* von Dani Levy', at www.shoa.de/rezensionen/185-filmrezensionen/620.html.
60 Michael Töteberg (ed.), *Dani Levy Mein Führer: Die wirklich wahrste Wahrheit über Adolf Hitler* (Hamburg, 2007), p. 143.
61 Ibid. p. 176.
62 Miller, *Child Rearing*, pp. 3–8.
63 Miller's book, which evaluated three extreme cases – Hitler, Christiane F. (*Wir Kinder vom Bahnhof Zoo*) and child killer Jürgen Bartsch – and refers specifically to studies by Katharina Rutschky (*Schwarze Pädagogik*, 1974), has been a consistent bestseller and has been translated into many languages.
64 Miller, *Child Rearing*, p. 195.
65 Ibid. p. 180.
66 Hitler biographer John Toland retells something related by a secretary. Paula, Hitler's younger sister, testified on questioning by American officers on 26 May 1945 that Hitler was beaten 'every day'. Paula Hitler was six years old when her father died. As any forensic expert knows, testimony by children can be but is not always credible. She told a very different story to the media, claiming that Hitler had not been punished enough. 'If he had been disciplined more as a child, he would probably not have become the most hated person in the world.' She went on to say that 'a couple of clouts in 1900 might well have prevented the outbreak of the Second World War.' Quoted in Wolfgang Zdral, *Die Hitlers: Die unbekannte Familie des Führers* (Frankfurt a. M., 2005), pp. 201f.
67 Miller, *Child Rearing*, p. 181. Miller's argumentation is still to be found in both a more refined and a more generalized form. Volker Elis Pilgrim, for example, thought Hitler, Napoleon and Stalin were mother's boys whose diabolical acts were attributable to their disturbed childhood, Volker Elis Pilgrim, *Muttersöhne* (Reinbek bei Hamburg, 1989), pp. 25–33. Pilgrim says of Alois Hitler: 'Hitler's father was a mother's boy, born illegitimately ... His mother, Maria Anna Schicklgruber, lived alone with her son for five years ... Adolf hated his father. Hate means ... not wanting to be like him

... Hitler's hatred of the Jews was derived from his hatred of his father. The father's mother ... worked in the household of a Jewish citizen ... had a child, her son Alois, whom her employer supported financially.' Pilgrim reiterates the assumption that spread after 1945 that Hitler's grandmother had been 'in service' in 1836 with a Jewish businessman by the name of Frankenberger in Graz and became pregnant by him or his son. Alois Hitler would then have been a 'half-Jew' and Adolf Hitler a 'quarter-Jew'. The entire Frankenberger myth comes from Hans Frank, who wanted to make the Jews partly responsible for their own extermination and sought to explain Hitler's anti-Semitism as a psychotic hatred of his own blood line. There was no Jew by the name of Frankenberger in Graz in 1836. In other words, the story was a complete fabrication on Frank's part.

68 The most coherent discussion is by the German-American psychiatrist and psychotherapist Helm Stierlin, who nevertheless presents little useful information. He saw his interpretation as a response to Erich Fromm's *The Anatomy of Human Destructiveness*, first published in the USA in 1973 and a year later in West Germany. See Helm Stierlin, *Adolf Hitler: Familienperspektiven* (Frankfurt a. M., 1975).

69 Hans Frank, *Im Angesicht des Galgens* (Munich-Gräfeling, 1953), p. 330. See the biography by Dieter Schenk, *Hans Frank: Hitlers Kronjurist und Generalgouverneur* (Frankfurt a. M., 2006).

70 See Werner Maser, *Adolf Hitler: Legende, Mythos, Wirklichkeit* (Munich, Esslingen, 1993).

71 This is the reason why a papal dispensation was required for the marriage of Alois Hitler and Klara Pölzl.

72 See Oliver Halmburg, Thomas Stahler, 'Familie Hitler – In Schatten des Diktators', broadcast on 3sat on 27 January 2006.

73 Jochmann, *Monologe* p. 357. Apparently Hitler was unaware of his family's history. He said in Werewolf, his Ukrainian headquarters, on 21 August 1942: 'I have no idea about my family history. I am completely ignorant in that area. When I was younger I didn't even know that I had relatives. I only discovered it after I became Reich Chancellor. I am not at all a family person ... I belong to my people.'

74 Werner Maser, *Das Ende der Führerlegende* (Munich, 1982), p. 252.

75 Personal statement by Traudl Junge, 1999.

76 Biological inbreeding has been observed in self-contained communities, on islands, in mountain valleys or in social ghettos, for example. Inbreeding and incest carry a risk of hereditary disease. Incest is sexual intercourse by close relatives, e.g. father and daughter, or siblings.

77 Hans-Albrecht Freye, *Humangenetik*, 5th reprint (Berlin, 1988), pp. 50–7. Freye notes that marriages between close relatives increase the likelihood of rare hereditary diseases.

78 Ibid. pp. 50 and 107.

79 Hamann, *Hitler's Vienna*; Zdral, *Die Hitlers*, p. 32. According to Sigmund, Johanna was a bit 'strange' but in no way feeble-minded. She managed a farm for Hitler's father Alois in Wörnhorts; see Anna Maria Sigmund, *Diktator*, p. 172.

80 A diabetic coma, caused by insulin deficiency, requires intensive medical care and even then it is not always possible to prevent death.

81 Annette Hinz-Wessels, 'Aloisia Veit: Ein "Euthanasie"-Opfer aus Hitlers

Familie', in Petra Fuchs et al. (eds), *'Das Vergessen der Vernichtung ist Teil der Vernichtung selbst' – Lebensgeschichten von Opfern der nationalsozialistischen 'Euthanasie'* (Göttingen, 2007), pp. 275–84.

82 See letters from Nissle to Morell on 5 and 8 August 1941. Morell had examined Hitler for the first time in 1936 and had noted eczema of the left leg that was 'apparently linked to a digestive disorder'. He treated the skin disorder with Mutaflor developed by the bacteriologist Nissle, who came from Freiburg in Breisgau (see Chapter 4). This soon settled Hitler's digestive problems and stopped the eczema. Hitler said later that Morell had asked for a year to treat him but that the eczema had disappeared after six months. Prior to that all consulting physicians had apparently failed to treat him successfully.

83 Morell's diary entry for 8 November 1944.

84 Personal statement by Professor Sterry, 2007.

85 Pschyrembel, *Klinisches Wörterbuch*, 257th edn (Berlin, New York, 1994), pp. 1261–2. In 50 per cent of cases psoriasis occurs before the age of twenty-five, with a second peak after the age of fifty. Its aetiology is multi factorial and it can be triggered by physical, chemical, mechanical or inflammatory stimuli or endogenous noxi.

86 *Lost* is named after the German chemists Lommel and Steinkopf (employees of Fritz Haber) who in 1916 suggested the use of the chemical bis(2-chloroethyl) sulphide as a poisonous gas, also known as mustard gas, yellow cross liquid, sulphur mustard or blistering agent. The NATO code is IID. It is in fact a liquid and is fired by an aerosol shell. It causes extensive chemical burning of the skin, particularly the mucous membranes, and attacks the eyes and lungs.

87 Maser, *Legende*, p. 92.

88 One example is the response to a publication by the American psychohistorian Rudolph Binion, *Hitler Among the Germans* (DeKalb, IL, 1984). Binion's observations regarding the relationship between Forster and Hitler were emphatically rebutted by Jan Armbruster, *Edmund Robert Forster (1876–1933): Lebensweg und Werk eines deutschen Nobelphysikers* (Husum, 2005).

89 Bernhard Horstmann, *Hitler in Pasewalk: Die Hypnose und ihre Folgen* (Düsseldorf, 2004). This subject had already been discussed in the 1960s when the neurologist and psychiatrist Johann Recktenwald also proposed, not uncontroversially, that Hitler had been suffering from hysterical blindness.

90 Pschyrembel, 25/th edn, p. 194.

91 Personal statement by specialist physician Karin Sallmon, Berlin, 2 June 2008.

92 Peter Riedesser, Axel Verderber, *Maschinengewehre hinter der Front: Zur Geschichte der deutschen Militärpsychiatrie* (Frankfurt a. M., 1996).

93 See Horstmann, who criticizes Maser's description of Hitler's gas poisoning. Maser describes the events on the basis of the contemporary witness account by Vincenz Müller, whom he met as a student and assistant to Ernst Niekisch at Humboldt University in East Berlin. Müller was a colleague of von Schleicher until 1933, and as officer in command of military district VII in Munich in 1934, when von Schleicher and von Bredow were shot, he was forced into silence by Hitler.

94 Ernst Weiss, *Der Augenzeuge* (Frankfurt a. M., 2000). Original title *Ich, der Augenzeuge.*
95 Horstmann, *Hitler in Pasewalk*, p. 112. The claim is based on an expert opinion by the psychologist Heidi Baitinger.
96 Ibid. p. 138.
97 According to a statement by Dr Rainer Striemer in 2008. Arthur Kronfeld, the most important hypnosis expert in the Weimar Republic, stated in 1924 that post-hypnotic suggestion had been observed in isolated cases up to four months or more after hypnosis but a lifelong trance situation was unheard of. See Arthur Kronfeld, *Hypnose und Suggestion* (Berlin, 1924), pp. 71f.
98 Edmund Forster, 'Der Krieg und die traumatischen Neurosen', in *Monatsschrift für Psychiatrie und Neurologie*, 38 (Berlin, 1915), 72–6.
99 Edmund Forster, 'Hysterische Reaktion und Simulation' in *Monatsschrift für Psychiatrie und Neurologie* 42 (1917), 298–324 and 371–80, particularly 317. In a reply he reiterated that it was not necessary to treat patients by suggestion: 'It is absolutely necessary in my opinion to tell these shell-shock victims that they are not sick but that they know very well themselves that their tremors are merely a bad habit designed to avoid going back to the front.' 'Zur Behandlung der Kriegszitterer' (comments on R. Hirschfeld's paper) in *Münchener Medizinische Wochenschrift* 34 (1917), Feldärztliche Beilage, 1126.
100 Forster thus agreed that hysteria was not a disease at all but a 'normal state'. See Armbruster, *Edmund Robert Forster*, pp. 159–74.
101 There is a noticeable difference in styles between the two volumes. Whereas volume I is a roughly structured and exaggerated mythologizing autobiographical narration, volume II is a systematic analysis of various political fields and may be read as a government programme. A detailed analysis can be found in Plöckinger, *Hitlers 'Mein Kampf'*.
102 Hitler, *Mein Kampf*, p. 187.
103 For detailed discussion including strong criticism of Maser's account, see Joachimsthaler, *Hitlers Weg*, pp. 186–97.
104 Joachimsthaler, *Hitlers Weg*, pp. 228–63. The author also discusses the confrontations between Karl Harrer, first NSDAP chairman, and Hitler, who was responsible for the party's publicity and propaganda.
105 Koch-Hillebrecht, *Homo-Hitler*, p. 71.
106 C. Fraenken (ed.), *Weyl's Handbuch der Hygiene*, particularly vol. 2 Bau- und Wohnungshygiene and vol. 4 Städtereinigung (Leipzig, 1912–14).
107 Otto von Schjerning (ed.), *Handbuch der Ärztlichen Erfahrungen im Weltkriege 1914/1915*, vol. 7 Hygiene, ed. Wilhelm Hoffmann (Leipzig, 1922).
108 German research responded to this need. Almost all of the researchers dealing with infectious diseases were deferred from military service during the Second World War as 'indispensable'. The barbaric human experiments in the concentration camps, regarding typhus for example, were justified by the defendants in the Nuremberg Doctors' Trial as a 'patriotic duty'.
109 The staff doctor and hygiene officer of the XIXth Army Corps wrote the following about his experiences: 'Every man has been instructed to wash his hands thoroughly after using the latrines with the prescribed amount of alcohol.' Erich Hesse, *Die Hygiene im Stellungskriege*, (Leipzig, 1915), p. 14.

110 Louis De Jong, 'Hat Felix Kersten das niederländische Volk gerettet?' in *Zwei Legenden aus dem Dritten Reich* (Stuttgart, 1974), p. 142.

111 Finding of the Medizinisch-Diagnostisches Institut Dr. med. A. Schmidt-Burbach, Morell's diary, 9 January 1940.

112 Hitler, *Mein Kampf*, p. 225.

113 This version was still being suggested in the 1980s by Simon Wiesenthal. Joachim Fest describes it as 'clearly inspired by literature' and going back to Thomas Mann. Fest, *Hitler*. The psychiatrist Langer, by contrast, conjectured in 1943 that Hitler's fear of syphilis was 'probably' due to a 'strong fear of castration'. He was unaware of the public discussion about the spread of venereal diseases. Langer, *Mind of Adolf Hitler*, p. 164–5.

114 For discussion of statistics, see Lutz Sauerteig, *Krankheit, Sexualität, Gesellschaft: Geschlechtskrankheiten und Gesundheitspolitik in Deutschland im 19. und 20. Jahrhundert* (Stuttgart, 1999), pp. 68–88.

115 In 1918 there were an estimated 25,000 syphilis sufferers in the army and 7,000 in the navy. Critics believed that these estimates were too low. See Sauerteig, *Krankheit*, p. 350.

116 A leading organization was the Deutsche Gesellschaft zur Bekämpfung der Geschlechtskrankheiten (German Society for Control of Venereal Diseases), founded in 1902, whose members included ministerial officials, university professors and medical policymakers. According to the medical historian Lutz Sauerteig, it soon became a policy influencing pressure group. See Sauerteig, *Krankheit*, pp. 89–125. Warning signs were also posted all over the front, and army doctors consistently cautioned troops about the risks. See Dyonys Fuchs, *Praktische Hygiene und Bekämpfung der Infektionskrankheiten im Felde* (Vienna and Leipzig, 1918), pp. 212f.

117 "German Hitler Parody Translated" http://www.youtube.com/watch?v=IUf4s3fgboo.

118 http://www.spiegel.de/panorama/leute/0,1518,591558,00.html; http://www.bild.de/BILD/news/vermischtes/2008/11/19/adolf-hitler-hoden/sanita eter-bestaetigung-aussage.html; http://www.bild.de/BILD/news/vermischt es/2008/11/19/lebensretter-von-adolf-hitler/lebte-in-angst-weil-er-von-hode nverletzung-wusste.html.

119 Eberle, Uhl, *Hitler Book*, p. 464. The post mortem report is printed in Lev Bezymenski, *The Death of Adolf Hitler* (New York, 1968).

120 Ibid. The integration of SMERSH in the NKGB was such that after a short time the former SMERSH officers were in charge. The secret service, now known as MGB (Ministry of State Security), gained in stature and importance. In 1953, after Stalin's death, its authority was cut back but quickly regained under its head Ivan Serov, with its name changed to KGB (Committee for State Security). It was further expanded after 1967 under Yuri Andropov.

121 Lev Bezymenski, *Operatsiya 'Mif' ili skolko raz khroronili Gitlera* (Moscow, 1995), p. 140.

122 The song, to the tune of the *Colonel Bogey March*, was written by the poet Toby O'Brien and modified anonymously many times during the war. In the original version, Hitler's ball was on the kitchen wall having been chopped off by his mother. It later moved to the Royal Albert Hall. Göring, Himmler and Goebbels were also said to have missing testicles. It is interesting to note that to say that someone has 'balls' means that he is courageous. A

person with 'no balls', by contrast, is cowardly and timid. The Allied propaganda did not change until Churchill's 'blood, sweat and tears' speech on 13 May 1940. It was only then, after the invasion of France, that Germany was regarded as a serious opponent. The song nevertheless remained popular among the troops.

123 See Maser's reproduction of Morell's protocol for Kempner in Werner Maser, *Fälschung, Dichtung und Wahrheit über Hitler und Stalin* (Munich, 2004), pp. 427–49.

124 Ron Rosenbaum, *Explaining Hitler: The Search for Origins of His Evil* (London, 1998), p. 148.

125 Ibid. p. 221.

126 Maser, *Legende*.

127 Redlich, *Diagnosis*, p. 211.

128 Hjalmar Schacht, *76 Jahre meines Lebens* (Bad Wörishofen, 1953), pp. 382f and 458f.

129 Fritz Wiedemann, *Der Mann der Feldherr werden wollte* (Velbert, 1964).

130 Personal statement by Traudl Junge, 1997.

131 Güstrow's real name was Dietrich Wilde. After escaping from East Germany he published under a pseudonym because the Ministry of State Security regularly pursued rebels and regime critics even after they had escaped to West Germany.

132 Wilde underwent a thorough denazification process as he was a candidate for the post of personnel director at the Martin Luther University of Halle. Information from Daniel Bohse, who was closely involved with denazification in Saxony Anhalt after 1945.

133 Dietrich Güstrow, *In jenem Jahren* (Munich, 1985) and *Tödlicher Alltag* (Munich, 1984).

134 See 'Hitler und seine Ärzte' in Rolf Hochhuth, *Neue Dramen, Gedichte, Prosa* (Reinbek bei Hamburg, 2003), pp. 773ff.

135 Hochhuth repeatedly presents facts and stories of this type in a media-friendly manner. For discussion of the motives for Hochhuth's 'moral maximalism' see Evelyn Finger, afterword to Hochhuth, *Neue Dramen*, pp. 1259–75.

136 Redlich, *Diagnosis*, pp. 325–6.

137 The ICD catalogue by the WHO, founded in 1948, systematically lists and assigns codes to diseases and causes of death. The ICD notations enable doctors' diagnoses to be understood internationally. In the ninth edition of the ICD in 1992 homosexuality was listed as a disease with the code 302.0. In the following edition, which is still valid today, it had been removed from the list.

138 Peter Jungblut, *Famose Kerle: Eulenburg – eine wilhelminische Affäre* (Hamburg, 2003).

139 Magnus Hirschfeld, *Berlins drittes Geschlecht*, edited with an afterword by Manfred Herzer (Berlin, 1991).

140 Because of the king's special relationship with his valet Michael Gabriel Fredersdorff, he was occasionally suspected of being homosexual. 'The fact that the king liked to surround himself with young hussars, whom he dressed in tight-fitting uniforms, and his unusual relationship to Fredersdorff may be regarded as indications of homosexual behaviour shown by 5 to 15 per cent of men', although not comparable with genuine homosexuality. It

is highly likely that Frederick the Great exhibited homosexual behaviour and permitted single-sex relations as a result, for the purpose of social camouflage if nothing else. The king was quite content that his unusual relationship with the dancer Barberina should arouse jealousy. See Hans-Joachim Neumann, *Friedrich der Grosse* (Berlin, 2000), pp. 40ff, 109.

141 Pschyrembel, 259th edn, p. 788. For definition and historical interpretation see Wikipedia and literary references, and Robert Aldrich (ed.), *Gay Life and Culture: A World History* (New York, 2006).

142 For general discussion of sexuality in the Nazi era see Dagmar Herzog, *Sex After Fascism: Memory and Morality in Twentieth-Century Germany* (Princeton, 2005), and Anna Maria Sigmund, *'Das Geschlechtsleben bestimmen wir' – Sexualität im Dritten Reich* (Munich, 2008).

143 *Brockhaus Konversationslexikon*, 14th edn (Leipzig, 1908).

144 *Knaurs Lexikon* (Berlin, 1939), p. 606. Although the Federal Constitutional Court stated that the increase in the severity of the law under the Nazis was constitutional in 1957, the law was amended in 1968. Section 175 in its current form results from the 29th Law Amending the Criminal Code of 31 May 1994.

145 The number of convictions under Section 175 rose steadily, from 853 in 1933 to 8,562 in 1938. Altogether more than 100,000 homosexuals were registered by the police and around 50,000 sentenced to imprisonment. Some 15,000 died in concentration camps, where only half survived. See Sigmund, *Geschlechtsleben*, pp. 196 and 209.

146 Decree by Hitler for the SA of 5 February 1931, quoted in Sigmund, *Geschlechtsleben*, pp. 189f.

147 Sigmund, *Geschlechtsleben*, p. 182.

148 The lively and open-ended discussion by the two major churches can be consulted on the Internet.

149 One indication of this is the letters from members of the public. Hitler did not receive letters of admiration suggesting a sexual connotation until after 1935. See Eberle, *Letters to Hitler*, p. 144 and pp. 153–4.

150 Lothar Machtan, *The Hidden Hitler* (New York, 2001).

151 Ibid. pp. 113–14.

152 Inasmuch as Ernst 'Putzi' Hanfstaengl can be taken seriously as a contemporary witness, his assertions about Hitler's sex life and homosexuality were the opposite of what Machtan later claimed.

153 Machtan, *The Hidden Hitler*, p. 220.

154 As far as we know, the proscription lists were drawn up not by Hitler but by Theodor Eicke, Reinhard Heydrich, Hermann Göring and others. The names of the victims were apparently decided in various SD and Gestapo committees. Hitler himself did not endorse the lists. See Heinz Höhne, *The Order of the Death's Head: The Story of Hitler's SS* (London, 1969), p. 101.

155 Sigmund, *Geschlechtsleben*, p. 55.

156 Maser, *Legende*.

157 Sigmund, *Geschlechtsleben*, p. 22.

158 August Kubizek, *The Young Hitler I Knew* (London, 2006), p. 36. Machtan describes Hitler's youthful friend as a complete fabricator and also as a homosexual, for which there is absolutely no evidence. Asked by Hitler biographer Werner Maser, Kubizek credibly stated that all allegations of

homosexuality were 'absolutely false'. They had even visited a brothel together.

159 Maser, *Legende*.
160 Mulders obtained the DNA samples voluntarily from one of Hitler's relatives. The others he acquired by collecting cigarette stubs and paper napkins. Fifteen markers on the Y chromosome were compared at the Life-ID laboratory. The Austrian and American samples corresponded in their entirety. Mulders found Loret's genetic material on stamps and envelopes that had been licked. See Jean-Paul Mulders, *Auf der Suche nach Hitlers Sohn: Eine Beweisaufnahme* (Munich, 2009).
161 Anna Maria Sigmund, *Frauen*, p. 728. Sigmund also reproduces the correspondence between Hitler and Reiter. He calls her 'my sweet child' and assures her how much he likes her. Ibid. pp. 1045–55.
162 Facsimile in Maser, *Legende*.
163 Ibid. p. 205.
164 In 2007, British newspapers speculated that Hitler might have had a son with Unity Mitford, an idea credibly refuted by Richard Evans in *The Times*. See http://einestages.spiegel.de/static/topicalbumbackground/2698/_heil_hitler_love_bobo.html and http://www.timesonline.co.uk/tol/news/uk/article3042944.ece.
165 In his criticism of Machtan's theory about Hitler's homosexuality, Maser repeats the spiteful remark by Ernst Hanfstaengl that he (Hanfstaengl) was meant to drown out Slezak's 'moaning' by playing loud piano music. Maser, *Legende*.
166 Testosterone was first isolated by the pharmacologist Ernst Laqueur, who also named it. Laqueur lost his professorship at the University of Amsterdam after the German occupation of the Netherlands. He was arrested on account of his Jewish descent and escaped death in 1944 only by luck.
167 The servant Linge noted in his diary for 22 November 1944 that Morell met Eva Braun privately from 1 p.m. to 8.35 p.m.
168 For Hitler's itinerary, see Franz W. Siedler and Dieter Zeigert, *Die Führerhauptquartiere: Anlagen und Planungen im Zweiten Weltkrieg* (Munich, 2004), particularly p. 330. For Eva Braun, who after the marriage of Hermann Fegelein to her sister Margarete on 3 June 1944 (witnesses: Himmler and Martin Bormann) 'officially' became part of Hitler's entourage, see Sigmund, *Frauen*, and sympathetically Johannes Frank, *Eva Braun: Ein ungewöhnliches Frauenschicksal in geschichtlich bewegter Zeit* (Coburg, 1997), pp. 269–79.
169 Morell's diary, e.g. at 11.50 a.m. on 29 September 1944.
170 Rudolph Binion, *Hitler Among the Germans*, pp. 15–17.
171 Ibid. p. 18.
172 Ibid. p. 56. It is clear that Binion was sincere in his search for an explanation for Hitler's personality. He told Ron Rosenbaum that his traumatic memory of his Jewish mother had made him sensitive to the issue. See Rosenbaum, *Explaining Hitler*, pp. 241–2.
173 See Wikipedia article on Eduard Bloch.
174 The most adamant is John Kafka, professor of clinical psychiatry and behavioural science at Washington University. See Rosenbaum, *Explaining Hitler*, pp. 245–50.
175 Hamann, *Hitlers Edeljude*, p. 92.

176 See Hamann, *Hitlers Edeljude*. Clinic directors did not usually accept married assistant doctors because they feared a lack of commitment and scientific ambition.
177 According to the safety data sheet of Chemische Werke Hommel, Ludringhausen, iodoform is classified as harmful to health. Protective clothing is therefore required when using it. It is also slightly flammable and must be disposed of as special waste. Present-day drugs with similar effect do not have these disadvantages.
178 Facsimile in Hamann, *Edeljude*, pp. 90f.
179 Johann Recktenwald, *Woran hat Adolf Hitler gelitten? Eine neuropsychiatrische Deutung* (Munich, 1963), p. 37.
180 Ibid. p. 13.
181 Ellen Gibbels, *Hitlers Parkinson-Krankheit: Zur Frage eines hirnorganischen Psychosyndroms* (Berlin, 1990), pp. 84 ff.
182 Currently 9 per cent of the German population agree with the statement that Nazism also had its good sides. See Oliver Decker and Elmar Brähler (commissioned by the Friedrich Ebert Stiftung), *Bewegung in der Mitte: Rechtsextreme Einstellungen in Deutschland 2008* (Berlin, 2009), p. 18.
183 In this case from Andernach to Hadamar near Limburg.
184 The court judged him innocent because no evidence could be produced of his involvement in the mass killing and believed Recktenwald's claim that by staying in his post he had prevented 'worse'. See www.mahnmal koblenz.de.
185 Peter Steinbach and Johannes Tuchel, *Georg Elser* (Berlin, 2008).
186 Walter Schellenberg, *The Schellenberg Memoirs* (London, 1956).
187 Michael A. Kater, *Doctors Under Hitler* (Chapel Hill, NC, 1989), pp. 128–9.
188 Schellenberg, *Memoirs*, p. 438.
189 Karlshof (Karolewo) has now been incorporated into Kętrzyn.
190 David Irving, 'Hitlers Krankheiten', in *Stern* 27 (1969), 44–6, and *Stern* 28 (1969), 40–5. At all events, Giesing was not inexperienced in neurology.
191 Schenck, *Patient Hitler*, pp. 505–10.
192 There is no 'yellow diary' in the file 'ED 100 Sammlung Irving' at the Institute of Contemporary History.
193 Written notification by Otto Günsche on 8 September 1998.

3 HITLER'S DOCTORS: PERSONAL PHYSICIAN MORELL AND OTHERS

1 Zdral, *Die Hitlers*, family tree in frontispiece.
2 Georg Franz-Willing, *Putsch und Verbotszeit der Hitlerbewegung: November–Februar 1925* (Preussisch Oldendorf, 1977), p. 114.
3 Schultze was charged on several counts for his involvement in the 'euthanasia' programme but was not convicted.
4 Quoted from Ottmar Katz, *Prof. Dr. med. Theo Morell, Hitlers Leibarzt* (Bayreuth, 1982), pp. 364f.
5 On 4 April 1932 Hitler gave speeches at the Lustgarten in Berlin, the Luftschiffhafen in Potsdam, the Sportpalast in Berlin and the sports ground in Berlin-Friedrichshain. See Max Domarus, *Hitler: Speeches and Proclamations 1932–1945*, vol. 1 (Mundelein, IL, 1990), p. 116.

6  25 June 1932 SS applicant, 25 July 1932 SS man, 31 July 1933 promotion to SS officer for special purposes.

7  The following information is based on the personal file in the Federal Archive, cf. BA (former BDC) SS-O NSDAP-OK 3200 (film 0014). Member no. H06473 of the NSDAP and originally 83632 of the SS, later corrected (31115). The SS number 27483 is obviously an error.

8  Personal file of Karl-Friedrich Dermietzel in BA Berlin (formerly BDC, SS-O archive).

9  3-methyl-1-butanol, formerly known as isoamyl alcohol, is a fusel oil found in all common spirits. It is often used as a solvent in cosmetics. See F. W. Klever GmbH Aham, *Die Ballistol-Story, Tipps und Wissenswertes über ein legendäres Öl* (undated), Gebrauchsinformation Neo-Ballistol, version 2001.

10  Hitler's dentist Johannes Blaschke claimed after 1945 to have been the first to recognize the substance as toxic. See Schenck, *Patient Hitler*, p. 301.

11  The complaint was described vividly by Albert Speer, although it is unlikely that the conversation was exactly as Speer wrote it. Albert Speer, *Inside the Third Reich* (New York, 1997), p. 104.

12  Grawitz killed himself and his family in 1945. For Grawitz's biography see Hubert Kolling, 'Grawitz, Ernst', in *Biographisches Lexikon zur Pflegegeschichte* (Munich, 2008), pp. 111–16.

13  David Irving, *Wie krank war Hitler wirklich? Der Diktator und seine Ärzte* (Munich, 1980), p. 135.

14  Personal statement by Traudl Junge, 1997.

15  Personal statement by Otto Günsche, 1998.

16  Schenck, *Patient Hitler*, p. 498. Schenck later revised this judgement and described Morell as a 'historical person'. Ernst Günther Schenck, *Dr. Morell: Hitler's Leibarzt und sein Pharmaimperium* (Schnellbach, 1998), p. 82.

17  Maser, *Legende*, pp. 214–15 and p. 230.

18  Fest, *Hitler*, pp. 672–3.

19  Bernd Freytag von Loringhoven, *In the Bunker with Hitler* (New York, 2005), p. 89.

20  Ibid. p. 116.

21  Hans-Dietrich Röhrs, *Hitler – Die Zerstörung einer Persönlichkeit: Grundlagen der Feststellungen zum Krankheitsbild* (Neckargemünd, 1965).

22  *Der Spiegel* 18 (1989), 94–7. The description of Morell's hygiene habits is cited in Hugh Trevor-Roper, *The Last Days of Hitler* (Chicago, 1992), p. 107.

23  Professor Dr med. Hanskarl von Hasselbach, 'Hitlers Mangel an Menschenkenntnis', 26 September 1945, BA Koblenz, Kl. Erw. 411–13.

24  Marginal note of 24 June 1948 on Morell's given names next to the entry in the register of births, marriages and death of Tegernsee registry office.

25  Even decades later Traudl Junge remained very enthusiastic about Morell's medical treatment. Personal statement, 1997.

26  According to Schenck the practice was in Fasanenstrasse, but in fact this was a later practice on the corner of Kurfürstendamm and Fasanenstrasse. Schenck, *Patient Hitler*, p. 474.

27  Claimed by Schenck, *Patient Hitler*, pp. 473f.

28  Katz, *Morell*, p. 34.

29  Statement by Karl Brandt, 19 September 1945, BA Koblenz, K. Erw. 411–3.
30  Letter by Nissle to Morell of 8 August 1941.
31  David Irving, *Secret Diaries*, p. 44.
32  Speer, *Inside the Third Reich*, pp. 105–6.
33  Schenck, *Pharmaimperium*, p. 78.
34  Eva Gruberova, 'Hitlers Hirte', in *Die Zeit* 40 (27 September 2007), 112.
35  Schenck, *Pharmaimperium*, pp. 95f. Tax returns from this time are not usually kept. As a frame of reference for Morell's salary, an ordinary university professor at this time received a basic salary of RM 12,000. The directors of medical clinics earned considerably more, however, from their private practices. The top earner at the University of Halle was the director of the eye clinic, which he had built up with his own funds. He earned around RM 100,000 before tax.
36  Schenck, *Pharmaimperium*. For details of the electron microscope, see ibid. pp. 211–23.
37  Katz, *Morell*, pp. 283f.
38  Schenck, *Pharmaimperium*, pp. 152–5.
39  Morell's diary entry for 16 November 1944.
40  It was difficult for Morell to find the right preparation for Hitler or to examine him at all because he was extremely shy. Morell's entry for 30 September 1944 provides eloquent testimony. It concerns a camomile enema that Hitler administered himself with an 'irrigator' sitting on the WC. 'I had to wait outside, in fact he even locked me out.'
41  Morell's diary entries for 20 April, 24 October and 25 October 1944.
42  Morell's diary entry for 1 October 1944.
43  Otto Günsche, whom Morell had known well since 1943, stressed in a letter of 4 September 1998 that Hitler's personal physician 'was in no way the charlatan that others regarded him as being'.
44  Personal statement by Traudl Junge, 1997.
45  Irving, *Wie krank war Hitler wirklich?*, pp. 15f.
46  Morell's diary entry for 8 November 1944.
47  Schenck, *Patient Hitler*, p. 462.
48  Written notification by the registrar, Tegernsee.
49  Morell's practice (and apartment) were at Kurfürstendamm 216 (at Fasanenstrasse intersection). Morell owned a house on Schwanenwerder, an island on the Havel river.
50  For details and an assessment of Brandt's life, see Ulf Schmidt, 'Die Angeklagten Fritz Fischer, Hans W. Romberg und Karl Brandt aus der Sicht des medizinischen Sachverstandigen Leo Alexander', in Angelika Ebbinghaus, Klaus Dörner (ed.), *Vernichten und Heilen: Der Nürnberger Ärzteprozess und seine Folgen* (Berlin, 2001), pp. 374–404.
51  Dr Brandt's membership application to the Nationalsozialistischer Deutscher Ärzteverbund e.V. of 27 January 1932.
52  Schenck, *Pharmaimperium*, pp. 31–3. Hitler's adjutant Wilhelm Brückner suffered serious head injuries as a result of the accident on 15 August 1933 that Dr Brandt treated.
53  The instruction was filed by Minister of Justice Franz Gürtner with the marginal comment: 'Given to me by Bouhler on 27 August 1940'. Illustration in Götz Aly (ed.), *Aktion T4 1939–1945: Die Euthanasiezentrale in der Tiergartenstrasse 4* (Berlin, 1989), p. 14.

54 Gerhard Jaeckel, *Die Charité: Geschichte eines Weltzentrums der Medizin von 1710 bis zur Gegenwart* (Munich, 2001), p. 14.

55 A further characteristic of the industrial-scale extermination of millions of people was the use of modern data processing and assessment systems to permit the comprehensive registration and effective selection of victims. For discussion of the transfer of technology on the use of gas, see Klee, *Euthanasie*.

56 This made Brandt a rival and effective superior of Reich Health Leader Leonardo Conti, whose competence Hitler increasingly questioned. Schmidt, 'Die Angeklagten', in Ebbinghauser, Dörner (ed.), *Der Nürnberger Ärzteprozess*, p. 400.

57 Speer, *Inside the Third Reich*, pp. 635–6.

58 Quoted from Schmidt, 'Die Angeklagten', in Ebbinghaus/Dörner, *Nürnberger Ärzteprozess*, p. 401.

59 Ernst Klee, *Das Personenlexikon zum Dritten Reich: Wer war was vor und nach 1945*, 2nd edn (Frankfurt a. M., 2007), p. 231.

60 The assessment by Volker Hess that the reputation of the University Accident Clinic suffered under Georg Magnus is somewhat harsh. See Volker Hess, 'Die medizinische Fakultät im Zeichen der "Führeruniversität"', in Christoph Jahr, *Die Berliner Universität in der NS-Zeit, vol. 1: Strukturen und Personen* (Stuttgart, 2005), pp. 46f.

61 Also known as thromboangiitis obliterans because it results in thrombosis and is frequently found among smokers. Hanskarl von Hasselbach, *Die Endangitis obliterans* (Leipzig, 1939).

62 Professor Dr. med. Hanskarl von Hasselbach, 'Hitlers Menschenkenntnisse', 27 September 1945, BA Koblenz, Kl. Erw. 411–13.

63 Personal statement, 1997.

64 Stumpfegger wrote a number of historical papers on the subject.

65 The Hohenlychen health facility was founded by the German Red Cross in 1902 as a sanatorium for tuberculosis sufferers but was transformed under its medical director Karl Gebhardt after 1933 into an SS sanatorium. It was no doubt Stumpfegger's personal ambition that took him to Hohenlychen.

66 Details from the handwritten curriculum vitae and personnel records in BA, SS-O, former BDC, no. 168-B (Stumpfegger personal file) and BA, RS (former BDC) G 0118 and MF OK W 0074.

67 BA Berlin (former Document Centre), SS-O no. 168-B, Stumpfegger, Ludwig personal file.

68 The wood wool from the car upholstery could not be removed from Heydrich's body.

69 Freya Klier, *Die Kaninchen von Ravensbrück: Medizinische Versuche an Frauen in der NS-Zeit* (Munich, 1994), pp. 161–83.

70 The pleadings by the defence council in the Doctors' Trial (Dr Alfred Seidel) imply that concentration camp inmates were not involved. See corresponding affidavits on www.nuremberg.law.harvard.edu. The testimony of Herta Oberheuser, who gave detailed answers during her questioning, however, is convincing. Her cooperation as a key witness probably resulted in her avoiding the death sentence and being sentenced to twenty years' imprisonment instead. The corresponding testimony is also now available online. On Stumpfegger, see Document NO-487, Pros. Ex. 208 on www.mazal.org/archive/nmt/01/NMT01-T393.htm.

71   A 'human bouillon' was prepared from the flesh of the dead inmates. Weber was not subsequently prosecuted and died as a free man in Homburg (Saar) in 1956. See Ernst Klee, *Auschwitz, die NS-Medizin und ihre Opfer* (Frankfurt a. M., 1997), pp. 58, 402ff, 43f.

72   BA Berlin (former Document Centre), SS-O no. 75.

73   Robert M. W. Kempner, *Das Dritte Reich im Kreuzverhör: Aus den unveröffentlichten Vernehmungsprotokollen des Anklägers* (Munich and Esslingen, 1969), pp. 63f.

74   Residence: Tauentzienstr. 7b.

75   No doctoral thesis by Blaschke has been found to date. It is possible that he was awarded the academic grades of Dr. med. dent. and professor as honorary titles.

76   BA Berlin (former Document Centre), SS-O, no. 75 (Blaschke personnel file).

77   www.hagalil.com/archiv/98/08/zahngold.htm.

78   According SS-Hauptsturmführer Bruno Melmer, who made the deposits, these precious metals and currency were called 'Melmer's gold'. See Independent Commission of Experts Switzerland – Second World War, *Gold Transactions in the Second World War: Statistical Review with Commentary, a contribution to the Conference on Nazi Gold*, London, 2–4 December 1997, p. 8. The total amount was put at 2.5 to 4 million US dollars at an exchange rate of 1 dollar for 4.2 reichmarks. The agreement was made between Heinrich Himmler and Reichsbank president Walter Funk, see 'Der grosse Raubzug', in *Der Spiegel* 22 (1998), 86.

79   Heusermann and Echtermann were subsequently arrested and transported to the Soviet Union. Bruck emigrated to the USA in 1947. For discussion of Bruck, see www.zm-online.de/m5a.htm?/zm/10_06/page2hist1.htm.

80   Stefan Doernberg (ed.), *Hitler's Ende ohne Mythos: Jelena Rshewskaja erinnert sich an ihren Einsatz im Mai 1945 in Berlin* (Berlin, 2005), p. 122.

81   Blaschke successfully convinced the interrogator Robert Kempner that he had been kept in the dark about many things precisely because he was Hitler's dentist. He had been treated 'like a raw egg' for fear that he might 'let something slip'. He continued: 'I am quite sure that with the exception of a small circle no one knew anything.' Kempner then directed the conversation to the staff of the Ministry of Finance, suggesting that they must have known something. Blaschke: 'They will have known.' Kempner, *Kreuzverhör*, pp. 58f. It would be wrong to accuse Kempner here of negligence. His task was to prepare the charge for the Wilhelmstrasse trial, an extremely heterogeneous matter. Moreover, in view of the start of the Cold War, his resources were limited and he realized that he should search for the main culprits. As far as he was concerned, Blaschke was a possible but unrewarding witness for the prosecution.

82   Tanja Rouenhoff, Carl Otto von Eicken, 'Vertreter der Hals-, Nasen- und Ohrenheilkunde in Giessen von 1910–1922', diss. (Giessen, 2004).

83   'Carl von Eicken (1873–1960): Otorhinolaryngologe an der Charité', in Konrad Haake, Anne Nischweitz (eds), *100 Jahre Hals-, Nasen- und Ohrenklinik an der Charité zu Berlin 1893–1993* (Berlin, 1993), p. 30.

84   'Carl Otto von Eicken (1873–1960): Amtzeit 1922–1951', in *Friedrich-Wilhelms-Universität* (Berlin, undated), 20–2.

85   With the fees for treating Hitler, initially RM 10,000 and later allegedly

209

RM 50,000, he financed the Von Eicken Foundation for the Promotion of Young German University Doctors; Rouenhoff, p. 103.

86 The liberal successor to the old William I suffered from laryngeal cancer and after months of incorrect treatment was saved only by a tracheotomy. He reigned as emperor for ninety-nine days but had to write his instructions on notepads. Hans-Joachim Neumann, *Friedrich III: Der 99-Tage-Kaiser* (Berlin, 2006).

87 The histology of Hitler's polyp is described in letters by Robert Rössle to Carl Otto von Eicken of 21 August 1935 and 25 November 1944. See Morell's diary.

88 Morell's diary entry for 22 November 1944.

89 According to Gerhard Jaeckel, Hitler was by this time 'just a nervous wreck kept going with difficulty by Morell's drugs'. Von Eicken brought relief 'by squeezing the tonsils and thoroughly irrigating the maxillary sinuses'. The latter remark was true but Hitler's destruction on account of Morell's drugs is conjecture. See Gerhard Jaeckel, *Charité*, p. 536.

90 Morell's penultimate entry at the end of 1944.

91 Doernberg (ed.), *Hitler's Ende*, pp. 118f.

92 www.bbaw.de, members of the precursor academies. It was originally established by Leibniz in 1700 as the Electoral Brandenburg Society of Sciences, becoming the Prussian Academy of Sciences and then until 1972 the German Academy of Sciences in Berlin. Today it is called the Berlin-Brandenburg Academy of Sciences. Its members have included Rudolf Virchow, Karl Gerhardt, Robert Koch, Ferdinand Sauerbach and Otto Warburg.

93 Unlike the eugenicist Fritz Lenz, for example. See Volker Hess, 'Die medizinische Fakultät im Zeichen der "Führeruniversität"', in Christoph Jahr, Rebecca Schaarschmidt, *Die Berliner Universität in der NS-Zeit, vol. 1: Personen und Strukturen* (Wiesbaden, 2005), p. 41.

94 Similar sterilization programmes also existed in other European countries and in the USA. The trials in Nazi Germany had the appearance of legality but were in fact part of an extermination programme directed at all elements of the population deemed to be racially 'worthless'. Some of the condemned were later to die in the gas chambers. For further details, see Gisela Bock, *Zwangssterilisation im Nationalsozialismus* (Opladen, 1986).

95 Andreas Malycha, 'Der Umgang mit politisch belasteten Hochschulprofessoren an der Medizinischen Fakultät Berlin in den Jahren 1945 bis 1949', in Rüdiger von Bruch, Uta Gerhard, Aleksandra Pawliczek (eds), *Kontinuitäten und Diskontinuitäten in der Wissenschaftsgeschichte des 20. Jahrhunderts* (Stuttgart, 2006), pp. 103f.

96 The combination of a public office with a higher university title was common among hygiene specialists in the first half of the twentieth century.

97 For indications and courses, see A. Nissle, 'Die antagonistische Behandlung chronischer Darmstörungen mit Colibakterien', in *Medizinische Klinik* 2 (1918), 29–37.

98 The most well-known example of a successful and recognized doctor and businessman is Nobel Prize winner Emil von Behring who marketed his diphtheria serum himself following disputes with Farbwerke Hoechst. Behring was also met with extreme hostility.

210

99  The Alfred-Nissle-Gesellschaft in Hagen explicitly recommends Mutaflor for chronic irritable bowel syndrome.

100  Ilya I. Mechnikov (1845–1916, Nobel Prize 1908), a Ukrainian who trained in western Europe, was appointed as a researcher with Louis Pasteur in 1887. He is regarded today as a pioneer in the study of the cellular immune system and also coined the term 'macrophage'.

101  The preparation referred to is 'Trocken-Koli-Hamma', which proved, however, to be ineffective.

102  Nissle discussed the usual 'racial hygiene' ideas on the long-term 'improvement of the hereditary gift of the German people'. See Alfred Nissle, *Richtlinien und Vorschläge für einen Neuaufbau der Kräfte und Leistungen unseres Volkes* (Freiburg, 1922), p. 14. The ideas of racial hygiene at the time and the question of sterilization were influenced by the Munich professor Fritz Lenz. See Fritz Lenz, *Menschliche Auslese und Rassenhygiene (Eugenik)* (Munich, 1932), pp. 267–307.

103  Eduard Seidler, 'Die Medizinische Fakultät zwischen 1926 und 1948', in Eckard John et al. (eds), *Die Freiburger Universität in Zeit des Nationalsozialismus* (Freiburg and Würzburg, 1991), p. 84.

104  In the literature Arthur Weber is often referred to as Alfred Weber and occasionally Karl.

105  Reprint from *Deutsches Archiv für klinische Medizin* 97 (Leipzig, 1909).

106  The electrical activity of the heart had been measured previously but it was not until 1903 that the Dutch physician Willem Einthoven presented the first interpretable electrocardiograph. In 1913 he produced the mathematical basis for the interpretation of cardiac surface potential maps as a prerequisite for calculating an electrocardiogram (ECG).

107  Dieter Klein, 'Arthur Weber (1879–1975) und das Balneologische Universitätsinstitut in Bad Nauheim von 1929 bis 1955', med. diss. (Giessen, 2005), pp. 135–56.

108  Arthur Weber, *Die Elektrokardiographie und andere graphische Methoden in der Kreislaufdiagnostik* (Berlin, 1948).

109  Letter by Morell to Weber, 13 May 1943.

110  According to Angelika Ebbinghaus and Karl Heinz Roth, see Ebbinghaus, *Vernichten und Heilen*, p. 215.

### 4 HITLER'S MEDICINE CHEST: THE DRUGS AND THEIR EFFECTS

1  Most drugs were listed in the official German pharmacopoeias (*Rote Liste* and GEHE Codex); some were in the process of registration.

2  Irving, 'Hitlers Krankheiten' in *Stern* 26 (1969), 42.

3  According to our evaluation of Morell's diary entries from 1941 to 1945 a total of eighty-two preparations would appear realistic.

4  *GEHE Codex der pharmazeutischen und organotherapeutischen Spezialpräparate ... umfassend deutsche und zahlreiche ausländische Erzeugnisse*, 7th rev. edn (Dresden, 1937).

5  *Rote Liste 1939: Preisverzeichnis deutscher pharmazeutischer Spezialpräparate*, 3rd edn (Berlin, 1939).

6  Schenk, *Pharmaimperium*.

7  This dye breaks down to form aromatic amines, which are carcinogenic.

8  Hans Eppinger, 'Pneumonie und Kreislauf', in *Deutsche Medizinische Wochenschrift* (1940), 867.

9  The ENT specialist Dr Erwin Giesing, who attributed Hitler's jaundiced look in September 1944 to the anti-gas pills, related his suspicion to Dr von Hasselbach, who in turn mentioned it to Dr Brandt. The criticisms were directed at Morell and led to a dispute between the doctors, in which Morell prevailed thanks to Hitler's protection.

10  Dr Carl Blumenreuter, SS Chief Pharmacist and head of the Chemical Pharmaceutical Office of the SS Health Department, analysed the strychnine content of the anti-gas pills and also checked other preparations at Morell's instigation. He informed Morell by telephone about the laxative Mitilax: 'It consists more or less solely of paraffin and has no damaging admixtures.'

11  Today tetracaine is used as a local anaesthetic instead of cocaine.

12  *Senna alexandrina* is a member of the Caesalpinioideae subfamily and was commonly used in the nineteenth century as a laxative. It is still used today by old people in Cyprus for this purpose and is also highly regarded as a folk remedy with various mythical powers.

13  Mutaflor contains viable bacteria of the strain *Escherichia coli*. Nissle had isolated the bacteria from the stool of a soldier in 1917 and developed the probiotic coliform preparation from it. It quickly became popular and is still on the *Rote Liste* today. Mutaflor was used less in hospital clinics than by outside doctors.

14  In *The Secret Diary of Hitler's Doctor*, David Irving wrote that Nateina was a 'mysterious haemostatic' used after the assassination attempt of 20 July 1944 (p. 271).

15  After the assassination attempt on Hitler at lunchtime on 20 July 1944, von Hasselbach was the first doctor on the scene. Morell then arrived and started his treatment with Nateina, which was said to help stop bleeding of all causes. Giesing saw Hitler only two days later, so it could not have been him who started the Nateina treatment. Cocaine is a painkiller and adrenaline a vasoconstrictor added to local anaesthetics. Haemophilia is a hereditary disease due to the deficiency of a blood coagulation factor. At the time there was no cure for it as the cause was not discovered until after the Second World War. Nateina was therefore ineffective in haemophilia. Hans-Joachim Neumann, *Erbkrankheiten in europäischen Fürstenhäusern* (Augsburg, 2002), pp. 256–9.

16  The frequency of the injections cannot be determined precisely, because Morell himself used only the term 'dann und wann' (now and then). In his records it is mentioned only once.

17  The antibiotic penicillin was discovered in 1928 by the British bacteriologist Alexander Fleming as a secondary metabolic product of *Penicillium notatum*, the mould from which penicillin is formed, and used medically from 1940 onwards. Fleming was awarded the Nobel Prize in 1945 for his revolutionary discovery. Morell's penicillin powder had no antibiotic effect. Penicillin was tested in German university clinics from 1943.

18  Methamphetamine was developed in Germany under the brand name Pervitin and was like the normal amphetamine but with the amino group methylated.

19 It may be assumed that Hitler used sedatives more often than noted by Morell.

20 Morell's head chemist Dr Kurt Mulli prepared the 'deluxe Vitamultin' with different ingredients on request. The precise composition remained unknown. The 'gold Vitamultin tablets' might have contained Pervitin (see Schenck, *Patient Hitler*, p. 447).

21 Schenck, *Pharmaimperium*, pp. 447–57.

22 *Rote Liste*, 1939 edn.

23 Yatren had a wide-ranging activity spectrum. It was recommended not only for amoebic dysentery but also to treat angina, stomatitis (inflammation of the oral mucosa) and gastrointestinal diseases.

24 Morell's daily records of 15 and 18 October 1944.

25 To strengthen Hitler's resistance and increase his performance, Morell devised a basic medicinal programme consisting of glucose, Tonophosphan and Vitamultin-Calcium, supplemented by other products. This approach may be described as one of irresponsible polypragmasia.

26 Substances causing addiction include alcohol, amphetamines, caffeine, cannabis, cocaine, hallucinogenics, hypnotics, nicotine, opiates and sedatives. Apart from addiction, there is also habitual use of substances that does not result in physical or psychological dependence. Hitler clearly used substances habitually and had an addictive attitude to drugs in general but this is not the same as an addiction or dependence.

27 Hitler, *Mein Kampf*, pp. 272–96 and pp. 598–607. The term 'Bolshevist' is inapplicable to the Stalinist dictatorship but that is not under discussion here. See Orlando Figes, *A People's Tragedy: The Russian Revolution 1891–1924* (London, 1996).

28 Georges Fülgraff, Dieter Palm, *Pharmakotherapie, Klinische Pharmakologie* (Stuttgart, 1997), p. 77.

29 Alfred Springer, 'Arzneimittelmissbrauch', in *Österreichische Apothekerzeitung* 25 (2001). Barbiturates are mildly stimulating but also sedative and ultimately soporific. Habituation occurs after a few days of regular intake, even with relatively low doses. With long-term intake the initial sedative effect can be replaced by a stimulating and euphoric effect, which is the main reason for barbiturate dependence. If the dose is continuously increased, emotional and physical dependence can occur. See Fülgraff, Palm, p. 77, and Pschyrembel, 257th edn, p. 159. Barbiturate withdrawal can create life-threatening situations. The use of barbiturates can damage various organs such as the liver, brain and nervous system, and can result in severely altered behaviour, confusion and psychosis.

30 Personal statement.

31 The slivovitz, a gift from the Croatian dictator Ante Pavelic, was analysed by Morell. The only questionable substance found in it was an insignificant amount of fusel oil.

32 Morell's diary entry for 3 November 1944.

33 Diary entries for 2 and 19 April 1943 and Morell's notes for January to April 1945.

34 *Gesetz über den Verkehr mit Betäubungsmitteln, Anlage III (zu § 1 Abs. 1), verkehrsfähige und verschreibungsfähige Betäubungsmittel*, BGBl. I (2001), pp. 1189–95.

35 Morell's diary entry for 18 April 1945.

36 Pschyrembel, 257th edn, p. 56.
37 Ralf Georg Reuth (ed.), *Joseph Goebbels: Tagebücher*, 5 vols (Munich, 1992), p. 1921.
38 Erik Eggers, 'Peppige Panzerschokolade', in *Die Tageszeitung* (28 December 2006).
39 *Der Spiegel* 43 (1999), 222.
40 Leonhard and Renate Heston, *The Medical Casebook of Adolf Hitler* (London, 1979), pp. 104 ff., rev. and expanded edn. Leonhard L. Heston, *The Medical Casebook of Adolf Hitler* (Lincoln, NE, 2007), pp. 62–74.
41 Gibbels, *Hitlers Parkinson-Krankheit*, p. 2.
42 Anton Joachimsthaler (ed.), *Christa Schroeder: Er war mein Chef* (Munich, 1985), pp. 205–8.
43 Personal statement, Traudl Junge, 1997.
44 Schenck, *Patient Hitler*, pp. 447ff.
45 Fest, *Hitler*, ppp. 672–3 and p. 739.
46 Ian Kershaw, *Hitler: 1936–1945: Nemesis* (New York, 2000), p. 728.
47 Schenck, *Patient Hitler*, pp. 447ff.
48 Ibid. pp. 446ff.
49 Morell's diary entry for 27 October 1944.
50 'An der Nadel', *Der Spiegel* 7 (11 February 1980), 84–90.
51 Schenck, *Pharmaimperium*, pp. 428ff.
52 Heston, *Medical Casebook*, p. 84.
53 Morell's diary entry for 27 October 1944. He was to refer to this change in dose again later in his diary.
54 Morell stated on 19 December 1944 that Hitler had asked him for Pervitin. Hitler was well aware of the public discussion surrounding this substance. It is possible that in his exhaustion he now wanted to try it out. Whatever the case, Morell mentioned it by name only once in his diaries. See entry for 19 December.
55 Schenck, *Patient Hitler*, p. 448.
56 Heston, *Medical Casebook*, pp. 39ff.
57 The *Hexenmittel* include incenses, bath oils, salves (e.g. marigold or St John's wort), elixirs and tinctures. St John's wort is the herbal medicine par excellence.
58 Seminars on *Hexenmittel* in homeopathy are offered by numerous institutions specializing in natural healing.
59 Lutz Roth, Max Daunderer, Kurt Kormann, *Giftpflanzen, Pflanzengifte* (Landsberg am Lech, 1994), pp. 509ff, 683–5.
60 Ernst Günther Schenck, 'Die Medikamente und die medikamentöse Therapie Dr. Th. Morells bei Hitler', report written for David Irving in 1969. See Irving, *The Secret Diaries*, p. 169.
61 Hans Eppinger, 'Pneumonie und Kreislauf', in *Deutsche Medizinische Wochenschrift* (1940), 867.
62 SS-Chefapotheker Carl Blumenreuter analysed the contents of the anti-gas pills to determine the amount of strychnine in them. Schenck, *Patient Hitler*, p. 201.
63 GEHE Codex, 7th edn (1937), p. 82.
64 Ibid. According to Blumenreuter, one pill contained 0.00029 g strychnine. According to the GEHE Codex, 120 anti-gas pills contained 0.5 g

strychnine and atropine in equal parts, so that one pill by this reckoning would contain 0.00416 g strychnine.

65 Louis Lewin, *Gifte und Vergiftungen: Lehrbuch der Toxikologie* (Berlin, 1929), p. 791.
66 Fülgraff and Palm, *Pharmakotherapie*, p. 77.
67 Morell's entries for Eukodal in 1943 and 1944.
68 Morell's diary entry for 30 October 1944.
69 'Oxycodon (Oxygesic®): Missbrauch, Abhängigkeit und tödliche Folgen durch Injektion zerstossener Retardtabletten, Bundeskammer Mitteilungen', in *Deutsches Ärzteblatt* 100, vol. 36 (5 September 2003), A 2326–7. Reference to SCRIP: Perdue to reformulate OxyContin, SCRIP No. 2669 (15 August 2001 c), 20.
70 Fülgraff, *Pharmakotherapie*, p. 77.
71 After the assassination attempt on 20 July 1944, Dr Erwin Giesing was summoned to treat the injury to Hitler's eardrum. He also took charge of treating the sinusitis that occurred in August 1944.

## 5  HITLER'S MEDICAL HISTORY

1 Three of Hitler's siblings died within a single year. His brother Gustav died of diphtheria on 8 December 1887 and his sister Ida of the same disease on 2 January 1888. Brother Otto died three days after birth.
2 Hitler, *Mein Kampf*, p. 16. According to Hitler, his father died at the age of sixty-five of a stroke. According to the register of deaths in Leonding (copy), Alois Hitler died on 3 January 1903 of 'bleeding of the lungs' (Bundesarchiv Koblenz NS 36/65, sheet 84). Kubizek wrote that Hitler's father collapsed silently in the local tavern and had died before a doctor or priest could be called (Kubizek, *Young Hitler*, p. 24).
3 Hitler's mother died on 21 December 1907. Hitler's grief at the loss of his mother is described by Dr Eduard Bloch, the family's Jewish doctor. Contrary to his customary practice of discarding mail from patients, Dr Bloch kept both of the greeting cards from Hitler 'as a souvenir of a brave and model son, who showed love and devotion for his stalwart mother', as he put it in a letter of 7 November 1938 (Bundesarchiv Koblenz NS 26/65, sheets 93–5). Bloch testifies to the close relationship between mother and son. Hitler's youthful friend Kubizek later confirmed Bloch's observation. 'Adolf really loved his mother. I swear to it before God and man … When we lived together in Vienna he always carried his mother's portrait with him.' Kubizek, *Young Hitler*, p. 19.
4 Maser, *Legende*.
5 Speer, *Inside the Third Reich*, p. 106.
6 Joachim Fest considered that this incessant fear of a premature death drove Hitler forward, and the haste with which Hitler prepared for war was dictated by this fear. Fest, *Hitler*, pp. 539 ff.
7 Schenck, *Patient Hitler*, pp. 294f.
8 Werner Maser, *Legende*, corrected in later editions.
9 Irving, *Wie krank war Hitler wirklich?*, p. 23.
10 David Irving, 'Hitlers Krankheiten', in *Stern* 25 (1969), 157; *Die geheimen Tagebücher des Dr. Morell*.

11 Maser, *Legende*. Morell noted in his examination in 1936: 'Scarring of the tonsils probably due to tonsillitis in childhood.'

12 On 4 October 1944, Morell noted: 'Staff doctor Giesing called because of ... redness of the tonsils ... which also (had) suppurating plugs.' Giesing pressed out the tonsils to remove the plugs and inflammatory residue.

13 Dr Eduard Bloch, 'My Patient Hitler', article in *Collier's Weekly*, 15 March 1941.

14 Ibid. 'Possibly his tonsils would be inflamed. He would stand obedient and unflinching while I depressed his tongue and swabbed the trouble spots.'

15 Unless a partial tonsillectomy was performed, which is unlikely.

16 Hitler, *Mein Kampf*, p. 17.

17 Schenck, *Patient Hitler*, pp. 294ff. 'His father's legacy, pulmonary phthisis, caught up with him.' Alois Hitler is supposed once to have had a pulmonary haemorrhage that might have been indicative of tuberculosis.

18 Hitler, *Mein Kampf*, p. 17.

19 Kubizek, *Young Hitler*, p. 29. 'As far as I can remember, his illness was actually some lung trouble. I know that for a long time afterwards he was plagued by coughs and nasty catarrhs.'

20 Heiko Magnussen and Georg Kanzow, 'Atemwege', in Heiner Greten, *Innere Medizin: Verstehen – Lernen – Anwenden*, 11th edn (Stuttgart, 2002), pp. 411–39. This article describes the causes, symptoms, diagnosis and treatment of pulmonary and respiratory diseases. The 'serious lung ailment' that Hitler claims to have had in 1905 cannot be identified and at best represents a subjective experience of a disorder or illness, but does not correspond to a specific pathology.

21 Kubizek, *Young Hitler*, p. 12.

22 Maser, *Legende*.

23 Maser, *Fälschung, Dichtung und Wahrheit*, p. 428.

24 Hans-Jürgen Stellbrink, Pramod M. Shah, 'Infektionskrankheiten', in Greten (ed.), *Innere Medizin*, p. 690.

25 Werner Maser, *Adolf Hitler: Das Ende der Führer-Legende* (Düsseldorf, 1980), pp. 351–66.

26 The diaries were made available to Werner Maser and published for the first time in 1975. Maser's footnotes clearly indicate that he was unaware of Dermietzel's identity and that here too he was obliged to give credence to Giesing's imagined explanation. Werner Maser (ed.), *Paul Devrient: Mein Schüler Adolf Hitler – Das Tagebuch seines Lehrers* (Munich, 2003).

27 Letters from the public, 1935, Russian State Military Archive (RGVA), Moscow, 1355 Opis 1 No. 15.

28 She is said to have had affairs among others with Rudolf Diels, the first head of the Gestapo, air force general Ernst Udet and Hitler's press secretary Ernst Hanfstaengl.

29 Archive of the Russian Ministry of Foreign Affairs, Hitler dossier.

30 Professor Rössle wrote to von Eicken on 21 August 1935: 'Finding: vocal cord polyp, confirmed benign and completely removed.' Six days later came a letter: 'I gratefully return the excised specimen for Adolf Müller. I examined some sections taken from the middle.' See Morell's notes.

31 Morell's diary entry for 17 November 1944.

32 Morell recorded the minor surgery in his diary: '11.30 a.m. F. feeling fine ... no discomfort. Injected 0.01 morphine and 0.0001 atropine

subcutaneously. 12.30 p.m. polyp operated on by von Eicken. Polyp as big as a lentil.'

33  Letter from Rössle to von Eicken, see Morell's records.

34  Irving, 'Hitler's Krankheiten', in *Stern* 26 (1969), 42–8.

35  Hans Adolf Jacobshagen (ed.), *Generaloberst Halder: Kriegstagebuch*, vol. 3, *Der Russlandfeldzug bis zum Marsch auf Stalingrad* (Stuttgart, 1964), p. 164.

36  Reuth (ed.), *Goebbels: Tagebücher*, p. 1653.

37  Nissle wrote to Morell on 8 August 1941 confirming receipt of the stool sample of 4 August and informed him of his findings: 'Manifold typical coliform bacteria cultures similar in properties to the original Mutaflor strain . . . no infectious bacteria.'

38  Morell's diary entry: Hitler was overcome by dizziness while in the map room on 7 August 1941. Morell was summoned and offered to give him a thorough examination, but Hitler refused saying he was fine. Morell was struck immediately by Hitler's tremor. Hitler also spoke of a constant buzzing in the left ear, but said that Professor von Eicken had found nothing. It is, of course, highly implausible that Morell was hearing about this buzzing for the first time if von Eicken had already been consulted.

39  According to Morell's diary entry for 7 August 1941, he started keeping a detailed record of his patient's daily state of health because Hitler had been looking tired and exhausted for some time; he was noticeably pale and also felt 'under the weather' in Ukraine. Hitler told his personal physician that he had recently been getting immensely worked up and had been feeling pretty low since then. The rows at the headquarters had got to his stomach and caused it to become upset again.

40  Dysentery is also known as shigellosis and is a reportable infectious disease caused by bacteria of the Shigella genus and mainly affecting the large intestine.

41  Irving, *Wie krank war Hitler wirklich?*, pp. 37f.

42  For an assessment of the persons involved see Erich von Manstein, *Lost Victories* (London, 2005), pp. 67–71.

43  Hans-Dieter Otto, *Lexikon fataler Fehlentscheidungen im Zweiten Weltkrieg: von Alpenfestung bis Zitadelle* (Munich, 2006), pp. 123–5.

44  Kershaw, *Fateful Choices*, pp. 263ff.

45  A rivalry existed between Morell and Giesing from the outset, because on their first meeting Giesing had failed to show the respect that Morell thought he was due as the Führer's personal physician.

46  According to Morell's records, Hitler caught a cold from his hairdresser on 15 rather than 17 August. He makes no mention of Giesing's almost daily cocaine treatment and in fact mentions Giesing himself only three times and never in connection with cocaine. Morell mentions cocaine but only as a 1 per cent eye drop solution. He was either unaware of Giesing's 10 per cent solution or chose to ignore it.

47  See Morell's diary entry for 20 September 1944. According to Morell, Hitler was X-rayed not on 19 September but a day later. He noted: 'Maxillary sinus X-ray, shadow left.' He did not have pansinusitis but just left-side 'acute maxillary sinusitis', which von Eicken treated by irrigation. The surviving X-rays today show a parietal shadow, indicative not of acute but rather chronic maxillary sinusitis. All of the other sinuses were clear. The folllow-up

X-ray on 21 October showed only a lateral shadow in the left maxillary sinus, prompting von Eicken to consider discontinuing the irrigation.

48 See Morell's diary entry for 27 September 1944. He said he wanted to examine Hitler on the following day, but was once again refused on 28 September. Instead Morell writes: '6.30 p.m. Führer sent for me, said he was suffering from violent spasms. Eukodal-Eupaverin injections', underlined in Morell's diary.

49 See Morell's diary entry for 29 September 1944. Morell did not share Giesing's suspicion of jaundice and was furious with the ear, nose and throat specialist. By confining Hitler to bed without visitors, he was able to keep the attendant physicians away. This also prevented Giesing from visiting Hitler, who apparently needed his cocaine treatment every day and was now in danger, according to Giesing, of becoming addicted. The fact that Hitler said nothing about Giesing's absence would appear to contradict the suggestion that he was dependent. Hitler demanded constant attention from Morell, summoning him at 1.30 a.m., 11.50 a.m., 4 p.m., 8.30 p.m. and 11.45 p.m. On the last visit Morell noted with satisfaction: 'He stayed confined to bed all day and ate nothing.'

50 See Morell's diary entry for 1 October 1944. It is clear that Morell was worried by Hitler's jaundiced appearance. He made a note of the way Hitler looked almost every day. He commented on an improvement at the end of September and wrote on 2 October: 'The yellow skin coloration has gone.'

51 See Morell's diary entries. On 6 September, before Hitler's jaundice, the urine values were normal. There were slight abnormalities on 3 October. The analysis on 10 November showed traces of urobilinogen (bile pigment; bilirubin by-product), while the analysis on 30 November was completely normal.

52 See Morell's diary entry for 3 October 1944. Brandt approached Morell on 30 September because he, like Giesing and von Hasselbach, believed that Morell was responsible for Hitler's intoxication symptoms. Morell noted the contents of his conversation with Brandt on 3 October 1944 in detail.

53 Greten (ed.), *Innere Medizin*, pp. 771–81.

54 Pschyrembel, 259th edn, p. 1752.

55 See Morell's diary entries for September and October 1944.

56 See Morell's diary entry from 10 December 1944: 'Führer (to von Eicken): Dr Giesing should have seen the polyps. Von Eicken somewhat embarrassed, told a story about a professor who had failed to treat Kaiser W. II correctly' and had left some of the polyp. He might have been referring to his father, Kaiser Frederick III, whose English doctor Morell Mackenzie mistook cancer for a polyp on the vocal cord.

57 Irving, *Secret Diaries*, p. 179.

58 Letter by Martin Bormann of 10 October 1944 to Reich Press Chief: 'Dear Dr Dietrich, Professor Dr Brandt left the Führer's service as an attendant physician because of his activity as Reich Commissar with effect from 10 October 1944, the same for Professor Dr von Hasselbach, who deputized for him for some time. The Führer has appointed SS-Obersturmbannführer Dr Stumpfegger as attendant physician with effect from 10 October 1944.'

59 Morell's diary entry for 13 October 1944.

60 Morell's diary entry for 8 November 1944.

61  Morell's diary entry for 14 October 1944. Morell used different letterheads. The infectious material he submitted for microbiological analysis was headed 'Prof. Dr. med. Theo Morell, Führer headquarters', whereas on other occasions he wrote 'Personal physician to the Führer'.
62  Morell's diary entry, 2 p.m. on 17 October 1944.
63  Irving, *Wie krank war Hitler eigentlich?*, p. 19.
64  Wolfgang F. Caspary, Till Wehrmann, 'Dünn- und Dickdarm', in Greten (ed.), *Innere Medizin*, pp. 741–3.
65  Pschyrembel, 259th edn, pp. 1370–1.
66  Wolfgang F. Caspary, Till Wehrmann, 'Dünn- und Dickdarm', in Greten (ed.), *Innere Medizin*, pp. 742f.
67  Pschyrembel, 259th edn, p. 1592.
68  This was the first form to be diagnosed, hence the name porphyria, the Greek word for purple. The red coloration occurs mainly with erythropoietic porphyria.
69  John C. G. Röhl, Martin Warren, David Hunt, *Purple Secret: Genes 'Madness' and the Royal Houses of Europe* (London, 1998). The British historian John Röhl shows that some family members of the royal houses of England, Hanover and Prussia have suffered for centuries from this hereditary disease. The English king George III, who went insane, was found in 1810 to have it, and porphyria can be traced back to James I (1566–1625). It was passed on to the house of Hanover by James' eldest daughter Elizabeth, whose eldest daughter Sophia married Prince Elector Ernest Augustus I of Hanover. Following the marriage of Sophia Charlotte to Prince Elector Frederick III of Brandenburg (later King Frederick I), the disease was passed on to Prussia. The first victim of the disease was probably the 'soldier king' Frederick William I. His eldest son, Frederick the Great, was also thought to have suffered from the disease. See Hans-Joachim Neumann, *Friedrich der Grosse* (Berlin, 2000), pp. 52ff.
70  Non-diagnosed diabetes can produce symptoms similar to irritable bowel syndrome.
71  Morell had Hitler's blood sugar checked (normal range according to Seiffert 90–120 mg/dl). Hitler's blood sugar was consistently in this range.
72  The request for stool analyses continued until 1945.
73  Heston, *Medical Casebook*. The Hestons do not indicate when Hitler became a vegetarian.
74  Susann Witt-Stahl (on behalf of the Vegetarierbund), *Tierschutz als Propagandawaffe* (2002).
75  Maser, *Legend*.
76  Ibid. p. 316. As related personally to Professor Werner Maser in 1967.
77  Personal written statement by Professor Dr Wolfgang Eisenmenger in 2007. When the Munich police district 5 was informed at 10.45 a.m. on 19 September 1931 that Angela Raubal had been found shot in her room on Prinzregentenplatz, the police investigation began by questioning all of the staff, but this inquiry produced no results. It is interesting to note that Hitler's pistol, which had been in an unlocked cupboard, was now missing. When the police forced the door open, they found Geli lying dead on the floor. Police doctor Dr Müller noted that death had occurred through a bullet to the lung that missed the heart. The body was released for burial by the public prosecutor's office on 21 September.

78 Personal statement in 1997 and written notification in 2002.
79 Schenk, *Patient Hitler*, pp. 34–42. If Hitler became a full vegetarian in 1931, he must have been a partial vegetarian before that. Ernst Hanfstaengl found Hitler's sweet tooth puzzling and spoke of his 'cake vegetarianism'. It is well known that Hitler tended towards a vegetarian diet from early on. The proprietor of the Elephanten in Weimar had created a Weimar bread soup specially for him, which Hitler highly appreciated.
80 Written notification by Cosima Wagner's biographer Oliver Hilmes on 19 January 2009, who claims that, like many other Wagner –isms, a lot was made of vegetarianism. They spoke of vegetarianism but ate poultry! In a work entitled *Religion und Kunst* published in 1880, Richard Wagner himself indicated ways of countering the 'degeneration of humanity'. Apart from a 'plant diet' and associations for the 'protection of animals' he recommended pacifism, socialism and art as means for 'restoring a lost paradise'. See Dieter David Scholz, *Richard Wagners Antisemitismus* (Würzburg, 1993), pp. 171f.
81 Hans-Jürgen Teuteberg, 'Zur Sozialgeschichte des Vegetarismus', in *Vierteljahrschrift für Sozial- und Wirtschaftsgeschichte* 81 (1994), 43ff. The term 'conservative revolution' coined by Armin Mohler is not under discussion here.
82 Written statement by Monika Gross in 2007.
83 Otto Strasser, *Hitler and I*, p. 5. A French translation of the charge against Hitler appeared in 1940 and contained several errors but interesting insights into Hitler's understanding of socialism.
84 Eugen Dollmann, *Dolmetscher der Diktatoren* (Bayreuth, 1963), p. 17.
85 Personal statement by Traudl Junge, 1997.
86 Eberle, Uhl, *Hitler Book*, p. 438.
87 Bovine spongiform encephalopathy (BSE) was widespread in the 1990s, particularly in Great Britain. It resulted in a prohibition on feeding cattle with animal protein – a prohibition that was later lifted by the EU – and a more professional approach to organic farming.
88 Written notification, 1998.
89 Hitler received letters of condolence from the population when political opponents poisoned his dog Wolf. See Eberle, *Letters to Hitler*, p. 89.
90 In autumn 1940 Hitler ordered a commission to seek a site for his new headquarters in the forest east of Rastenburg (now Kętrzyn) in East Prussia close to the Soviet border. The site on the northern edge of the Masurian Lake District was also suitable in terms of security because the dense old mixed forest away from major transport routes and the large Masurian lakes from Angerburg (Węgorzewo) to Johannisburg (Pisz) formed a natural barrier. The original headquarters, codenamed Chemische Werke Askania, were built by Organisation Todt (O. T.), which was set up in 1938 and named after Reich Minister Fritz Todt, General Inspector for German Roadways. See Seidler, *Führerhauptquartiere*, n. 128, p. 378.
91 Irving, *Wie krank war Hitler wirklich?*, pp. 36f.
92 Oedemas are painless non-reddened swellings caused by the accumulation of fluid in the intercellular tissue space in patients with cardiac insufficiency. In the case of right ventricular failure they are found above all on the ankles and in front of the tibia; with left ventricular failure they occur in the form of pulmonary oedema.

93 Morell's diary entry for 14 August 1941.
94 A glycoside that has a positive inotropic effect on the heart (in the event of insufficiency, for example). It is obtained from the common foxglove (*Digitalis purpurea*).
95 Letter from Professor Arthur Weber of 20 August 1941 to Professor Morell with the ECG findings.
96 Classification of arterial hypertension (according to Chobanian et al., 2003); European Society of Hypertension/European Society of Cardiology Guidelines Committee, 2003. For introduction see Holger Reinecke, Thomas Budde, Günter Breithardt, 'Koronäre Herzkrankheit', in Greten, *Innere Medizin*, pp. 31–54.
97 Professor Arthur Weber's report with accompanying letter to Morell on 17 May 1943.
98 Weber's last ECG report in Morell's diary entry for 4 December 1944.
99 Personal statement by Dr Swertlana Möller, 2008.
100 See classification of arterial hypertension (according to Chobinian et al., 2003). European Society of Hypertension European Society of Cardiology Guidelines Committee, 2003.
101 Pschyrembel, 259th edn, p. 746.
102 Blood pressure is measured in Europe in millimetres of mercury using a sphygmomanometer developed by Scipione Riva-Rocci (RR). A pressure of 1 mmHg is equivalent to 1 torr, named after Evangelista Torricelli, a student of Galileo Galilei. In SI units, 1 mmHg or 1 torr is equivalent to around 1.33 hectopascals.
103 WHO Guidelines Subcommittee 1999, *Guidelines for treatment of arterial hypertension*, Deutsche Hochdruckliga e V; Deutsche Hypertoniegesellschaft.
104 Morell's diary entries, blood pressure readings, 1944.
105 This incorrect assessment caused tension in the Allied headquarters because it was the Americans who had stopped the offensive. Montgomery's assumptions in general often proved to be wrong and arrogant with respect to the Americans. Gerhard L. Weinberg, *A World At Arms: A Global History of World War II* (Cambridge, 1994), pp. 768 ff.
106 Morell's diary entry for 15 and 18 August 1941.
107 Expert opinion by Dr Joseph Brinsteiner (family and district doctor) of 8 January 1924 to the administration of Landsberg prison. See Katz, *Morell*, pp. 346f.
108 See Gibbels, *Hitler's Parkinson-Krankheit*.
109 Personal statement, 1997.
110 Ellen Gibbels, 'Hitlers Nervenleiden – Differentialdiagnose des Parkinson-Syndroms', in *Fortschritte der Neurologie – Psychiatrie* 57 (Stuttgart, 1989), 505–17.
111 Report by Professor Dr. med. Karl Brandt: Theo Morell (Oberursel, 19 September 1945). See BA Koblenz, Kl. Erw. 411–3.
112 See Morell's diary entries for 1941–5.
113 Heston, *Medical Casebook*, pp. 96–100.
114 Gibbels, 'Hitlers Parkinson-Krankheit', pp. 91f.
115 Linge, *Bis zum Ende*, p. 40.
116 Albert Zoller, *Hitler privat nach den Aufzeichnungen seiner Sekretärin* (Düsseldorf, 1949), p. 3.

117 Joachimsthaler (ed.), *Christa Schroeder*, p. 71.
118 Personal statement, 1997.
119 Hanskarl von Hasselbach: comments on Hugh R. Trevor-Roper's book *The Last Days of Hitler*. Quoted in Schenck, *Patient Hitler*, p. 304.
120 Jochen von Lang (ed.), *Henry Picker und Heinrich Hoffmann, Hitlers Tischgespräche im Bild* (Stuttgart, Hamburg, 1969), pp. 39, 54 and 59.
121 Irving, 'Hitlers Krankheiten', in *Stern* 26, 27 (1969).
122 When the Führer's Chancellery was offered a Continental typewriter with extra-large type by Wanderer-Werke Chemnitz in 1936, the adjutant's office replied that it was not required because it already had a similar machine. These typewriters were normally designed for speech manuscripts. RGVA Moscow Fund 1355 Opis 1 Delo 15, sheet 282f.
123 Diary entry for 22 July 1942.
124 Personal statement by Karin Sallmon, ophthalmologist, Berlin.
125 Letter to Professor Morell and eye examination findings by Professor Walter Löhlein of 2 March 1944.
126 Professor Löhlein's report on Hitler's eye examination on 7 April 1945.
127 Joachimsthaler, *Hitlers Ende ohne Mythos*, pp. 380f.
128 BA Berlin (former Document Centre), SS-O no. 75, personal file Blaschke, Hugo.
129 Bezymenski, *Death of Adolf Hitler*; Blaschke quoted in Schenck, *Patient Hitler*, pp. 311ff.
130 For the state of dentistry at the time see Georg Axhausen, *Allgemeine Chirurgie in der Zahn-, Mund- und Kieferheilkunde*, 3rd edn (Munich, 1947) and Wolfgang Rosenthal, Walter Hoffmann-Axhelm, Alexander Bienengräber, *Spezielle Zahn-, Mund- und Kieferchirurgie*, 2nd edn (Leipzig, 1963).

**6 HITLER'S HEALTH AND THE WAR**

1 Kershaw, *Hitler Myth*, pp. 151–68.
2 Andreas Hillgruber, *Hitlers Strategie: Politik und Kriegsführung 1940–1941* (Munich, 1982); Stefan Scheil, *Die Eskalation des Zweiten Weltkriegs* (Munich, 2005).
3 Hubatsch, *Hitlers Weisungen*, pp. 84f.
4 Discussion on the number of victims continues. The precise number of deaths in the war between the German Reich and the Soviet Union has still not been determined because Russian historians believe that the victims of Stalin's repressive measures were included with the deaths at the hands of the Germans. At the same time, the number of victims was scaled down in Soviet statistics so that the extent of the disaster would not be apparent. The research by Russian historians is not likely to reduce the number of victims of the war in Europe as a whole – on the contrary.
5 Schenck, *Patient Hitler*, pp. 21f; Trevor-Roper, *Last Days*, p. 105.
6 Hitler, *Mein Kampf*, p. 620.
7 Morell's diary entries from 7 August 1941 onwards.
8 Morell's diary entry for 7 August 1941.
9 Nicolaus von Below, *At Hitler's Side: The Memoirs of Hitler's Luftwaffe Adjutant, 1937–1945* (London, 2001), p. 109.

10 In 1989 Ernst Günther Schenck claimed that there was a remote hint in Morell's notes of 7 August regarding 'facial spasms with rush of blood to the temples' to back von Below's assertion, although there is no mention whatsoever of a stroke. Schenck, *Patient Hitler*, pp. 336f.
11 Morell's diary entry for 8 August 1941.
12 When Hermann Göring once addressed him jokingly as the 'Reich Injection Master', Morell was unsure whether it was meant ironically or as a compliment. At all events he didn't like it.
13 Morell's diary entry for 8 August 1941.
14 Morell's diary entry for 9 August 1941.
15 Morell's diary entry for 11 August 1941.
16 Ibid.
17 Morell's diary entry for 14 August 1941 including thorough examination of Hitler and ECG.
18 Morell's diary entry for 18 August 1941. Morell mentioned the poor conditions in the bunkers on several occasions, but he was powerless to do anything about them.
19 Morell's diary entries for 19 and 20 August 1941.
20 Morell's diary entries for 21 to 25 August 1941.
21 Morell's diary entry for 29 August 1941.
22 Friedländer, *Years of Extermination*, p. 251.
23 See Chapter 2.
24 Peter Bor, *Gespräche mit Halder* (Wiesbaden, 1950), p. 201.
25 Geoffrey P. Megargee, *Inside Hitler's High Command* (Lawrence, KS, 2000), p. 133; Kershaw, *Hitler*, pp. 641–8.
26 It was not in fact until 19 July 1941 that the Stavka Verkhovnovo Glavkomandovaniya – headquarters of the supreme high command – was headed by Stalin, who was appointed People's Commissar for Defence on this date. The military command of the war was assumed by his deputy Marshal Georgi Konstantinovich Zhukov, who also took the salute at the victory parade in Red Square in 1945. The Soviet Union thus implemented the principle of politico-military dual leadership that many high-ranking German generals also regarded as an ideal form of organization.
27 Other authors plausibly claim that the German army simply underestimated the effects of the mud, in other words that the timetable for the operation was also overly optimistic. See Heinz Magenheimer, *Hitler's War: Germany's Key Strategic Decisions 1940–1945* (London, 1998), pp. 114–15.
28 Megargee, *Inside*, pp. 142–70.
29 Geoffrey Roberts, *Stalin's Wars: From World War to Cold War, 1939–1953* (Hartford, 2008), p. 112.
30 Hans-Dieter Otto, *Lexikon*, pp. 141–7.
31 Magenheimer, *Hitler's War*, p. 120.
32 Kershaw, *Fateful Choices: Ten Decisions that Changed the World* (London, 2007), p. 329.
33 Magenheimer, *Hitler's War*, p. 130.
34 Roberts, *Stalin's Wars*, p. 116.
35 Hubatsch, *Hitlers Weisungen*, pp. 183f.
36 Roberts, *Stalin's Wars*, pp. 121–6.
37 Carbolineum is a mixture of coal tar components. It contains phenols and

other aromatic hydrocarbons. It is now seldom used because of its carcino-genicity and the frequently observed skin irritations associated with it.

38 Morell's diary entries in July 1942.

39 'Weisung Nr. 45, Fortsetzung der Operation "Braunschweig"', in Hubatsch, *Hitlers Weisungen*, pp. 196ff.

40 Quoted in Torsten Dietrich, *Paulus: Das Drama von Stalingrad* (Paderborn et al., 2008), p. 223.

41 As commander of Army Group F, von Weichs abandoned Yugoslavia in autumn 1944 but stated that the retreat was caused by the enemy troops.

42 Dietrich, *Paulus*, pp. 224ff.

43 Unlike Hitler, who interfered increasingly in the planning, Stalin left the organization of the counter-offensive to Zhukov and the general staff, reserving the right only to make the final decision. See Richard Overy, *Why The Allies Won* (New York, 1997), pp. 87 ff.

44 Manstein, *Lost Victories*, pp. 369 ff.

45 Morell's diary entries for 9 and 15 December 1942.

46 Morell's diary entry for 17 December 1942.

47 This opinion was voiced in an interview in 1949 with the secretary Christa Schroeder by Albert Zoller, who subsequently proceeded to publish an unauthorized version of her memoirs.

48 Reuth, *Goebbels: Tagebücher*, p. 1904.

49 Manstein, *Lost Victories*, pp. 407 ff.

50 In view of Germany's geographical position in the centre of Europe, the German general staff had always contemplated a war on two fronts. The corresponding scenarios allowed for the high risk required for a possible or probable but then often spectacular success. The Schleiffen Plan in the First World War was one occasion when the risk failed to pay off. The campaign in France, by contrast, was an example of a successful venture.

51 Reuth, *Goebbels Tagebücher*, p. 1907.

52 Ibid.

53 Magenheimer, *Militärstrategie*, pp. 210–34.

54 Roberts, *Stalin's Wars*, pp. 165–8.

55 Bernd Wegner, 'Die Genese der Kursker Schlacht', in Frieser (ed.), *Die Ostfront*, pp. 61–79.

56 Morell's diary entry for 28 May 1943.

57 Morell's diary entry for 20 June 1943.

58 Frieser, 'Die Schlacht im Kursker Bogen', in Frieser (ed.), *Ostfront*, p. 83.

59 Quoted in Magenheimer, *Militärstrategie*, p. 220.

60 Frieser, 'Die Schacht im Kursker Bogen', pp. 83–203.

61 Eberle, Uhl, *Hitler Book*, p. 219.

62 Andreas Hillgruber (ed.), *Staatsmänner und Diplomaten bei Hitler*, vol. 2 (Frankfurt a. M., 1970), pp. 287–300.

63 Morell's diary entry for 19 July 1943.

64 Lutz Klinkhammer, *Zwischen Bündnis und Besatzung: Das nationalsozia-listische Deutschland und die Republik von Salò* (Tübingen, 1993).

65 Reuth, *Goebbels Tagebücher*, p. 1956; Morell's diary entries for September 1943.

66 Morell's diary entry for 27 January 1944; Eberle, Uhl, *Hitler Book*, pp. 238f.

67 Morell's diary entries for 11 and 22 February 1944.

68 Ulrich Chaussy, Christoph Prüschner, *Nachbar Hitler: Führerkult und Heimatzerstörung am Obersalzberg* (Berlin, 2004); Bernhard Frank, *Geheime Regierungsstadt Hitlers – Obersalzberg* (Berchtesgaden, 2004).

69 Although it is not possible here to discuss the development of a German atomic bomb, Hitler was also optimistic about its prospects. See Rainer Karlsch, *Hitlers Bombe: Die geheime Geschichte der deutschen Kernwaffenversuche* (Munich, 2005).

70 Overy, *Why the Allies Won*, pp. 5–6. Luftwaffe adjutant von Below cited even higher losses in production (von Below, *At Hitler's Side*, pp. 193–4). Several regional research projects are currently in progress on the transfer of the German armaments industry to underground factories.

71 Frieser, 'Der Zusammenbruch im Osten', in Frieser (ed.), *Ostfront*, p. 522.

72 Führerbefehl Nr. 11, Hubatsch, *Hitlers Weisungen*, p. 243.

73 Waldemar Erfurth, *Die Geschichte des Deutschen Generalstabes 1918–1945* (Hamburg, 2001), reprint of 1960 edn, p. 297.

74 Morell's diary entry for 9 May 1944.

75 Morell's diary entry for 23 May. 1944.

76 For discussion of Operation Neptune, see Horst Boog (ed.), *Germany and the Second World War, Volume VII: The Strategic Air War in Europe and the War in the West and East Asia 1943–44/45* (Oxford, 2006); John Keegan, *Six Armies in Normandy: From D-Day to the Liberation of Paris* (Harmondsworth, 1982).

77 Eberle, Uhl, *Hitler Book*, p. 264.

78 Reuth, *Goebbels Tagebücher*, p. 2065f.

79 Overy, *Why the Allies Won*, p. 134–80.

80 Frieser (ed.), *Ostfront*, p. 533ff.

81 The fact that the Soviet troops stopped before Warsaw has frequently been seen to have set the course for the future Communist dominion in Poland. Stalin is thought to have ordered the swing northwards to enable the Germans to put down the Warsaw uprising. Military objectives must also have played a role, however.

82 Erfurth, *Generalstab*, p. 297.

83 Zone defence called for the front-line troops to retreat to secondary positions in the face of enemy artillery fire. This caused the enemy to move out of the range of its own artillery into the opponent's ideal firing range. A classic example of the astonishing success achieved by this tactic in the Second World War is the Battle of Seelow Heights in April 1945, in which Marshal Zhukov's troops ran right into the General Gotthard Heinrici's 'drawn sword'. See Frieser (ed.), *Ostfront*, p. 524.

84 Hoffmann, *German Resistance*, p. 404.

85 Below, *At Hitler's Side*, p.196.

86 In this way, for example, Arthur Nebe, head of the Office of the Reich Criminal Police, had already heard of the failed attempt by 1.15 p.m. He took advantage of this advice to obliterate any links connecting him with the conspirators.

87 Domarus, *Speeches and Proclamations*, vol. 4, p. 2925.

88 Admiral Wilhelm Canaris, long-standing head of the Abwehr, died in Flossenbürg concentration camp. His successor Georg Hansen was sentenced to death on 10 August 1944 by the People's Court along with Erich

Fellgiebel, Fritz Dietlof Graf von der Schulenburg and Berthold Graf von Stauffenberg.

89  Domarus, *Speeches and Proclamations,* vol. 4, p. 2926.
90  There are several versions of this comment by Hitler. This quote comes from David Irving, *Hitler's War* (London, 2002), p. 710.
91  Personal statement by Traudl Junge, 1997. Other authors also cite similar comments by Hitler.
92  According to Schenck this examination took place not in Rastenburg but in the Führer headquarters with a portable X-ray machine.
93  Hermann Jung, *Die Ardennen-Offensive 1944/45: Ein Beispiel für die Kriegführung Hitlers* (Göttingen, 1992), p. 101.
94  Warlimont, *Im Hauptquartier der deutschen Wehrmacht 1939–1945* (Augsburg, 1990), p. 505; Jung, *Ardennen-Offensive,* p. 102.
95  Around 400,000 British, French and Belgian troops had been cut off at Dunkirk in May 1940, although the British managed to evacuate 300,000 members of their expeditionary force.
96  Jung, *Ardennen-Offensive,* p. 104.
97  See Chapter 5.
98  Morell's diary entries for 29 September and 6 December 1944.
99  Morell's diary entries for 1 a.m. on 1 October 1944.
100  Morell's diary entry for 9 p.m. on 2 October 1944.
101  Morell's diary entries for 14 to 31 October 1944.
102  Morell's diary entry for 30 October 1944.
103  In spite of the tense psychological situation, on 7 November Hitler stood up and pointed proudly to his shrunken abdomen. Göring's corpulence and lack of attention to himself clearly irritated him.
104  Seidler, *Die Führerhauptquartiere,* p. 324f.
105  Reuth, *Goebbels Tagebücher,* p. 2115.
106  Morell's diary entry for 10 December 1944.
107  The remains of the detonated headquarters were used to build the first houses in Wiesental, today part of the town of Butzbach in Hessen.
108  *Die Wehrmachtsberichte 1939–1945,* vol. 3, 1 January 1944 to 9 May 1945 (Cologne, 1989), p. 370f.
109  Morell's diary entry for 12 January 1945.
110  *Bekenntnisschrift* of 1812 in Hans Rothfels (ed.), *Carl von Clausewitz: Politische Schriften und Briefe* (Munich, 1922), p. 85.
111  Bernd Wegner, 'Choreographie des Untergangs', in Frieser (ed.), *Ostfront,* p. 1199–209.
112  Helmut Heiber (ed.), *Hitlers Lagerbesprechungen: Die Protokollfragmente seiner militärischen Konferenzen 1942–1945* (Stuttgart, 1962), p. 620.
113  Kershaw, *Hitler,* p. 852.
114  The deployment of powerful fighting units to Hungary appeared sensible from a military point of view as the territories, which had not been conquered until 1938, were in danger there. A further important consideration, however, was probably the fact that the deportation of Jews from Hungary had not yet finished, and Hitler repeatedly insisted on the complete extermination of the Hungarian Jews. See Longerich, *Holocaust,* pp. 405–10. Also Hitler's discussions with Prime Minister Sztójay on 7 June 1944, in Andreas Hillgruber (ed.), *Staatsmänner und Diplomaten bei Hitler,* vol. 2 (Frankfurt a. Main, 1970), p. 460–8.

115 Because of its fundamental importance, Hubatsch included this Führer command, although not described as such, in his list; see Hubatsch, *Hitlers Weisungen*, p. 300.

116 Irving, *Hitler's War*, p. 802.

117 Domarus, *Speeches and Proclamations*, p. 3008.

118 Hermann Giesler, *Ein anderer Hitler* (Leoni am Starnberger See, 1978), p. 478ff.

119 Irving, *Hitler's War*, p. 775.

120 Joachim Fest, Bernd Eichinger, *Der Untergang: Das Filmbuch* (Reinbek bei Hamburg, 2004).

121 Fest, 'Der Untergang: Eine historische Skizze', in ibid. p. 26.

122 Martin Moll, *'Führer-Erlasse' 1939–1945* (Stuttgart, 1997), p. 486f.

123 Ibid. p. 489f.

124 Morell's diary entry, Löhlein's findings, for 7 April 1945.

125 Morell's diary entry for 21 April 1945.

126 Eberle, Uhl, *Hitler Book*, p. 386.

127 Joachimsthaler, *Hitlers Ende*, p. 163.

128 The investigation reports by SMERSH were published on CD-ROM in 1995. See *Unknown Pages of the History of World War II: Hitler – Documents from KGB Secret Archives* (Moscow, 1995). The final report by the NKVD for Stalin was discovered in 2003 by the German historian Matthias Uhl. See Eberle, Uhl, *Hitler Book*, p. 465–84.

129 The film earned worldwide revenues of 92 million US dollars for producer Bernd Eichinger and it was seen in German cinemas by over 4.5 million people. It attracted seven million viewers when broadcast for the first time on television.

130 Eberle, Uhl, *Hitler Book*, p. 271.

131 NKVD investigation file of 31 May 1946, GARF 9401/552, sheet 552.

132 Eberle, Uhl, *Hitler Book*, p. 283.

133 According to Ernst Günther Schenck the capsules were made in the Waffen-SS Medical Service under Dr Carl Blumenreuter and not in Sachsenhausen concentration camp. See Schenck, *Patient Hitler*, p. 444f. Blumenreuter himself did not use the poison. He was released from British imprisonment in 1946 and worked as a hospital pharmacist in Schleswig-Holstein; Klee, *Personenlexikon*, p. 55.

134 Strasser, *Hitler and I*, p. 231.

135 Langer, *A Psychological Profile*.

136 Knuth, *Conhbnln Tagehiiehen*, p. 721.

137 Fest, *Hitler*, p. 747.

138 Personal statement by Traudl Junge, 1997; facsimile of will in Werner Maser, *Hitlers Briefe und Notizen – Sein Weltbild in handschriftlichen Briefen und Notizen* (Graz, 2002), pp. 357–75.

139 Dönitz naturally refused to accept highly compromised cabinet members and distanced himself from Hitler. (Dönitz, *Memoirs*, p. 446).

## 7 CONCLUDING DIAGNOSIS

1 Judgement by the Senate of the Federal Social Court of 30 October 1972, ref. 3RK93/71 Senate No. 3, in BSGE, vol. 35, pp. 10, 12.

2 Preamble to the Constitution of the World Health Organization signed on 22 July 1946.
3 This result comes from a representative nationwide survey in West Germany. Given the enduring attitudes, it is likely that a similar survey in East Germany would have produced comparable results. See E. Noelle, E. P. Neurmann, *Jahrbuch der öffentlichen Meinung 1947–1955* (Allensbach, 1956), p. 276.
4 Friedländer, *Years of Persecution*, pp. 111–12.

# SELECTED BIBLIOGRAPHY

ARCHIVES

BA Koblenz Nachlass Morell N 1348/4: The diaries of Hitler's personal physician Professor Theodor Morell
BA Koblenz Kleine Erwerbung: Statements by Brandt and von Hasselbach
BA Berlin (former Berlin Document Center) SSO: Personal documents on Hugo Blaschke, Dr Ludwig Stumpfegger
State Archive of the Russian Federation (GARF) Moscow Fund 9401, Opis 2: NKVD investigation on Hitler

Aly, Götz, *Hitlers Volksstaat: Raub, Rassenkrieg und nationaler Sozialismus* (Frankfurt a. M., 2005); available in English as *Hitler's Beneficiaries: Plunder, Racial War, and the Nazi Welfare State* (New York, 2006)
——(ed.), *Volkes Stimme: Skepsis und Führervertrauen im Nationalsozialismus* (Frankfurt a. M., 2007)
Aly, Götz and Susanne Heim, *Vordenker der Vernichtung: Auschwitz und die deutschen Pläne für eine neue europäische Ordnung* (Frankfurt a. M., 1997); available in English as *Architects of Annihilation: Auschwitz and the Logic of Destruction* (Princeton, 2002)
Arendt, Hannah, *The Origins of Totalitarianism* (Cleveland, 1958, first pub. 1950)
Armbruster, Jan, *Edmund Robert Forster (1878–1933): Lebensweg und Werk eines deutschen Nobelphysikers* (Husum, 2005)
*Arzneimittelkursbuch: Fakten und Vergleiche für mehr als 10 000 Medikamente* (Berlin, 1992)
*Arzneimittelverzeichnis*, 22nd edn (East Berlin, 1988)
Bajohr, Frank and Dieter Pohl, *Massenmord und schlechtes Gewissen: Die deutsche Bevölkerung, die NS-Führung und der Holocaust* (Munich, 2006)
Below, Nicolaus von, *Als Hitlers Adjutant 1937–45* (Mainz, 1980); available in English as *At Hitler's Side: The Memoirs of Hitler's Luftwaffe Adjutant, 1937–1945* (Barnsley, UK, 2006)
Benz, Wolfgang, *Die Juden in Deutschland 1933–1945: Leben unter nationalsozialistischer Herrschaft* (Munich, 1996)

229

——(ed.), *Dimension des Völkermordes: Die Zahl der jüdischen Opfer des Nationalsozialismus* (Munich, 1996)

Benz, Wolfgang and Werner Bergmann (eds), *Vorurteil und Völkermord: Entwicklungslinien des Antisemitismus* (Bonn, 1997)

Benz, Wolfgang et al., *Enzyklopädie des Nationalsozialismus* (Munich, 2001)

Benz, Wolfgang and Walter H. Pehle (eds), *Lexikon des deutschen Widerstandes* (Frankfurt a. M., 2001)

Bezymenski, Lev, *The Death of Adolf Hitler* (New York, 1968)

——*Stalin und Hitler: Das Pokerspiel der Diktatoren* (Berlin, 2006)

Boberach, Heinz (ed.), *Meldungen aus dem Reich 1938–1945: Die geheimen Lageberichte des Sicherheitsdienstes der SS*, 17 vols. (Herrsching, 1984)

Bräuninger, Werner, *Hitlers Kontrahenten in der NSDAP 1921–1945* (Munich, 2004)

Broszat, Martin, *Der Staat Hitlers: Grundlegung undEntwicklung seiner inneren Verfassung* (Munich, 2000, first pub. 1969); available in English as *The Hitler State: The Foundation and Development of the Internal Structure of the Third Reich* (London, 1981)

Browning, Christopher, *The Origins of the Final Solution: the Evolution of Nazi Jewish Policy, September 1939 – March 1942* (Jerusalem, 2004)

Dahrendorf, Ralf, *Versuchungen der Unfreiheit: Die Intellektuellen in Zeiten der Prüfung* (Munich, 2006)

Domarus, Max, *Hitler: Reden und Proklamationen 1932–1945, kommentiert von einem deutschen Zeitgenossen* (Munich, 1965); available in English as *Hitler: Speeches and Proclamations 1932–1945* (Mundelein, IL, 1990)

Ebbinghaus, Angelika and Klaus Dörner (eds), *Vernichten und Heilen: Der Nürnberger Ärzteprozess und seine Folgen* (Berlin, 2001)

Eberle, Henrik and Matthias Uhl, *Das Buch Hitler: Geheimdossier des NKWD für Josef W. Stalin, zusammengestellt aufgrund der Verhörprotokolle des Persönlichen Adjutanten Hitlers, Otto Günsche und des Kammerdieners Heinze Linge Moskau 1948/49* (Bergisch Gladbach, 2008, first pub. 2005); available in English as *The Hitler Book: The Secret Dossier Prepared for Stalin from the Interrogations of Hitler's Personal Aides* (London, 2005)

Evans, Richard J., *The Coming of the Third Reich* (New York, 2003)

——*The Third Reich in Power* (New York, 2005)

Falter, Jürgen, *Hitlers Wähler* (Munich, 1991)

Fest, Joachim C., *Das Gesicht des Dritten Reiches: Profile einer totalitären Herrschaft* (Munich, 2006)

——*Hitler: Eine Biographie* (Hamburg, 2007, first pub. 1973); available in English as *Hitler* (Boston, 2002)

Frank, Johannes, *Eva Braun: Ein ungewöhnliches Frauenschicksal in geschichtlich bewegter Zeit* (Coburg, 1997)

Freye, Hans-Albrecht, *Humangenetik*, 5th reprint (Berlin, 1988)

Friedländer, Saul, *Nazi Germany and the Jews: The Years of Extermination 1939–1945* (New York, 2007)

——*Nazi Germany and the Jews: The Years of Persecution, 1933–1939* (New York, 1997)

Fuchs, Gerd A., *Die Parkinsonsche Krankheit: Ursachen und Behandlungsformen* (Munich, 2003)

Fülgraff, Georges and Dieter Palm, *Pharmakotherapie, Klinische Pharmakologie* (Stuttgart, 1997)

Funke, Manfred, *Starker oder schwacher Diktator? Hitlers Herrschaft und die Deutschen* (Düsseldorf, 1989)

Gibbels, Ellen, *Hitlers Parkinson-Krankheit: Zur Frage eines hirnorganischen Psychosyndroms* (Berlin, 1990)

Goodrick-Clarke, Nicholas, *The Occult Roots of Nazism: Secret Aryan Cults and Their Influence on Nazi Ideology* (New York, 1992)

Greten, Heiner (ed.), *Innere Medizin: Verstehen – Lernen – Anwenden* (Stuttgart, 2005)

Hamann, Brigitte, *Hitlers Edeljude: Das Leben des Armenarztes Eduard Bloch* (Munich, 2008)

——*Winifried Wagner oder Hitlers Bayreuth* (Munich, 2003); available in English as *Winifred Wagner: A Life at the Heart of Hitler's Bayreuth* (Orlando, FL, 2005)

Heer, Hannes, *Vom Verschwinden der Täter: Der Vernichtungskrieg fand statt, aber keiner war dabei* (Berlin, 2005)

——*Hitler war's: Die Befreiung der Deutschen von ihrer Vergangenheit* (Berlin, 2008)

Heiden, Konrad, *Hitler*, vol. 1 (Zurich, 1936), vol. 2 (Zurich, 1937); available in English as *Der Führer* (New York, 1999, first pub. 1944)

Herzog, Dagmar, *Sex After Fascism: Memory and Morality in Twentieth-Century Germany* (Princeton, 2005)

Heston, Leonard and Renate, *The Medical Casebook of Adolf Hitler* (London, 1979)

Hilberg, Raul, *The Destruction of the European Jews* (New York, 1985)

Hoffmann, Peter, *Widerstand, Staatsstreich, Attentat: Der Kampf der Opposition gegen Hitler* (Munich, 1969); available in English as *The History of German Resistance 1933–1945* (London, 1977)

Höhne, Heinz, *Der Orden unter dem Totenkopf: Die Geschichte der SS* (Bindlach, 1990, first pub. 1966); available in English as *The Order of the Death's Head: The Story of Hitler's SS* (London, 2000, first pub. 1969)

——*'Gebt mir vier Jahre Zeit': Hitler und die Anfänge des Dritten Reiches* (Berlin, 1999, first pub. 1996)

Horstmann, Bernhard, *Hitler in Pasewalk: Die Hypnose und ihre Folgen* (Düsseldorf, 2004)

Hubatsch, Walther (ed.), *Hitlers Weisungen für die Kriegsführung (1939–1945): Dokumente der Oberkommandos der Wehrmacht* (Utting, undated – reprint, 1983); partially available in English as *Hitler's War Directives 1939–1945* (London, 1964)

Irving, David, *Hitler's War* (London, 2002)

——*Wie krank war Hitler wirklich? Der Diktator und seine Ärzte* (Munich, 1980)

Jaeckel, Gerhard, *Die Charité: Geschichte eines Weltzentrums der Medizin von 1710 bis zur Gegenwart* (Munich, 2001)

Jochmann, Werner (ed.), *Adolf Hitler: Monologe im Führerhauptquartier 1941–1944, aufgezeichnet von Heinrich Heim* (Munich, 2000)

Jung, Hermann, *Die Ardennen-Offensive 1944/45: Ein Beispiel für die Kriegführung Hitlers* (Göttingen, 1992)

Junge, Traudl, *Bis zur letzten Stunde: Hitlers Sekretärin erzählt ihr Leben* (Munich, 2002); available in English as *Until the Final Hour: Hitler's Last Secretary* (London, 2005)

231

Kater, Michael A., *Doctors Under Hitler* (Chapel Hill, NC, 1989)
Katz, Ottmar, *Prof. Dr. med. Theo Morell, Hitlers Leibarzt* (Bayreuth, 1982)
Kellerhoff, Sven Felix, *Hitlers Berlin: Geschichte einer Hassliebe* (Berlin, 2005)
Kershaw, Ian, *Fateful Choices: Ten Decisions That Changed The World 1940–1941* (London, 2007)
——*Hitler* (Harlow, 1991)
——*Hitler: 1936–1945: Nemesis* (New York, 2000)
——*The 'Hitler Myth': Image and Reality in the Third Reich* (Oxford, 1987)
Klee, Ernst, *Auschwitz, die NS-Medizin und ihre Opfer* (Frankfurt a. M., 1997)
——*Das Personenlexikon zum Dritten Reich: Wer war was vor und nach 1945,* 2nd ed. (Frankfurt a. M., 2007)
——*Das Kulturlexikon zum Dritten Reich: Wer war was vor und nach 1945* (Frankfurt a. M., 2007)
Klier, Freya, *Die Kaninchen von Ravensbrück: Medizinische Versuche an Frauen in der NS-Zeit* (Munich, 1994)
Köhler, Joachim, *Wagners Hitler: Der Prophet und sein Vollstrecker* (Munich, 1999); available in English as *Wagner's Hitler: The Prophet and His Disciple* (Cambridge, UK, 2000)
Kopperschmidt, Josef (ed.), *Hitler der Redner* (Munich, 2003)
Kretschmer, Ernst, *Physique and Character: An Investigation of the Nature of Constitution and the Theory of Temperament* (London, 1999, first pub. 1925)
Kubizek, August, *Adolf Hitler: Mein Jugendfreund* (Graz, 1953); available in English as *The Young Hitler I Knew* (London, 2006)
Kulka, Otto Dov and Eberhard Jäckel (eds), *Die Juden in den geheimen NS-Stimmungsberichten 1933–1945* (Düsseldorf, 2004); available in English as *The Jews in the Secret Nazi Reports on Popular Opinion in Germany, 1933–1945* (New Haven, 2010)
Lang, Jochen von, *Der Sekretär: Martin Bormann – Der Mann, der Hitler beherrschte* (Herrsching, 1990); available in English as *Bormann: The Man Who Manipulated Hitler* (London, 1979)
Lange-Eichbaum, Wilhelm and Wolfram Kurth, *Genie, Irrsinn und Ruhm* (Munich, 1967, first pub. 1942)
Langer, Walter C., *The Mind of Adolf Hitler: The Secret Wartime Report* (London, 1973)
Large, David Clay, *Where Ghosts Walked: Munich's Road to the Third Reich* (New York, 1997)
Lewin, Louis, *Gifte und Vergiftungen: Lehrbuch der Toxikologie* (Berlin, 1929, first pub. 1885)
Longerich, Peter, *Hitlers Stellvertreter: Führung der Partei und Kontrolle des Staatsapparates durch den Stab Hess und die Parteikanzlei Bormann* (Munich, 1992)
——*Heinrich Himmler: Biographie* (Munich, 2008); available in English as *Heinrich Himmler* (Oxford, 2012)
——*Die braunen Bataillone: Geschichte der SA* (Augsburg, 1999)
——*'Davon haben wir nichts gewusst!' Die Deutschen und die Judenverfolgung 1933–1945* (Munich, 2006)
——*Politik der Vernichtung: Eine Gesamtdarstellung der nationalsozialistischen Judenvernichtung* (Munich, Zurich, 1998); available in English as *Holocaust: The Nazi Persecution and Murder of the Jews* (Oxford, 2010)

232

Lukacs, John, *The Hitler of History: Hitler's Biographers on Trial* (London, 2000)

Machtan, Lothar, *The Hidden Hitler* (New York, 2001)

Magenheimer, Heinz, *Die Militärstrategie Deutschlands 1940–1945: Führungsentschlüsse, Hintergründe, Alternativen* (Munich, 1997); available in English as *Hitler's War: Germany's Key Strategic Decisions, 1940–1945* (London, 1998)

Malinowski, Stephan, *Vom König zum Führer: Deutscher Adel und Nationalsozialismus* (Frankfurt a. M., 2004)

Manstein, Erich von, *Verlorene Siege* (Bonn, 1955); available in English as *Lost Victories* (London, 2000, first pub. 1958)

Marks, Stephan, *Warum folgten sie Hitler? Die Psychologie des Nationalsozialismus* (Düsseldorf, 2007)

Maser, Werner, *Adolf Hitler: Das Ende der Führer-Legende* (Munich, 1982)

——*Adolf Hitler: Legende, Mythos, Wirklichkeit* (Munich, 1971)

——*Fälschung, Dichtung und Wahrheit über Hitler und Stalin* (Munich, 2004)

Matussek, Paul, Peter Matussek and Jan Marbach, *Hitler: Karriere eines Wahns* (Munich, 2000)

Megargee, Geoffrey P., *Inside Hitler's High Command* (Lawrence, KS, 2000)

Menasse, Eva, *Der Holocaust vor Gericht: Der Prozess um David Irving* (Berlin, 2000)

Militärgeschichtliches Forschungsamt, *Das Deutsche Reich und der Zweite Weltkrieg* (Munich, 1979–2008)

Mohler, Armin, *Die Konservative Revolution in Deutschland 1918–1932: Ein Handbuch* (Graz, 1999)

Mosse, George L., *The Crisis of Ideology: Intellectual Origins of the Third Reich* (New York, 1988)

Neumayr, Anton, *Krankheiten grosser Diktatoren* (Wiesbaden, 2007, first pub. 1995)

Nolte, Ernst, *Der Faschismus in seiner Epoche* (Munich, 2000)

Overesch, Manfred and Friedrich Wilhelm Saal, *Chronik deutscher Zeitgeschichte: Politik, Wirtschaft, Kultur* (Düsseldorf, 1982)

Overy, Richard, *Why The Allies Won* (New York, 1997)

——*The Dictators: Hitler's Germany, Stalin's Russia* (New York, 2004)

Pätzhold, Kurt and Manfred Weissbecker, *Rudolf Hess: Der Mann an Hitlers Seite* (Leipzig, 1999)

Pilgrim, Volker Elis, *Muttersöhne* (Reinbek bei Hamburg, 1989)

——*'Du kannst mich ruhig Frau Hitler nennen': Frauen als Schmuck und Tarnung der NS-Herrschaft* (Reinbek bei Hamburg, 1994)

Plöckinger, Othmar, *Geschichte eines Buches: Adolf Hitler 'Mein Kampf' 1922–1945* (Munich, 2006)

Poliakov, Leon, *The Aryan Myth: A History of Racism and Nationalist Ideas in Europe* (London, 1974, trans. from French)

Pschyrembel, *Klinisches Wörterbuch*, 257th edn (Berlin, 1994)

——*Klinisches Wörterbuch*, 259th edn (Berlin, 2004)

Read, Anthony, *The Devil's Disciples: The Lives and Times of Hitler's Inner Circle* (London, 2004)

Redlich, Fritz, *Hitler: Diagnosis of a Destructive Prophet* (Oxford, 1999)

Ricardi, Hans-Günter, *Hitler und seine Hintermänner: Neue Fakten zur Frühgeschichte der NSDAP* (Munich, 1991)

233

Roberts, Geoffrey, *Stalin's Wars: From World War to Cold War, 1939–1953* (Hartford, 2008)

Rose, Olaf (ed.), *Julius Schaub – in Hitlers Schatten: Erinnerungen und Aufzeichnungen des Chefadjutanten 1925–1945* (Stegen/Ammersee, 2005)

Rosenbaum, Ron, *Explaining Hitler: The Search for Origins of His Evil* (London, 1998)

Sauerteig, Lutz, *Krankheit, Sexualität, Gesellschaft: Geschlechtskrankheiten und Gesundheitspolitik in Deutschland im 19. und 20. Jahrhundert* (Stuttgart, 1999)

Schenck, Ernst Günther, *Dr. Morell: Hitler's Leibarzt und sein Pharmaimperium* (Schnellbach, 1998)

——*Patient Hitler: eine medizinische Biographie* (Augsburg, 2000)

Schmölders, Claudia, *Hitlers Gesicht: Eine physiognomische Biographie* (Munich, 2000); available in English as *Hitler's Face: The Biography of an Image* (Philadelphia, 2006)

Schroeder, Christa (with Anton Joachimsthaler), *Er war mein Chef* (Munich, 1985)

Sigmund, Anna Maria, *Des Führers bester Freund: Adolf Hitler, seine Nichte Geli Raubal und der 'Ehrenarier' Emil Maurice – eine Dreiecksbeziehung* (Munich, 2003)

——*'Das Geschlechtsleben bestimmen wir' – Sexualität im Dritten Reich* (Munich, 2008)

——*Die Frauen der Nazis I–III* (Munich, 1998–2005); partially available in English as *Women of the Third Reich* (Richmond Hill, ON, 2000)

——*Diktator, Dämon, Demagoge: Fragen und Antworten zu Adolf Hitler* (Munich, 2006)

Smelser, Ronald et al. (eds), *Die braune Elite* (Darmstadt, 1999)

Speer, Albert, *Inside the Third Reich* (London, 1995)

Steffahn, Harald, *Hitler* (Reinbek bei Hamburg, 1999)

Stierlin, Helm, *Adolf Hitler: Familienperspektiven* (Frankfurt a. M., 1975)

Süss, Dietmar und Winfried (eds), *Das 'Dritte Reich': Eine Einführung* (Munich, 2008)

Toellner, Richard, *Illustrierte Geschichte der Medizin* (Salzburg, 1990)

Trevor-Roper, Hugh (ed.), *The Testament of Adolf Hitler: The Hitler–Bormann Documents* (London, 1961)

Ueberschär, Gerd R., *Für ein anderes Deutschland: Der deutsche Widerstand gegen den NS-Staat* (Frankfurt a. M., 2006)

Ueberschär, Gerd R. and Winfried Vogel, *Dienen und Verdienen: Hitlers Geschenke an seine Eliten* (Frankfurt a. M., 2006)

*Die Wehrmachtsberichte 1939–1945*, reprint (Cologne, 1989)

Weinberg, Gerhard L., *A World At Arms: A Global History of World War II* (Cambridge, 1994)

Weiss, Hermann (ed.), *Biographisches Lexikon zum Dritten Reich* (Frankfurt a. M., 1999)

Welzer, Harald, *Das kommunikative Gedächtnis: Eine Theorie der Erinnerung* (Munich, 2008)

——*Täter: Wie aus ganz normalen Menschen Massenmörder werden* (Frankfurt a. M., 2005)

Wiedemann, Fritz, *Der Mann, der Feldherr werden wollte: Erlebnisse und*

*Erfahrungen des Vorgesetzen Hitlers im Ersten Weltkrieg und seines späteren Persönlichen Adjutanten* (Velbert, 1964)

Wildt, Michael, *Generation des Unbedingten: Das Führungskorps des Reichssicherheitshauptamtes* (Hamburg, 2003)

——*Volksgemeinschaft als Selbstermächtigung: Gewalt gegen Juden in der deutschen Provinz 1919 bis 1939* (Hamburg, 2007)

Wistrich, Robert, *Who's Who in Nazi Germany* (London, 1982)

Witte, Peter (ed.), *Der Dienstkalender Heinrich Himmlers 1941/42* (Hamburg, 1999)

Zdral, Wolfgang, *Die Hitlers: Die unbekannte Familie des Führers* (Frankfurt a. M., 2005)

Zetkin and Schaldach, *Lexikon der Medizin* (Wiesbaden, 1999)

Zitelmann, Rainer, *Hitler: Selbstverständnis eines Revolutionärs* (Munich, 1998)

# INDEX